Carol
Smith

HOW

NATIONS

NEGOTIATE

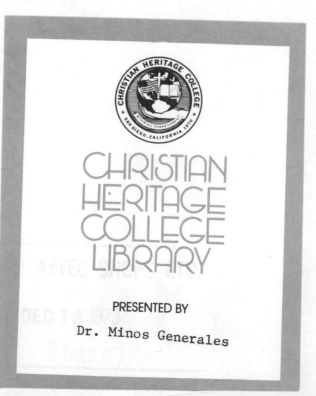

Written under the auspices of
THE CENTER FOR INTERNATIONAL AFFAIRS
Harvard University

HOW
NATIONS
NEGOTIATE

FRED CHARLES IKLÉ

FREDERICK A. PRAEGER, *Publishers*
New York · Washington · London

FREDERICK A. PRAEGER, *Publishers*
111 Fourth Avenue, New York, N.Y. 10003, U.S.A.
    5, Cromwell Place, London S.W.7, England

Published in the United States of America in 1967
by Frederick A. Praeger, Inc., Publishers

Second printing, 1968

© 1964 by Fred Charles Iklé.

The original edition of this book was published in 1964 by Harper & Row, Publishers, Inc. Minor additions and corrections have been made for this paperback edition.

Library of Congress Catalog Card Number: 67-22334

Printed in the United States of America

TO DORIS

CONTENTS

STATES HAVE NEGOTIATED SINCE THE BEGINNING OF HISTORY— as they have fought wars. Compared with the changes in methods of warfare, however, the methods of negotiation have remained much the same. Of course, negotiation and war are not mutually exclusive. States can live in peace without negotiating at all, they may start to fight while they are negotiating, and if their leaders are prudent, they will continue to negotiate even though they are at war.

Nor is negotiation intrinsically good just because war can be so evil. In the nuclear age, when a single battle can bring total disaster, negotiation has acquired the nimbus of Salvation that will protect the world from destruction and eventually deliver it from the terrible engines of war. But negotiation is only an instrument: it can be used on the side of the angels as well as by the forces of darkness. It may settle dangerous conflicts short of war, divert governments from the use of force, and terminate fighting before destruction becomes complete. Yet, it may also exacerbate hostilities, strengthen an aggressor, prepare the way for his attack, and erode the legal and moral foundations of peace.

Although negotiation has happily been more prevalent in the relations of states than war, it has never been studied with the same incisiveness. From antiquity on, the strategies and tactics of the battlefield have been analyzed more systematically and with greater precision than the strategies and tactics of diplomacy.

The same discrepancy can be found in the present period. During the last fifteen years, while the writings both on warfare and on diplomatic bargaining have been multiplying rapidly, a rigorous intellectual effort has been devoted only to the problems of war and of preventing it through deterrence and arms control. Our understanding of these problems has been raised far above intuition and common sense. It is based on carefully developed ideas which all hang together, such as active vs. passive deterrence, the functions of uncertainty and credibility, the connection between vulnerable forces and accident-proneness, the interdependence between strategic choices and the efficient allocation of resources, and the dilemma of common interests in disarmament and incentives for violating agreements.

A comparable intellectual development centering on the subject of negotiation has not yet occurred. There are, to be sure, comparable categories of literature in each of these fields. Thus, diplomatic histories of particular countries might be considered analogous to the histories of armies and navies; both are rich in interesting illustrations but rarely deal systematically with the process by which opponents interact. Memoirs of negotiators and case studies of specific conferences find their counterpart in the memoirs of soldiers and in accounts of particular battles; both are full of exciting material essential for any further analysis. And the treatises on diplomatic practices correspond to the field manuals of the military. But little has been written on the strategies and tactics of negotiation that would be equivalent in precision and coherence to the better studies on military defense, deterrence, and arms control. The few books instructing diplomats how to be good negotiators (written mostly a long time ago) do not meet the standard; they compare rather with those homilies that advise soldiers to be obedient, brave, alert, and resourceful.

When this book was completed, early in 1964, several of the negotiations discussed in it had not yet been terminated. The development of these negotiations since then can be used here to reexamine some of the ideas contained in the chapters below.

West Berlin is no longer an issue of conflict between the United States and the Soviet Union—at least for the time being. Under Khrushchev's leadership, the Soviet government waged a seven-year diplomatic offensive against West Berlin and Western access to that city. There was some change in the status quo in 1961, when the Western powers quietly accepted the Berlin Wall. The fact that this wall prevented the escape of people from East Germany may have made it easier for the Soviets to abandon their aims regarding West Berlin. For the larger part, however, the status quo was preserved without any new agreement—confirming the view expressed in this book that the Berlin crisis was nothing but the echo of Khrushchev's threats. As in all "redistribution" negotiations (a term explained below), the issue was settled as soon as the threat had vanished—or more precisely, a settlement became unnecessary since the issue then disappeared. The outcome disproved the claims widely made in the West that the Western powers ought to exert themselves and take initiatives to reach a new agreement on Berlin (see pp. 34–35, 46).

The new issue that now absorbs the central attention of negotiators in Washington and throughout the world is the problem of terminating the war in Vietnam. However, public discussions of this issue, both in official speeches and in the news media, frequently focus on unimportant aspects or nebulous ideas. For example, the question is often raised whether one or the other side is "negotiating in good faith" or would be willing to do so, without any clarification as to which of the many possible meanings of this phrase is meant (see pp. 111–14).

Also, too much is being made of the distinction between the bargaining before the parties meet at the conference table, on the one hand, and the bargaining at a conference (either secret or public) on the other. Both sides in the war in Vietnam have proposed terms for a settlement at least since 1965, both have continued to advance supporting arguments for their positions, and both have occasionally revised their terms. Surely this ought to be considered as being part of "negotiation." A conference or informal meetings may not add much to the essential bargaining process. It is only when the parties want to settle details of some complicated agreement that a conference becomes necessary, or at least useful.

This book takes a wider view of "negotiation" in order to put diplomatic conferences and informal diplomatic meetings into their proper context. It considers the entire bargaining process between governments as long as it is aimed at an explicit agreement. In this process the diplomatic conference may be only a minor phase, if it takes place at all. The moves that are important for the outcome— such as threats, commitments, and other actions to influence the opponent—often take place outside the conference room.

The impact of negotiations between two parties on a third party is dealt with below (pp. 55–58) as one of the "side effects" of negotiation. A new instance is provided by the United States–Soviet negotiations on an agreement against nuclear proliferation. These negotiations may turn out to be more important in further isolating Communist China than in curbing the spread of nuclear weapons.

In a triangle, such as that involving Washington, Moscow, and Peking, where all three powers are more or less antagonistic toward each other, almost any negotiations between two parties will have a strong impact on the relationships with the third party. Of course, negotiations between Washington and Peking have long remained limited to a restatement of incompatible positions and to the exchange of old warnings and threats, but this is likely to change.

Since dictatorships can execute sudden shifts in their alliances, such power triangles are highly unstable. A switch that ushered in World War II was the Nazi-Soviet pact of August, 1939, consummated while the British and French were trying to negotiate an agreement with the Soviet Union (pp. 55–56). Today Moscow may fear a sudden Peking-Washington pact as much as Washington ought to be concerned about the possibility of a new Sino-Soviet alliance. In order to appreciate fully the possibilities for switches in alliances, we must be aware of the fact that "minimum positions" and "unacceptable demands" are unstable. The evaluations of parties keep shifting in purely bilateral negotiation (Chapter 10), and in a triangular relationship they can shift even faster.

F.C.I.

Cambridge, Mass.
March, 1967

ACKNOWLEDGMENTS

I FIRST BECAME INTERESTED IN STUDYING INTERNATIONAL negotiation some three years ago while working on problems of disarmament at the RAND Corporation. Ever since, Nathan Leites has continued to take an active role in my work. Those who know Nathan Leites' own writings on negotiation will easily recognize part of my debt to him. My full debt only those will understand who have similarly benefited, in intellectual collaboration with him, from his exceptional ability to encourage clear thinking and to enliven one's own drabness with his fresh insights.

It is to Thomas Schelling that I owe most for the theoretical foundation. If his work on bargaining had not preceded, my study would have been left without a larger context and been deprived of many essential concepts and incisive details. But not only did I have the pleasure of reading Thomas Schelling; I constantly profited from his advice and encouragement while writing this book at the Harvard University Center for International Affairs.

Robert Bowie, Director of the Center, and Henry Kissinger, one of its Faculty Members, contributed more than they might realize. Prolonged conversations with Robert Bowie taught me a great deal about the complex realities of negotiation and inspired my attempt to capture the meaning of its diverse outcomes. Henry Kissinger, both through his writings and in numerous discussions, gave me a better perspective and deeper understanding of Western diplomacy, past and present.

To Philip Mosely I am doubly indebted. His help and encouragement were decisive in broadening my research beyond the perusal of books and documents, so that I could learn from the practitioners of negotiation. And his superb analysis of his own important negotiating experience served me as an indispensable guide.

My gratitude also goes to Paul Kecskemeti, for his careful review and important comments; and to Harold Jacobson, Roger Fisher, and Martin Shubik for many valuable suggestions.

The working environment at the Center for International Affairs was ideal. Each year a group of senior civil servants from all over the world come to the Center. Straddling two academic years, I had the opportunity to expose my ideas to the thoughtful criticism of two such groups. Among them I wish to thank in particular Risto Hyvarinen, Ernst Jung, Louis Kunzig, and David Mark for having commented extensively on my manuscript. Many of my chapters have been greatly improved by expert advice from Morton Halperin, Karl Kaiser, James Richardson, Kenneth Waltz, and Ciro Zoppo, all past or present Research Associates at the Center.

The manuscript gained immeasurably from editorial help by Max Hall and Robert Erwin. They had the skill to ferret out not only weakness in language but also weaknesses in the thoughts behind it. Joseph Tulchin ably assisted me in the historical research and, in addition, contributed many pertinent examples and expert suggestions. Most of the typing and preparation of the manuscript was done by Connie Griffith, to whom I owe a great debt for cheerfully devoting her unflagging care to this task.

The Center for International Affairs generously supported the larger part of this study, while the initial phase was financed by the RAND Corporation with additional assistance from the Rockefeller Foundation. The grant from the Rockefeller Foundation enabled me to conduct extensive interviews of European diplomats and to study the negotiating techniques in the European Communities.

To RAND I am grateful for much more than unstinting financial support. At RAND I learned that relations between modern states can be subjected to systematic analysis and calculation without at all neglecting the emotional and irrational components of human behavior. It was at RAND that I acquired a clearer understanding of the constraints and opportunities for governments in coping with uncertainty, allocating scarce resources, and interacting with friend and foe. And it was from my former RAND colleagues that I received the initial stimulation and encouragement to tackle my difficult topic. Hans Speier and Alexander George have been particularly warm supporters, and Herbert Goldhamer imparted to me unique insights from his personal experience in negotiations.

For some months in 1962 I had the pleasure of working on this study as the guest of the Council on Foreign Relations in New York. This afforded me a welcome opportunity to exchange ideas with many experienced diplomats. And the staff of the Council thoughtfully advised me on my research and writing. In particular, George Franklin, Executive Director, and W. Phillips Davison went out of their way to be helpful.

My acknowledgments must remain incomplete. Many experienced diplomats in Washington, London, Paris, and in the European Communities have most generously granted me interviews offering insights, factual information, and an understanding of the art of diplomacy that I could never have acquired by reading. I feel it best accords with their wishes if I express my gratitude to them without revealing their identity. Without this cooperation from the Negotiators, my study on negotiation would not have been possible.

F.C.I.

Cambridge, Massachusetts
March 1964

CHAPTER 1

WHAT IS NEGOTIATION?

CERTAIN SUBJECTS SEEM QUITE CLEAR AS LONG AS WE LEAVE them alone. The answers look obvious until we ask questions, the concepts appear to be well understood until we wish to define them, causes and effects are easily recognized until we seek to explain them, and all the rules pass for valid until we try to prove them. The social scientist, alas, shares the honor with the philosopher of often moving in his inquiries from the obvious to the obscure. Of course, he hopes to go beyond and to emerge with a clearer view of the whole and a better knowledge of the details than he first had on the basis of folklore and common sense. But to begin with, he must challenge the old answers with new questions.

Negotiation is a subject on which much has been said and written that seems self-evident until examined more closely. To resolve conflict and avoid the use of force, it is said, one must negotiate (Is this always the best way to settle conflict?). Negotiation requires a willingness to compromise (Why?), and both sides must make concessions (According to which law?). Neither side can expect to win all it wants (Not even if its objectives are modest?). If both sides negotiate in good faith (Who judges "good faith"?), they can always find a fair solution (And what is "fair"?). If there is a conflict about many issues, the less controversial ones should be solved first because agreement will lead to further agreement (Or will the postponed issues become harder to solve?). A negotiator should never make a threat he is not prepared to carry out (What is wrong with successful bluffing?). Each side has its minimum beyond which it cannot be moved (But how about moving the opponent's minimum?).

This book is concerned with the process and effects of negotiation between governments; in particular, it seeks to relate the *process* of negotiation to the *outcome*. To begin with, two elements must normally be present for negotiation to take place: there must be both common interests and issues of conflict. Without common interest there is nothing to negotiate for, without conflict nothing to negotiate about.

There are many ways in which governments—always subject to change, idiosyncrasy, and pressure from within—relate their common interests to their conflicting interests. They may be isolationist and try to stay apart to avoid all conflict, while sacrificing the pursuit of possible common interests. Or they may simply follow habits and rules that regulate their interests and conflicts automatically without bargaining. The observance of some diplomatic practices is of this character. (So is routine buying and selling at fixed prices.) But usually a government takes account of the fact that its interests and its ability to pursue national objectives are influenced by decisions of other nations. Likewise it realizes that these other nations will be affected by its own decisions. It may try to coordinate this interaction without explicitly saying so—a process of "tacit bargaining." Or it may communicate with other governments for the explicit purpose of working out a particular combination of conflicting and common interests; that is, to reach an agreement.

One should perhaps distinguish between two kinds of common interests: an *identical common interest* in a single arrangement or object, and a *complementary interest* in an exchange of different objects. In the identical common interest, the parties want to share the *same* object or benefit from the same arrangement, which, however, they can bring about only by joining together. Hence they have to agree on the object's characteristics (concerning which they may have different preferences) and on the division of the costs and gains (where their interests are likely to conflict). Examples of agreements on such identical common interests are the U.S.-Canadian treaty on the St. Lawrence Seaway, international fishery agreements to protect the supply of fish, and, in a sense, cease-fire agreements.

When parties are interested in an exchange, they want *different* things. These they cannot obtain by themselves but can only grant to each other. The clearest examples are barters and sales. Similarly, commercial aviation agreements, where each country wants to have its planes fly to the other country, have the purpose of settling an exchange. So do agreements for mutual tariff concessions.

In reality, however, most negotiations embrace a combination of identical common interests and complementary interests. When the six European countries set up the European Economic Community, they had complementary interests in the exchange of tariff concessions and common interests in a large, unified European market. The nuclear test-ban treaty between the United States and the Soviet Union can satisfy the complementary interest in slowing down the opponent's development of new weapons and the common interest in preventing an increase in radioactive fallout or in discouraging the proliferation of nuclear weapons. Whether the identical common interests or the complementary interests dominate depends on how the purposes of the agreement are defined.

The process by which two or more parties relate conflicting to common interests is the warp and woof not only of international relations but of human society; individuals, groups, and governments engage in it all the time. We become aware of it only when we call it something special—like Molière's Monsieur Jourdain when he discovered that for forty years he had been speaking "prose." There seems to be no established term for all the ways in which parties with conflicting and common interests interact—whether explicitly or tacitly—though "bargaining" is sometimes used that broadly.

"Negotiation" in a narrower sense denotes a process that is different from tacit bargaining or other behavior that regulates conflict. As used here, *negotiation is a process in which explicit proposals are put forward ostensibly for the purpose of reaching agreement on an exchange or on the realization of a common interest where conflicting interests are present.* Frequently, these proposals deal not only with the terms of agreement but also with the topics to be discussed (the agenda), with the ground rules that ought to apply, and with underlying technical and legal issues. It is the confrontation of explicit proposals that distinguishes negotiation (as here defined) from tacit bargaining and other types of conflict behavior. Beyond this confrontation appear other moves that the negotiating parties make to strengthen their own position, to weaken that of the opponent, or to influence the outcome in other ways. The subject matter of this book includes all these moves and the ways in which they relate to the outcome. That is, bargaining moves are included in the broader sense, to the extent that they serve pending or ongoing negotiations where explicit proposals are being put forward.

Only part of the frequent changes in relations between countries are the result of negotiation. Governments often revise their expectations and attitudes toward other countries as a result of unilateral actions or tacit bargains. Military and technological developments, growth or decline in economic strength, and internal political changes continually cause the rearrangement of conflicting and common interests between nations, and this happens whether or not diplomats negotiate.

There is no simple rule as to when negotiation is needed, and when tacit bargaining or even less conscious confrontations are more effective to restructure international relations. For certain arrangements negotiation clearly cannot be dispensed with; for others it is optional; and there are some issues which are better settled without it.

Negotiation is necessary for any arrangement that establishes complicated forms of collaboration, such as a joint war effort or Britain's attempted entry into the Common Market. (In contrast, the entry of, say, the Ivory Coast into the United Nations did not require significant negotiations.) Negotiation is needed for most exchanges, such as exchanges of prisoners or the granting of mutual consular facilities, and for all transactions involving monetary compensation, as in the payment of oil royalties or the leasing of air bases. Negotiation is, of course, necessary for the setting up of formal international institutions and for any arrangement where an _explicit_ agreement is essential, such as a peace treaty or an alliance system.

On the other hand, certain undertakings are arrived at in such a delicate way that explicit proposals might interfere with the process. The mutually observed restrictions in the Korean War (for instance, no attacks on the supply lines leading into North and South Korea) is an example of arrangements that would not have been facilitated or might even have been upset by negotiation. The very uncertainties of a tacit understanding may have made these restrictions more stable, because both sides were unwilling to probe and push toward the limits of the "bargain," lest it all be upset. The negotiation of an explicit _quid pro quo_ might have given rise to new demands and invited more haggling and tugging than the arrangement which the parties never discussed and never explicitly settled. Furthermore, while soldiers were being killed fighting the enemy, negotiations to establish rules and restraints for the battle or on the interdiction of supplies would have clashed with domestic opinion and perhaps adversely affected the morale of the troops.[1]

Likewise, if there is a deep-seated hostility between the populations of two countries, governments may be unable to negotiate because of public opposition but may work out some arrangements of mutual interest through tacit bargaining. The relationship between Jordan and Israel is an example.

In the field of arms control and disarmament, where we have become so accustomed to large and formal conferences, important understandings can at times be arrived at without negotiation. Formal talks might, in fact, make it more difficult to harmonize some arms policies insofar as they inevitably introduce political issues or questions of prestige and legal precedents.[2]

[1] A pioneering analysis of the role of tacit bargaining in limited war is given by Thomas C. Schelling, _The Strategy of Conflict_ (Cambridge, Mass.: Harvard University Press, 1960), chap. iii and appendix A. The delicate interaction of tacit limitations on air-attacks in the Korean War is discussed by Morton H. Halperin, _Limited War in the Nuclear Age_ (New York: John Wiley, 1963), pp. 53–55.

[2] On the importance of tacit bargaining for arms control, see Thomas C. Schelling and Morton H. Halperin, _Strategy and Arms Control_ (New York: Twentieth Century Fund, 1961), pp. 77–82.

Negotiation plays an important role in formalizing turning points in international relations, in catalyzing or at least clarifying changes that were caused by tacit bargaining or other processes, and in working out those finer shades in new arrangements between nations that the brute interplay of latent strength cannot define.

Although negotiation is necessary for any new relationship that is based on explicit agreement, an explicit agreement is usually only part of the outcome of negotiation. Negotiation may change the positions of the parties and their mutual relations in many other ways. The outcome may include, for example, tacit understandings between the parties, a clarification of the points of disagreement, a reorientation of national objectives, new commitments to third parties (allies, domestic groups, or world opinion), and propaganda effects. Many of these results may outweigh in importance whatever explicit agreement is arrived at. And even agreements themselves vary widely in their degree of specificity and the amount of disagreement that they leave unsettled.

CHAPTER 2

AGREEMENT AND DISAGREEMENT

AN AGREEMENT BETWEEN GOVERNMENTS CAN BE DEFINED AS an exchange of conditional promises, by which each party declares that it will act in a certain way on condition that the other parties act in accordance with their promises. Sanctions supported by higher authority cannot be invoked in case of a violation as they can for contracts under domestic law. Nonetheless, these promises are significant, since the parties have an interest in living up to them for other reasons.

First, as long as governments find an agreement attractive *on balance,* they will want to keep their own part of the bargain if that is the condition for the other parties' fulfillment of their promises.

Second, governments have a certain interest in keeping agreements as a matter of principle, apart from preserving the advantages of a particular bargain. If they violate an agreement, they may find it more difficult to reach other agreements in the future and will reduce the good will they might have enjoyed with other governments. Among allied or friendly countries, the desire to maintain good will is an exceedingly important motive for keeping agreements. Like a businessman's credit rating, the reputation of fulfilling the treaty obligations toward one's allies is too important to be sacrificed for one-time gains except in the case of dire emergency. Among more hostile countries there may be little good will to lose, but the threat of reprisals can help to discourage the breach of agreements. This threat is reinforced by the fact that parties that suffer from a violation have an interest in increasing the penalty to discourage others from similar violations. In other words, actual or potential victims of violations have a stake in making the breach of agreements unattractive.

Third, where a breach of an agreement necessitates a clear-cut action requiring complicated decisions, democratic governments may encounter institutional obstacles to a violation. The burden of proof would lie with those government officials who advocate that the agreement should be broken; they would have to overcome tendencies to inaction, moral and legal objections, and conflicting appraisals as to the consequences.[1]

There is no simple relationship between the process of negotiation and its outcome. Usually, the outcome is not simply an agreement which settles in clear-cut terms all the issues of conflict that were dealt with. Even if one ignores side-effects of negotiation, the explicit terms of agreement tell only part of the story. Important issues may have been settled only in ambiguous terms or in general principles. Other parts of the settlement may consist in tacit understandings. Frequently, there is no explicit agreement at all, but the negotiating process may have created new attitudes toward the issues of disagreement or a new common understanding as to what the disagreement consists of.

THE ROLE OF SPECIFICITY

The West has often been warned against concluding ambiguous agreements or "agreements in principle" with the Communists, because it has been the experience, when it came to work out the details of such agreements, that the Communists would renege on the understanding the Western diplomats thought they had reached. As Philip Mosely pointed out:

One of the main pitfalls in wartime Anglo-American negotiations with the Soviet Union was the tendency to rely upon reaching an "agreement in principle." . . . At Yalta the Soviet government agreed, after

[1] For an exposition of this and other factors that make governments comply with rules, see Roger Fisher, "Constructing Rules that Affect Governments," in *Arms Control, Disarmament, and National Security,* ed. Donald G. Brennan (New York: Braziller, 1961), pp. 56–67.

very lengthy argument and stubborn resistance, to participate in a reconstruction of the Polish government which would, it appeared, permit the survival of some political freedom for the great non-Communist majority of the people. By delays and quibblings over the execution of the "agreement in principle" during the next few months, the Soviet government secured about ninety per cent of the original position with which it had come to Yalta and thus strengthened beyond challenge the small Communist minority in its dominant control of the country.[2]

We should distinguish two different risks inherent in agreements in principle. First, the parties may conclude such an agreement, unaware that their interpretations of the implicit parts of the bargain are in conflict. Second, there is the risk of deliberate violation; that is, one party violates what it *knows* the other party thought was a mutual—though tacit or unwritten—understanding as to how the general guidelines were to be carried out.

In the case of unintentional misunderstanding, one or the other side will feel cheated when it comes to carry out the agreement later on. The remedy against this is greater specificity; but to make agreements more specific is often too time-consuming and may lead to rigid agreements that will soon become obsolete. A case might be made that the Yalta agreements, in part, involved unintentional misunderstanding rather than deliberate violation. Stalin's view of the world may have led him to believe that the Western leaders expected him to exercise total political control wherever they let him maintain *de facto* military control. He may have thought that the agreed principles contradicting this were only for domestic consumption in the West and that the leading Western statesmen could not be so naïve as to expect him to tolerate Capitalist parties in areas that they left to his sole control. Therefore, when he set out to collect what (he could have thought) had been implicitly granted to him at Yalta, he may have felt that the disappointment of the Western leaders was feigned. More likely, however, Stalin knew that most Western leaders expected him to act differently.

The second risk, that of deliberate violation, is of course not confined to agreements in principle—the most explicit details may be violated, too. But as long as an agreement in principle is

[2] Philip E. Mosley, *The Kremlin and World Politics* (New York: Vintage Books, 1960), pp. 25–26.

being observed in letter though not in spirit, the government of
the aggrieved country will find it more difficult to prove intentional
violation, both to satisfy itself and to convince its allies or domestic
opinion.

Winston Churchill may have sensed this difficulty in the spring
of 1945, when he tried to convince President Harry Truman that
American forces in Germany should not be withdrawn to the
occupation line previously agreed to with the Soviet Union, until
Soviet behavior in Eastern Europe conformed better to the Western
understanding of the Yalta agreement. On May 12, Churchill
cabled to the President: "I have always worked for friendship with
Russia, but, like you, I feel deep anxiety because of their misinterpretation of the Yalta decisions. . . . Surely, it is vital now to
come to an understanding with Russia, or see where we are with
her, before we weaken our armies mortally or retire to the zones
of occupation."[3]

Churchill's recommendation might have found greater support
within the American government had he been able to list a number
of clear-cut violations of the Yalta agreement instead of having to
refer to Soviet "misinterpretation." For example, there was a
White House meeting on April 23, 1945, where the Secretary of
State, Edward Stettinius, said that the Russians had "receded"
from the Yalta agreement on the Polish question and that their
insistence on having the Communist Lublin group accepted as the
Polish government was "directly contrary to the Yalta understanding." But not all those advising President Truman in this meeting
agreed with Secretary Stettinius' interpretation. According to
Charles Bohlen's notes of the meeting, Admiral Leahy said that
"he had left Yalta with the impression that the Soviet government
had no intention of permitting a free government to operate in
Poland, and that he would have been surprised had the Soviet
government behaved any differently than it had. He thought the
agreements were susceptible to 'two interpretations'. . . and that
a break would be serious, but that 'we should tell them that we
stood for free and independent Poland.' "[4]

[3] Winston S. Churchill, *Triumph and Tragedy* (Boston: Houghton Mifflin,
1953), pp. 573–74.
[4] Walter Millis (ed.), *The Forrestal Diaries* (New York: Viking, 1951), pp.
49, 51.

There is further evidence that the ambiguity of the Yalta agreement inhibited the American government from opposing the Soviet take-over in Poland more forcefully along the lines suggested by Churchill. At the end of May, 1945, prior to the Potsdam Conference, President Truman sent Joseph E. Davies, former U.S. Ambassador in Moscow, on a special mission to see Churchill. Davies, according to his own report of this mission, told Churchill that the President "wanted to know exactly what the engagements and agreements with the Soviets were. If there was disagreement as to what they were, he wanted to clarify that situation definitely, if possible." After having listened to Churchill's complaints about Russian violation, Davies gave him his personal reaction, that "it was not the facts, so much as the interpretation of the facts, which might have a destructive effect upon all hope for a decent, just peace structure for humanity. . . ." Davies added that, in his opinion, "American armies would promptly be withdrawn to the occupational zones agreed upon. . . . If agreements now entered into were clearly defined between the three great Powers and if such agreements were violated in such a way as to establish clearly that any great Power was bent on world domination hostile to the American way of life, then and only then, would the American people accept the possibility of having their armed forces fighting in Europe."[5]

One should not confuse, however, the risks inherent in agreements in principle with the risks of exchanging possession for a promise. The exchange of possession for a promise played an even more important role in the Western disappointment with the wartime and early postwar agreements with the Soviet Union. Or more precisely, many of these agreements compounded the two risks: possession (or potential possession) was exchanged for a promise that had been spelled out only in general principles. Had the promise at least been specific, it would have been easier to halt the exchange (as Churchill had urged in vain).

[5] U.S. Department of State, *Foreign Relations of the United States: The Conference of Berlin (Potsdam) 1945* (Washington, 1960), I, 68, 71, 73–74.

DISPUTES ABOUT SPECIFICITY

Western diplomats, having learnt the dangers of ambiguous agreements with Communist governments, usually insist on detailed and specific language in any new agreement. Since Communist negotiators tend to resist specificity, this can lead to prolonged disputes as to how specific the text of an accord should be made.

However, such disputes are essentially a symptom of disagreement about the substance, not the form, of the settlement. This is the reason why they are so common and take up such an inordinate amount of time in East-West negotiations, whereas they are rare between Western nations. For if nations are agreed on a bargain they wish to conclude, there should, on the one hand, be little objection to spelling it out in detail and, on the other, somewhat less interest in recording the details. When the Soviet delegate in disarmament conferences protests against the Western efforts to specify control provisions, he is right in saying that there ought to be trust to make such detailed commitments unnecessary. If there was trust, however, there would be not only less interest in specificity on the Western side but also fewer objections to specificity by the Soviets. By refusing to have an agreement recorded in detail, the Soviets indicate that agreement on these points, in fact, does not exist.

The government opposed to specificity expects that it might later want to give the agreement another meaning than that which the opponent tries to read in; but during the negotiations it does not want to avow the latent disagreement. (If the latent disagreement was avowed, the dispute on how specific the treaty should be made would turn into a dispute about substance.) The government in favor of specificity expects to make a violation of its understanding of the agreement less likely, or at least less costly to itself. The very fact that the opponent explicitly subscribed to the understanding will make it somewhat harder for him not to comply. The more flagrant the violation, the easier it is for the victim to rule out misunderstanding and to enlist some support from those who believe—for moral or political reasons—that agreements should generally be kept.

In agreements between Western governments, a high degree of specificity is sometimes desired, not so much to discourage violations or to prevent misunderstandings, but to clarify the domestic consequences of the international undertaking and to enable government officials to implement the accord in full detail. In contrast to East-West negotiations, however, the details can usually be settled in drafting committees or by groups of experts, since the original lack of specificity in the preliminary accord is merely an expedient and does not cover up some fundamental disagreement. Within the European Communities, the specification of details in agreements-in-principle is an important function of the supranational institutions (such as the Commission of the Common Market). The ministers of the Six (participating countries) prepare the broad outlines of an accord and settle the essential bargains, after which the supranational executives take over to complete a draft agreement.

Although Communists are known for exploiting ambiguities in agreements, they do not always prefer less specificity than Westerners. The nuclear test-ban conference provides not only examples of issues on which the Soviet Union wanted ambiguous language but also examples where the West preferred ambiguity.

In the fall of 1958, at the very beginning of the test-ban conference, the American and British delegates fought hard (and successfully) to win Soviet consent for inclusion into the draft treaty of many articles containing specific control provisions. On other articles in the test-ban treaty, however, it was Tsarapkin, the Soviet delegate, who fought for more specific language. For example, in January, 1959, the British delegate proposed that an article be worded so that "each of the parties" to the treaty would agree to the installation of the detection system. Tsarapkin objected to the phrase "each of the parties" and asked that it be replaced with a specific listing of the three original parties. "An attempt to avoid naming in the treaty the Powers assuming the principal obligation . . . ," Tsarapkin warned, "cannot fail to raise serious doubts about the real purpose of our talks."[6]

[6] Conference on the Discontinuance of Nuclear Weapon Tests, Verbatim Record of the 33d Plenary Meeting, Jan. 9, 1959 (GEN/DNT/PV. 33), p. 5; 35th Plenary Meeting, Jan. 13, 1959, p. 21.

Similarly, in a later phase of this conference, agreement had been reached that the Western powers, the Soviet Union, and the non-nuclear powers should each provide exactly one-third the staff in every control post. Tsarapkin did not want to leave the selection of the last third to the discretion of the chief administrator of the detection system. He demanded more specific language according to which the last third was to be subdivided into three parts between nationals from Communist, Western, and non-aligned countries: "We cannot rely on spoken words. Of course, you speak fine words, Mr. Wadsworth, about not seeking advantages for yourselves. . . . Let us put these fine words—we agree with them—into the treaty."[7]

There is a special reason why Western and Soviet negotiators took alternating roles in the test-ban conference, in demanding specific treaty language on issues where the opponent preferred ambiguity. In the 1958–60 version of the test-ban treaty, many of the articles had the purpose of influencing the action of an arbiter.

In contracts under domestic law, specificity can predetermine the court's interpretation in case of dispute. At least, it will make the court's decision more predictable; and the more predictable the outcome in court, the less likely is litigation to begin with. The situation is similar between governments. Specificity can be used to bind an arbiter to the preferred interpretation of an agreement, while ambiguous language leaves him more freedom. Some international arbiters are reluctant to become involved in disputes between governments and often choose an easy way out by claiming that the issue is beyond their jurisdiction. If a party fears that this might happen, it will try to spell out or make mandatory those actions by the arbiter that are in its interest. In the Laos conference of 1961–62, this objective lay behind the Western insistence on a detailed description of the rules of access and reporting functions of the International Control Commission.

On the other hand, a negotiator may be basically distrustful of an arbiter, fearing that he might assume too much power in pursuit of his own ambitions or favor the opponent. In this case, specificity will be demanded in order to reduce the arbiter's freedom and to

[7] 164th Plenary Meeting, Feb. 2, 1960, p. 19. (This was before the Soviet Union withdrew its agreement to a single neutral administrator.)

curtail his discretion. This is what Tsarapkin had in mind in the above example, when he objected to leaving the selection of the last third of control personnel to a neutral administrator, albeit with the unwritten understanding that Communist, Western, and neutral nationals should be equally represented.

CONSENSUS ON AMBIGUITY

Two consequences of ambiguity have been distinguished so far: (1) the parties have an honest misunderstanding about implications that the agreement fails to spell out; or (2) one party, while knowing what its opponent expected of the bargain, may pretend that it had a different understanding of it (i.e., the ambiguities are exploited to cover up a deliberate violation). There is a third possibility: the parties to the agreement know that the ambiguous terms mean different things to each of them. It may be more appropriate to call this *equivocality* than ambiguity. Equivocal language is used to cover up disagreement on issues which must be included for some reason in a larger settlement or which must be dealt with as if there was agreement. An equivocal agreement is similar to a partial agreement that leaves certain undecided issues for future negotiation, with the difference that the equivocal terms serve to cover up differences rather than mark them for future resolution.

According to a French saying, international agreements would be impossible without conflicting mental reservations. Indeed, there is often complicity in creating the alleged misunderstanding. The parties knowingly choose equivocal terms so that they can pretend to agree even where they continue to disagree. As Lester Pearson recalled from his diplomatic experience:

I know that there have been occasions, and I have been concerned with one or two, when, as the lesser of two evils, words were used in recording the results of negotiations or discussion whose value lay precisely in the fact that they were imprecise, that they could be interpreted somewhat freely and therefore could be used not so much to record agreement as to conceal a disagreement which it was desired to play down and which, it was hoped, would disappear in time. It is a practice, however, which is only rarely justified.[8]

[8] Lester B. Pearson, *Diplomacy in the Nuclear Age* (Cambridge, Mass.: Harvard University Press, 1949), pp. 47–48.

A recent example may be the reference to a possible link between the partial test-ban treaty and a non-aggression pact, which the Western and Soviet negotiators put into their joint communiqué of July 25, 1963, when they announced that the treaty had been initialed. The Soviets had tried to link the test ban with a non-aggression pact between NATO and the Warsaw Treaty countries, but the United States and Great Britain were opposed. When Khrushchev finally realized that he could not exploit the Western desire for a test ban with such a tie-in, he must have wanted to conceal his failure. The Western powers possibly cooperated in saving him embarrassment (perhaps they thought it was the price for the test ban) by agreeing to the following equivocal language in their communiqué: ". . . the three delegations discussed the Soviet proposal relating to a pact of nonaggression. . . . [They] have agreed fully to inform their respective allies in the two organizations concerning these talks and to consult with them about continuing discussions on this question with the purpose of achieving agreement satisfactory to all participants."

Incidentally, one should not confuse this use of equivocal terms in agreements with equivocal negotiating positions. Ambiguity and equivocality in negotiating positions serve other purposes, such as to maintain flexibility during the bargaining process or to probe the opponent's position.

RESIDUAL DISAGREEMENT

Even an agreement whose terms are explicit often leaves some issues unsettled, despite the fact that they are neither extraneous to its subject matter nor trivial. However, these issues may have been clarified by the negotiations that led to such a partial agreement. The residual disagreement can be explicit in the sense that certain issues are marked "for future negotiation," implicit in the agreement's equivocal language, or latent if differences originally ignored or viewed as unimportant later turn into serious disputes.

Residual disagreement is by no means universal. With the benefit of historical hindsight we are able to identify a number of negotiations that settled in a definitive way all issues with which they were concerned. Examples can be found among the voluntary transfers of territory, such as Secretary Seward's negotiations for the purchase of Alaska, or the U.S.-Danish negotiations in 1916 and 1917 for the purchase of the Virgin Islands.

Other agreements left issues unsettled both explicitly and implicitly. For example, the Hague agreement of 1949 between the Netherlands and Indonesia explicitly reserved the disposition of West New Guinea for future negotiations.[9] Most agreements fall into this middle group where a number of important issues are settled but a significant amount of disagreement is left.

On the other extreme there are those pseudo-agreements which do not settle any of the important conflicts at issue. An example, now almost forgotten because the treaty was so meaningless, is the Four-Power Pact of 1933 between Germany, France, Great Britain, and Italy, committing the signatories—among other things—"to make every effort to pursue, within the framework of the League of Nations, a policy of effective cooperation . . . [and] to ensure the success of the Disarmament Conference." Some contemporary observers recognized the emptiness of this treaty. For example, the London *Times* reported from Paris: "It is no doubt true that the Four-Power Pact in its final form adds little to the existing machinery of consultation, and commends itself to some of its critics chiefly on the ground that it seems harmless." But an editorial of the *New York Times* was slightly less discerning: "To have induced France and Great Britain, Germany and Italy to underwrite the peace of Europe for ten years is a wonderful achievement, full of reassurance. . . . It is an agreement dovetailed into the existing international organization for peace, and designed to strengthen it. Thus it embraces and must keenly interest the whole world in its scope and effect."[10]

A more recent example of an agreement in which the residual

[9] Article II of The Hague agreement reads: "With regard to the residency of New Guinea it is decided: (a) in view of the fact that it has not yet been possible to reconcile the views of the parties . . . that the Status Quo of the Residency of New Guinea will be maintained with the stipulation that within one year from the date of the transfer of sovereignty the question of the political status of New Guinea be determined through negotiations between . . . Indonesia and the Netherlands."

[10] *Times* (London), June 7, 1933; *New York Times,* June 3. The text of the Pact can be found in Hamilton Fish Armstrong, *Hitler's Reich* (New York: Macmillan, 1933), pp. 67 ff.

disagreement outweighed the issues that were settled is the U.S.-Soviet Joint Statement of Agreed Principles on disarmament, negotiated between John McCloy and Valerian Zorin during the summer of 1961. Of course, as its name suggests, this Joint Statement was never meant to settle details. But even as a broad framework for later negotiation, it contained more issues of dispute and disagreements on concepts than genuine understandings on principles. In part, it covered up differences by avoiding specificity; in part, it expressed agreement on general and complete disarmament which can at best be a distant goal of which East and West must have a totally different conception; and in part, the residual disagreement (about verification) was made clear. Paradoxically, this last aspect—the agreement on disagreement—seemed the most important result of this Joint Statement. As McCloy himself put it: "True, the issue of inspection and control remains unsettled; but the McCloy-Zorin exchanges brought into the open for the first time the essential difference between the Soviet and Allied concepts of inspection and control, and as a result it should now be possible to attack the realities rather than the semantics of the problem."[11] However, the subsequent course of disarmament negotiations has shown that the agreement on disagreement did not make it easier "to attack the realities"; all it did—and this may have been worthwhile—was to clarify the dispute for the benefit of allied and non-aligned nations.

Agreements on disagreement might serve other purposes, apart from focusing future negotiations on the crucial disputes. They can be used to isolate unsettled issues so as to facilitate agreement on other matters. In peace conferences, refractory disputes are often reserved for future negotiations in order to expedite the conclusion of a treaty. It is true that such leftovers sometimes sour postwar relations for years or decades or even become the cause of another war. The fate of Trieste, left in the unresolved state of a "Free

[11] John J. McCloy, "Balance Sheet on Disarmament," *Foreign Affairs* (April, 1962), p. 358. Actually, the disagreement on verification was expressed in a subsequent exchange of letters between McCloy and Zorin rather than in the Joint Statement itself. The Soviet position was that only the demolition of arms need be verified. The United States maintained that verification must also be used to guard against exceeding the agreed level of armament by clandestine replacement or other means.

City" in the Italian peace treaty after World War II, disturbed Italian-Yugoslav relations until 1954. The disposition of the Saar territory between France and Germany was left somewhat indeterminate after both world wars. After World War II, this issue stood in the way of a French-German *rapprochement* until a final settlement could be reached in 1955. Frequently, however, any agreement would be impossible without the separation of refractory conflicts. The Antarctica Treaty of 1959, which reserves this polar region for non-military uses, states explicitly (Article IV) that the treaty shall not affect any of the previous claims to territorial sovereignty. Had the old territorial claims and disputes not been exempted, Argentina, Chile, and perhaps some of the other signatories could not have been brought into accord. Similarly, the Treaty of Rome establishing the European Economic Community (the Common Market) could, in all likelihood, not have been concluded without postponing agreement on a common agricultural policy until the end of the first phase in this three-phase program for economic integration.

What negotiators often fail to realize is that they may settle an issue inadvertently, even though they formally exempt it from an agreement or explicitly reserve it for future negotiations. The Yugoslav and Western occupation zones in the Free City of Trieste closely predetermined the final partition of the city; the Antarctica Treaty will probably weaken the territorial claims notwithstanding the special exemption; and the Potsdam Conference of 1945, by leaving "the final delimitation" of the German-Polish frontier to "the peace settlement," carried the administrative boundaries of Poland from the fluid postwar situation into an indefinite future at which time the *de facto* borders will have become as rigid as state frontiers agreed to in a treaty.

Churchill, for one, realized at the Potsdam Conference that the postponement of a settlement for Poland's western frontier might, in fact, make the existing administrative boundaries permanent. The minutes of the session at which this issue was discussed record that "the President said he did not see the urgency of the matter. It would be helpful to have a preliminary discussion and the matter would not finally be settled until the peace conference." Churchill, however, now arguing more with Truman than with Stalin, said (according to these minutes) "that with great respect he wished to explain the urgency of the matter. If the settlement of the question were delayed the present local situation would be consolidated. Poles would be digging themselves in and taking effective steps to make themselves the sole masters of this territory. The longer the problem waited the more difficult it would be to settle it."[12]

In other negotiations, it is more appropriate to regard a settlement with important residual disagreements as a phase in a continuing confrontation of the same powers. The residual conflict is not so much postponed as channeled into new directions, and new rules for handling it are agreed upon. For example, the 1954 agreement on Indochina left Laos' position between the Communist camp and the West uncertain. (Laos' fate was undetermined because the 1954 agreement linked it to the then unpredictable internal power-struggle between Communist and anti-Communist forces, although some of the signatories, particularly Great Britain, expected that it would be neutral.) As a result, East-West bargaining about Laos continued almost without pause for another eight years, both at the negotiating table and through the confrontation of military forces in the field.

To recapitulate the various forms of residual disagreements, we might distinguish among five different reasons why negotiators may settle for an incomplete agreement. First, the parties may want to clarify what they disagree about so as to better focus future negotiations on the unsettled dispute. Second, they may want to postpone refractory disputes for future negotiations in order not to hold up agreement on related issues that are ripe for settlement. Third, they may want to clarify their disagreement in order to contain it—to keep their broader relations, as it were, uncontaminated. Fourth, they may use their partial agreement to place the residual

---

[12] *Foreign Relations of the United States: The Conference of Berlin* (*Potsdam*) *1945*, II, 249. This view was also expressed in a British aide-memoire to the American government: "If the British and the United States governments allow the permanent settlement of the frontier to be postponed indefinitely, only putting their views on record for the present, the difficulties of settlement at a later date will be aggravated. . . . In these circumstances the assurance given by M. Vyshinsky to the effect that the presence of Polish Administration does not prejudice the fate of German territory, which is for discussion at the Peace Conference, is of little practical value" (*ibid.*, I, 778–79).

dispute into a new context where it can be handled more safely or more cheaply. Fifth, they may be interested in certain symbolic or hidden implications of having a signed agreement, even though it fails to settle anything.

To clarify this last category, the formality of concluding an agreement must be distinguished from its content. The term *pseudo-agreement* will be used here to designate a pact which is all formality, which does not record any new settlement. That is to say, a pseudo-agreement contains no new exchanges of complementary interests or new combinations of common interests. Nonetheless, the parties may read certain implications into it. If all parties had the same hidden content in mind and were mutually aware of this, they would in fact have concluded a tacit bargain for which the pseudo-agreement might serve as a symbol. But in international relations such a meeting of minds is rare. Usually the parties attribute no significant bargains to a pseudo-agreement, and if they do, their attributions are likely to differ. For example, in 1933 Mussolini may have promoted the Four-Power Pact simply because he felt that he was gaining in prestige by concluding a treaty with the other leading European powers, although it was only a façade.

The conclusion of a pseudo-agreement among powers whose relations are strained is sometimes construed as though these powers had exchanged promises to be more accommodating toward each other in the future. A non-aggression pact between NATO and the Warsaw Pact countries might be an example.

Similarly, statesmen may read into a pseudo-agreement a mutual commitment to reach significant agreements in the future. According to this view, the pseudo-agreement will act as a catalyst for some real settlements. Many Westerners felt this way about negotiations with the East—in the 1950s more so than today. Agreements with the Russians were sought after, not for their content, but "to make further agreement easier." Henry Kissinger pointed out the dangers of this view:

> The inevitable consequence of such a conviction is that more ingenuity is expended in finding things to agree on, no matter how trivial, than in coming to grips with the issues that have caused the tensions. In the process, a curious distortion takes place. The difficulties which are

"ironed out" are often soluble only because they are inconsequential. But the mere fact that they are settled is taken as a proof of the possibility of "progress."[13]

Sometimes there is an additional factor which accounts for the interest in agreement as a formality apart from content. As will be discussed in more detail later, those who are involved in negotiations may come to feel that their efforts failed should the conference end without an agreement, particularly if the negotiations have been going on for a long time. Consequently, they become anxious to reach some kind of a formal accord because they regard this formality as a token of success, independent of the terms of the agreement.

CARRY–OVER FOR FUTURE NEGOTIATIONS

The amount of agreement reached and the residual disagreement left do not encompass the entire outcome of negotiations. In addition, there may be latent effects which impinge on the course of subsequent negotiations. Even if a conference ends without any agreement—neither an explicit nor a tacit one, neither a specific nor an ambiguous one—the issues dealt with may have been permanently altered. This effect of negotiation is latent, since it materializes only if a future conference leads to an agreement on the same issues.

Carry-over effects result from the fact that a government normally changes its position between the beginning and the end of a conference—that is, a negotiating position is rarely totally inflexible. If the conference ends without agreement and the same issue is taken up again in later negotiations (perhaps with some new participants), the government is likely to start out with a position that is closer to the one it held at the end than at the beginning of the previous conference. There are three reasons for this.

First, there is often considerable justification in viewing the prior and succeeding conferences as a single negotiation. Given such a view, a government may feel that it would be improper to

[13] Henry A. Kissinger, *The Necessity for Choice* (New York: Harper, 1961), pp. 189–90.

abandon its final position from the initial conference, in the same sense that it may be considered improper to withdraw an offer after it has been accepted or to revert to a harder position from a more conciliatory one during a single negotiation.

Second, the terminal position in the original conference may become part of a government's propaganda stance or of its public image, thus acquiring a certain rigidity, like a dogma. Officials often tend to become personally committed to certain views as to what the goals and negotiating positions of their government should be, and these commitments may survive into the next negotiation.

Third, the internal decision-making process in a government may suffer from inertia or work at cross-purposes, so that the only internally agreed position for the new conference is the one left over from the previous one. Also, broad objectives and definitions of issues have a certain inertia, because revising them would require changes in official terminology, doctrine, budget allocations, or related policies—all of which are hard to push through without the pressures of ongoing negotiations.

East-West disarmament negotiations, ever since 1946, produced a considerable carry-over effect from one conference to the next, both on specific positions and on broad objectives and definitions of issues. Although the London disarmament conference of 1957 did not result in any agreement, it predetermined important positions for the test-ban conference which began a year later.[14] And on general disarmament, the United States became increasingly committed between 1959 and 1962 to the principle of "general and complete disarmament," as a result of negotiatory pressures from the Soviet Union. By 1962, this commitment had acquired a permanence that is likely to survive from conference to conference, as if it had been an original American objective of long standing.

Some observers of the Geneva disarmament talks feel that the Russians, too, are not merely revising their proposals occasionally

[14] This carry-over has been analyzed by Ciro E. Zoppo, *The Issue of Nuclear Test Cessation at the London Disarmament Conference of 1957: A Study in East-West Negotiation* (RAND Corporation Research Memorandum 2821 [Santa Monica, Calif., 1961]).

but are gradually changing their objectives and doctrine, learning that they indeed have some common interest in the disarmament objectives advanced by the West. At the present time, it remains to be seen whether this education toward a new doctrine will permeate from the Soviet delegation in Geneva to the inner decision-making councils in Moscow.

The question of carrying over a position from one phase of negotiation into the next became important in connection with a Western proposal on the Berlin issue. Toward the end of the Geneva Foreign Ministers' Conference in 1959, the three Western powers advanced a proposal for a five-year interim arrangement, providing (among other things) for East German "agents" of the Soviet Union to control traffic and for curbs on propaganda and intelligence activities in Berlin. The Soviet Union rejected this. Half a year later the three Western Powers and the German Federal Republic made a declaration in Paris which abandoned the interim proposal. The Bonn government was reported to be jubilant that this position would not be carried over into the negotiations in 1960, since it considered the political curbs on West Berlin and the partial recognition of East Germany quite dangerous. In January, 1960, Adenauer stated very bluntly, not only that it would be false to resume summit negotiations at the point where the Foreign Ministers' Conference was broken off, but also that the Western proposal had been rejected and therefore "no longer existed."[15]

There are other long-term effects from negotiation, in addition to the carry-over of positions and objectives into subsequent conferences. A government may reveal its estimate of the balance of power by the way in which it negotiates, and this will affect its bargaining strength in the future. Also, the tactics that it uses will be remembered by other parties and influence their expectations when they deal with this government again. This "bargaining reputation" will be discussed later, but first we have to analyze why governments enter negotiations.

For negotiations to start on some issue, one of the parties, or a mediator, must take the initiative. There has to be an explicit

[15] Quoted from Hans Speier, *Divided Berlin, The Anatomy of Soviet Blackmail* (New York: Praeger, 1961), p. 80.

proposal to hold a conference, to begin diplomatic talks, or at least the new issue has to be introduced into ongoing discussions. Negotiations do not start accidentally or through forces of nature. Therefore the government taking the initiative must have an objective in mind for starting them, and the governments joining in must have their reasons for participating.

CHAPTER 3

FIVE OBJECTIVES

As the richness of diplomatic history illustrates, there is an enormous diversity in international negotiations. Governments are constantly engaged in diplomatic bargaining, ranging from casual contacts to large formal conferences. In order to bring out common traits and render this variety more manageable, one must distinguish among different purposes for which the parties negotiate. The aims or objectives of governments in international negotiations can be classified adequately into five types: (1) extension agreements, (2) normalization agreements, (3) redistribution agreements, (4) innovation agreements, and (5) effects not concerning agreements. In reality, the negotiating parties always pursue a mixture of several of these types of objectives, although one of them may predominate. Moreover, in one and the same negotiation, the dominant objective of one party is often of a different type from that of the other party.

Negotiations for the purpose of an *extension* agreement are meant to continue the "normal"; that is, to prolong existing arrangements which are acceptable to some, if not all, parties involved. Examples are the extension of tariff agreements, the renewal of rights to maintain an overseas military base, or the replacement of important officials in international organizations. Negotiations for the purpose of a *normalization* agreement are meant to terminate the abnormal or to formalize arrangements tacitly arrived at, such as to stop fighting through a cease-fire or truce, to re-establish diplomatic relations, or to end a temporary occupation in exchange for a military alliance and regularize other postwar uncertainties through a peace treaty.

Negotiations for the purpose of a *redistribution* agreement are characterized by a demand of an offensive side for a change in its favor, at the expense of a defensive side, the change consisting of a new distribution of territory, political influence, institutional powers and rights, economic and military assets, or the like. Essentially, what the offensive side gains, the defensive side loses; hence the offensive side has to couple its demand with the threat of causing worse consequences if the demand is refused. Negotiations for the purpose of an *innovation* agreement deal with the setting up of new relationships or obligations between the parties, with the founding of a new institution, or with a new arrangement for controlling objects and areas. In contrast to redistribution, the change supposedly works to the advantage of all parties concerned, though not necessarily to equal advantage.[1] Finally, parties that negotiate for the sake of other *effects not concerning agreement* are interested in such results as propaganda, intelligence, or dissuading the opponent from the use of force.

EXTENSION

The following recent negotiations are examples in which the extension type of objective predominated for both sides: the renewal of cultural exchange agreements between the United States and the Soviet Union, the extension of status-of-forces agreements between the United States and some of its allies, the renewal of the agreement for the sharing of financial burdens within NATO, and the replacement of Trygve Lie by Dag Hammarskjöld as Secretary-

---

[1] Thomas C. Schelling (*The Strategy of Conflict*, p. 21) introduces the distinction between the "efficiency" aspect of bargaining and the "distributional" aspect: the former consists of exploring for mutually profitable adjustments; in the latter the better bargain for one party means less for the other. Innovation negotiations are clearly dominated by "efficiency" bargaining, while redistribution negotiations are dominated by "distributional" bargaining. In extension and normalization negotiations, these two aspects are usually mixed. There are, of course, many gradations between a pure redistribution and innovation negotiation, ranging from exclusively "distributional" negotiation, through mixed "distributional-efficiency" bargaining, to purely "efficiency" cases.

General of the United Nations. The outcome of such negotiations may be an agreement that simply confirms the status quo or one that makes slight changes in the existing relationship. (If there are major changes, the outcome represents a redistribution or innovation.) The initiative to negotiate might be taken by any one of the parties or by an international institution.

If no agreement is reached, the result is a change from the status quo; that is, there will be an interruption of customary relations between the parties or a discontinuation of the existing arrangements that were based on earlier agreements. Sometimes this interruption is avoided by a tacit understanding to extend the status quo temporarily; or to put it differently, the negotiations result in a tacit extension. The principal incentives to agreement are the disadvantages of interrupting existing arrangements, as for example, the economic losses from an expired trade agreement, the inconvenience of an unfilled vacancy in an international organization, or the military disadvantage to one side and financial loss to the other if an agreement for a foreign base is not extended.

An important characteristic of negotiation for an extension is the strong influence exercised by the previous agreement. The old agreement limits the area of dispute, introduces weighty precedents, and may even provide specific means for settling differences regarding the renewal. For the replacement of officials in an international organization, for example, the institutional framework often circumscribes the choices and methods of negotiation quite narrowly. Sometimes there are arbitration procedures to bring in third parties if the original parties fail to reach agreement among themselves.

NORMALIZATION

Examples of negotiations where the main objective of all parties was a normalization agreement, are Litvinov's talks in Washington in 1933 leading to American recognition of the Soviet Union, the negotiations for the peace treaty with Japan in 1951, the negotiations between Egypt, Israel, and United Nations mediators on the armistice of 1949, the Panmunjom conference on the Korean armistice, and (to a large extent) the 1961–62 Geneva conference on Laos. At peace conferences, however, the principal parties frequently have other objectives, apart from normalization. The Paris Peace Conference of 1919–20 and the Potsdam Conference with its sequels from 1945 through 1946, for example, served purposes of redistribution and innovation as well as normalization. The League of Nations, an important issue at the Paris Peace Conference of 1919, is an example of an innovation.

In situations where fighting will continue or threatens to resume unless agreement is reached, public opinion and other domestic forces may exert considerable pressures on the negotiators to agree. Often, there are important asymmetries in the susceptibility to such pressures. American negotiators at Panmunjom and their superiors in Washington felt very strongly the yearning back home for an end to the fighting, but their Chinese and North Korean opponents —while sensitive to the military weakness of their side—remained relatively immune to popular sentiment in their countries.

Apart from these pressures for agreement, negotiations for the purpose of normalization are strongly influenced by the *instability* of the "abnormal" situation they are supposed to settle. If fighting continues while negotiations are prolonged, one side may gain through force what it failed to gain through bargaining. Or, at least, it may shake the opponent's confidence in his ability to defend his military position and thus make him anxious to reach an agreement. After a temporary suspension of fighting, however, the threat of a resumption of hostilities tends to become less effective for bargaining purposes, unless supported by existing military capabilities or preparations that make a new offensive both likely and dangerous to the opponent.

The Korean armistice negotiations would probably have led to an agreement much sooner, or on terms more favorable to the United Nations side, if the latter had been able to demonstrate to the Communist side that it might launch a major offensive. In the spring of 1953, when General Mark Clark as the UN Commander in Korea met President Dwight D. Eisenhower, he had prepared "a detailed estimate of the forces and plans required to obtain military victory in Korea should the new administration decide to take such a course." But according to General Clark, the newly elected President showed no interest in using the threat of such an offensive to exert pressure on the truce negotiations: "The question of how much it would take to win the war was never raised."[2]

In the event that no normalization agreement is reached, the "abnormal" situation will initially continue; but because of its instability, further changes usually ensue in short time. After the failure of cease-fire negotiations, continued fighting will change the fortunes of war; after the failure of truce negotiations, the cease-fire may erupt again into fighting. Conversely, hostilities may gradually subside despite the failure of negotiations, so that a tacit truce will in fact be established.

REDISTRIBUTION

Negotiation for the purpose of redistribution is characterized by a clear and permanent division between an offensive side and a defensive side. The demand by the offensive side is often directed against one of the weaker or more exposed allies on the defensive side. In the most acute form of this type of negotiation, the offensive side presents its central demand in the form of an ultimatum (that is, a position put forward as final), with only ancillary issues left for bargaining, and it not only makes its threat highly specific but also announces that the threat will be carried out at a definite date unless the central demand is satisfied.

If the offensive side is successful, agreement in this type of negotiation will lead to a change in the status quo, as the defensive side complies with all or part of the demand. The classic illustrations are the Munich agreement and its sequel in March, 1939, when President Hácha of Czechoslovakia was forced to surrender the rest of his country to Hitler. There are other illustrations, however, of a far less aggressive character and an entirely different political tenor. For example, Iceland's claim in 1958 to a twelve-mile zone for exclusive fishery was backed up by the threat of force against British vessels. After some resistance, Great Britain, as the defensive side, essentially complied with the Icelandic demands.

If the offensive side is unsuccessful, an agreement may still re-

[2] Mark W. Clark, *From the Danube to the Yalu* (New York: Harper, 1954), p. 233.

sult, whereby the defensive side consents to exchange some face-saving formula for a formal withdrawal of the demand. For example, the negotiations for the lifting of the Berlin blockade of 1948–49 resulted in an agreement by which the Western powers consented to a Foreign Ministers' conference with the Soviet Union, which was to start eleven days after the termination of the blockade and discuss problems regarding Germany and Berlin. (This conference reached no agreement of substance.) However, if either side is stubborn, redistribution negotiations may end without any agreement. In this case, there are two basic outcomes: either the status quo is preserved tacitly, which means that the offensive side gives in completely, or the offensive side carries out its threat or part of it. When the Soviet-Finish negotiations in the fall of 1939 failed to induce Finland to cede the territories demanded by Russia, the Russians carried out their threat and attacked Finland.

There are some distinguishing features between negotiations for a redistribution and those for an innovation. In redistribution, the conflicting interest is the principal topic of negotiation, whereas the common interest remains tacit or is shunted into peripheral bargaining. The conflicting interest simply stems from the demand by the offensive side. The common interest lies in the mutual desire to avoid violence; that is, the offensive side would rather keep its gains more modest than carry out its threat, and the defensive side would rather relinquish something than challenge the threat. Occasionally, a complementary interest in an exchange is added to this basic common interest, such as the formal withdrawal of a threat in exchange for a face-saving formula, or the preservation of long-term friendship in exchange for a modest concession. (This was the idea of the British government when Mussolini demanded a free hand in Abyssinia: to buy Italy's friendship by granting Mussolini part of what he asked for.)

In negotiations for an innovation, on the other hand, it is the common interest, or alleged common interest, which constitutes the primary topic, while the conflicting interests are relegated to the details. Threats are scarcely used for innovations. But for redistributions, the offensive side must always threaten, or at least issue strong warnings.[3]

[3] A distinction between "threats" and "warnings" is developed in chap. 5.

A demand for institutional changes in an international organization may have the objective of a redistribution of political power. In contrast to institutional innovations, such changes are clearly to the disadvantage of the defensive side. They are the issue of conflict, while the common interest, if any, is extraneous to them. An example is the Soviet demand that the United Nations Secretariat be headed by a "troika" instead of by a single, independent Secretary-General. Since this change was firmly opposed by many UN members, including all the other permanent members of the Security Council who had the power to veto it, the Soviet negotiators had no chance of success unless they could find an effective threat.

After the sudden death of Dag Hammarskjöld in 1961, it seemed as if the opportunity for such a threat had come. As expected, the Soviet negotiators tried to tie their demand for a "troika" to the threat that they would veto the replacement of the single UN Secretary-General. In other words, they tried to link a redistribution agreement on the "troika" with an extension agreement for the staffing of the UN Secretariat. In the former they were opposed by parties that could veto the redistribution; in the latter they, in turn, could veto the kind of staffing that the same parties wanted. In principle, a tie-in between an extension and a redistribution agreement can be very effective—the offensive side trades its consent to the extension in exchange for the demanded redistribution. (This is the essence of labor-management negotiations.) In this particular case, however, the tie-in could have been used for a compromise only, since the "troika" could not be traded for the replacement of a *single* Secretary-General, the two being incompatible. As it turned out, the Soviet negotiators lacked the skill to advance their cause significantly by a compromise. (They might have succeeded, for instance, in obtaining a "troika" of powerful Deputy Secretaries, in exchange for their consent to the election of a single Secretary-General.)

There is an interesting difference in the reaction of public opinion to negotiation for normalization and for redistribution. A cease-fire, armistice, or peace treaty—the ostensible goal of negotiation for normalization—is usually supported by public opinion on both sides, and the publicized dispute concerns only the terms for settlement. (An exception is the propagandistically important opposition of Egypt and other Arab countries to a peace treaty with Israel.) In negotiation for redistribution, on the other hand, the offensive side usually appears in the public eye as the disturber of peace—unless the redistribution is aimed at the liberation of occupied areas or colonies. In modern times, if liberation or decolonization can be neither the true objective nor a plausible pretext, it takes someone as bold as Hitler to admit unashamedly that he is making a demand for a change entirely to his advantage. Although Hitler still used the pretense of liberating the Sudeten Germans in the Munich conference, he felt no embarrassment that he had to do without a pretext in the subsequent negotiations with Hácha.

Characteristically, Khrushchev says that his demands for West Berlin aim not for a change of the status quo to his advantage but for a normalization of the aftermath of World War II. As part of this tactic to enlist public support, Khrushchev argues that what he is after in West Berlin is merely to clear up old business: "The need to do away with the vestiges of World War II by signing a German peace treaty."[4] On the surface, Khrushchev's demands for a "free city" of West Berlin could be viewed as a normalization. But the Western powers fear that Khrushchev's real goal is a redistribution: to detach West Berlin from the Federal Republic of Germany—the ally of the West—and gradually to incorporate the city into the Communist bloc. The history of Eastern Europe since World War II gives ample ground for this interpretation.

WHY DOES THE DEFENSIVE SIDE NEGOTIATE AT ALL?

In examining the motives of the defensive side for entering redistribution negotiations, one must distinguish two possibilities. In certain cases, the defensive side may have concluded that it is better to yield, for if it did not, the offensive side would in all likelihood carry out the threat, and this would result in greater losses than yielding would. Here negotiation has the purpose of cutting the losses—for instance, by obtaining a face-saving arrange-

---

[4] *Tass* statement of July 12, 1962. This is a constantly recurrent theme in the Soviet statements on Berlin.

ment or some small compensation, or by improving the prospects for friendly long-term relations with the offensive side.

A recent example is the transfer of West New Guinea in 1962 from Dutch administration to Indonesia. It appeared very likely to the Netherlands and the United States (the latter being largely responsible for the settlement) that Sukarno would carry out his threat and attempt to take West New Guinea by force. Sukarno might, in fact, have welcomed a "war of liberation" to rally his people and cover up economic mismanagement at home. Although the Dutch might have successfully defended the territory (certainly if given American naval help), the losses from doing so seemed greater to the American government than the losses from giving up the territory, because West New Guinea was an economic burden for the Netherlands, and a war with Indonesia would have been costly and might have driven Sukarno closer to the Communists. (Of course, as in all appeasements, there was the question whether it might not do greater harm by setting a bad precedent and encouraging Sukarno to make further territorial demands.)

On the other hand, in many redistribution negotiations the defensive side has concluded that it is better not to yield, either because the costs of yielding seem greater than the costs from whatever the offensive side threatens or because it seems unlikely that the threat will be carried out. In such situations, why should the defensive side want to negotiate at all?

This very question has been a source of prolonged differences between Washington and London on one side and Paris on the other in connection with Khrushchev's demands for Berlin. The French government maintained that it was unwise for the Western powers to enter into or show interest in negotiations. In a speech to the French Parliament in December, 1961, the Foreign Minister, Couve de Murville, explained some of the objections to negotiating on Berlin:

This problem, paradoxically, is whether the French, the Americans, and the British should take the initiative to propose to the Russians the setting-up of a four-power conference. I say "paradoxically" because, after all, it is the Russians who have raised the question of a change of status quo. Looking at it differently, it would mean that we should ask them to discuss their conditions for our staying in Berlin; that is, to discuss the concessions we would have to make to them so that they agree, to a certain extent and perhaps for a certain time only, that our troops can stay and that the freedom of West Berlin thus will remain more or less guaranteed.[5]

One can be more specific about the risks that the defensive side runs by negotiating on a redistribution demand. First, the negotiators of the defensive side might feel they ought to demonstrate flexibility; therefore they offer concessions that go some way toward satisfying the offensive demand. Second, they might lower their expectations and adapt their image of the status quo so as to bring it closer to the opponent's position (a process to be discussed later). Third, their view of the character of the negotiations may gradually change from a redistribution to a normalization. That is, they may come to regard a situation that has been the subject of prolonged negotiations as abnormal. Ergo, they will deem it appropriate to change the status quo so as to normalize it.

Despite these risks of negotiating, the governments of the defensive side may have countervailing reasons for meeting with their opponents, even though they conclude that they need not yield. They may be in favor of negotiation because they think that it has certain advantageous effects unrelated to any agreement. That is, they pursue side-effects. In addition, some Westerners when faced with certain offensive demands favor negotiation in order to find out what the opponent "really" wants. Thus they imply that the opponent could not be so brutish as to want what he in fact keeps demanding. They feel the opponent's true goal must be more reasonable or more realistic, and then a solution satisfactory to both sides could be found.

INNOVATION

Negotiations with the objective of innovation are meant to create a new relationship or new undertakings between parties. They are exemplified by the conferences on the Treaties of Rome to set up

[5] *Journal Officiel de la République Française* (Sénat), Dec. 5, 1961, p. 2297.

the Common Market and Euratom, the discussions on the treaty demilitarizing Antarctica, the conference for the statute for the International Atomic Energy Agency, and the marathon talks for a nuclear test ban. Disarmament negotiations normally pursue a mixture of objectives in which this type predominates.

As to the initiative, it is usually quite clear which party has made the first move proposing the innovation. Sometimes, this initiator continues to push for agreement; at other times, the initiative for the innovation may shift from one side to the other (in contrast to redistribution negotiations, where it is always the offensive side that wants the change). For example, in the nuclear test-ban negotiations it was at first clearly the Soviet Union that was pressing for a ban while the United States remained reluctant; but since 1960 or 1961 these roles have been reversed.

What pressures are available to the parties primarily interested in an innovation, to induce reluctant partners to agree? An important way of exerting pressure is the mobilization of domestic political support among the prospective partners. Jean Monnet's Action Committee for the United States of Europe has been instrumental in rallying the support of important political groups among the Six behind the Treaties of Rome and subsequent steps toward European integration. One of the important functions of the European Parliamentary Assembly in Strasbourg (the parliament of the Six) is the domestic support that it can generate within the member states to strengthen the hand of the European Executives on innovations advancing integration.[6] For innovations in the disarmament field, the initiators seek to exert pressures through public opinion within the countries of reluctant opponents as well as through neutral countries. (In part, these pressures may be designed to make the opponent disarm unilaterally, rather than to force an agreement on him.)

To win over those who hesitate to go along with an innovation, the warning of exclusion is often more effective than pressures

[6] These three Executives (the High Authority of the Coal and Steel Community and the Commissions of the Common Market and Euratom) use resolutions by the European Parliament to defend their position in the Council of Ministers (which represents the six governments). The ministers normally do not want to disregard the views of the European parliamentarians, who are also members of their home parliaments.

of public opinion. A party that is at first reluctant or indifferent toward an innovation may join merely because it is afraid of becoming an outsider.

When President Eisenhower first proposed the creation of an International Atomic Energy Agency in December, 1953, he said that "the United States would be more than willing—it would be proud to take up with the others 'principally involved' the development of plans [for such an agency]. Of those 'principally involved,' the Soviet Union must, of course, be one."[7] The United States government followed up this invitation in a diplomatic exchange with Moscow, but the Soviet government took a negative attitude. Nine months after his initial proposal, President Eisenhower therefore declared: "Although progress in this plan has been impeded by Soviet obstruction and delay, we intend to proceed—*with* the cooperation and participation of the Soviet Union if possible, *without* it if necessary."[8] This warning was given weight by a number of American initiatives: among them the exploratory talks with seven other friendly nations and the rapid expansion, early in 1955, of bilateral agreements between the United States and twenty-four countries for aid on peaceful uses of atomic energy. A year later, the Soviet Union joined in establishing the International Atomic Energy Agency, after it obtained certain concessions modifying the original American design.[9]

In April, 1945, when Molotov came to see President Truman a few days before the United Nations was to be launched at San Francisco, it seemed uncertain whether the Russians would cooperate in creating the new world organization, since deep differences had already arisen over the Yalta agreements. President Truman told Molotov that the United States was determined to go ahead with plans for the world organization, or as the President put it privately to his advisers, that he "intended to go on with

[7] Address by President Eisenhower to the United Nations, Dec. 3, 1953.
[8] The President's press release at the signing of the Atomic Energy Act, Aug. 30, 1954.
[9] In the fall of 1955 the Soviet Union entered the negotiations on the preparation of the statute for the Agency, and in October, 1956, the revised Statute was finally adopted by 81 nations. For an excellent history see Bernard G. Bechhoefer, "Negotiating the Statute of the International Atomic Energy Agency," *International Organization*, XIII (Winter, 1959), 38–59.

the plans for San Francisco and if the Russians did not wish to join us they could go to hell. . . ."[10]

The warning of exclusion, however, is ineffective against a government which thinks the innovation will not be successful (or would not succeed without its participation). A cardinal error of British foreign policy during the 1950s was the belief that European integration would not succeed. In 1950, the British turned down the Franco-German invitation to participate in the negotiations which translated the Schuman Plan into the Coal and Steel Community, and in 1955 they stayed away from the Conference of Messina which established the principles for the European Economic Community and Euratom. Subsequently they sent only an observer to the committee of experts which, on the basis of the Messina principles, prepared the report that led to the Treaties of Rome. And they soon withdrew their observer again when pressed to assume a positive attitude toward European integration.[11]

While the initiator of an innovation will want to have essential parties included, he has to be careful lest his efforts to win over reluctant participants jeopardize his basic goals. In the negotiations for the implementation of the Schuman Plan, Jean Monnet removed the principle of a supra-national authority as a topic of dispute and compromise by making its acceptance the condition for participation in the negotiations. The British refused to meet this condition.[12] It has occasionally been said that such a condition is contrary to diplomatic practice among friendly nations. With perhaps more validity, however, it might be argued that, without violating diplomatic standards, initiators of a new proposal who invite others to discuss its implementation may define the agenda so as to exclude alternatives incompatible with their proposal.

There are many situations where the initiator of an innovation

[10] Harry S Truman, *Memoirs* (Garden City, N.Y.: Doubleday, 1955), I, 80; and Walter Millis (ed.), *The Forrestal Diaries,* p. 50. Three days earlier, however, the President was less sanguine; when Harriman asked him whether America would go ahead with the United Nations plans even if the Russians dropped out, Truman replied the truth of the matter was that without Russia there would not be a world organization (*Memoirs,* I, 72).

[11] Karl Kaiser, *EWG und Freihandelszone* (Leiden: Sythoff, 1963), p. 37.

[12] According to Anthony Nutting (*Europe Will Not Wait* [London: Hollis & Carter, 1960], p. 29), this condition merely provided the British government with the excuse it wanted for staying out.

cannot use the warning of exclusion to win over reluctant parties. The participation of certain countries may be so essential that their exclusion would make negotiations meaningless. In any disarmament negotiation of a global scope, the United States and the Soviet Union, of course, play such a role. So would Communist China and several other powers, if disarmament progressed beyond the initial phase.

Other situations do allow the warning of exclusion to be used against essential parties. An interesting example is the Antarctica treaty. In spite of the fact that Soviet participation was essential for an agreement to *demilitarize* the region, the United States, as the initiator, did have a warning of exclusion available. If the Soviet government had obstructed agreement (for example, by objecting to inspection), the United States could have switched from the demilitarization project to a project for *regional security* based on the exclusion of the Soviet Union. (The only countries close to Antarctica are U.S. allies and South Africa, and all claims to Antarctic territory were made by allies, with the only unclaimed sector generally recognized as a potential U.S. claim. Given allied cooperation—an important qualification! the Soviet Union could have been effectively excluded, for example, through a condominium.) This possibility never came into the open during the negotiations, in part because the conflict of interest was relatively mild—unlike the usual feeling in disarmament negotiations. Nonetheless, as a latent threat it may have contributed significantly to the successful conclusion of the Antarctica treaty.

The warning of exclusion can be ineffective for two reasons: either the innovation is meaningless without the participation of those who oppose it, or it requires approval by an international organization in which the opponents have a veto. It is for the latter reason that initiatives for revising the United Nations Charter have made so little headway.

There are cases, however, when even the obstacle of the veto has been overcome. The treaty of the European Economic Community provided that a common agricultural policy be gradually established according to certain principles, but it left all the important details to future negotiations. France expected to be the chief beneficiary of the integration of agriculture, while Germany stood to lose; and without German consent, agricultural integration would have been held up.[13] Initially it seemed that the French negotiators had no leverage to win German consent. But when the transition of the Common Market from its first to its second stage came up for negotiation in 1961, the French refused to agree to it unless agricultural integration was included. This created sufficient pressure on the Germans, since they were generally interested in the transition to the second stage (as were the other members of the Common Market). This *iunctim,* as the Germans call such a tie-in, combined two innovations: one (the transition to the second stage) in the interest of all the parties, and another (agricultural integration) in the interest of only some of the essential parties.

The French government was less interested than the other members of the Common Market in the transition to the second stage as such, apart from the integration of agriculture. Or at least it gave the appearance of being less interested, which was made easy by its well-known coldness toward the majority voting provided in the second stage. This lack of interest was an essential aspect of the *iunctim,* because it made credible the French threat to veto the transition. The *iunctim* also had the advantage of offsetting the domestic strength of the German farmers, who were opposed to agricultural integration, with the strength of industrial and other groups in Germany that wanted to have the Common Market move into its second stage.

Incidentally, the history of the provision in the Common Market treaty which enabled France to veto the second stage illustrates how negotiators sometimes acquire a bargaining advantage by accident or for the wrong reason. This provision was requested by France and reluctantly accepted by the other five member-countries in 1956 in the belief that the French economy might need an escape from rapid integration. But in 1961 the French could use this escape clause for almost the opposite purpose: to prevent the Germans from escaping a more rapid integration of agriculture.

[13] After the first two stages of the Common Market, the agricultural policy could have been adopted by majority vote. From the French vantage point in 1961, not only would this have meant considerable postponement, but in view of the possible entry of Great Britain and other countries, the opposition to agricultural integration might also have become stronger.

FIVE OBJECTIVES OF NEGOTIATION

	Extension Agreement	Normalization Agreement	Redistribution Agreement	Innovation Agreement	Side-Effects
Subject of negotiation	Continuation of normal (renewals or replacements).	Termination of abnormal (cease-fire, truce, resumption of diplomatic relations).	New distribution in favor of offensive side (surrender of territory, liberation of colonies).	New institutions or other arrangements of mutual interest.	The less likely the agreement, the more important the side-effects.
Main characteristics of negotiating process	Strong influence of previous agreement: as a precedent, and in limiting area of dispute.	Strong influence of situation at time of negotiations. Domestic or third-party pressures toward normalization.	Continuous division between offensive and defensive side. Continuous open threat of offensive side.	Inducement of mutual benefits, and risk of exclusion. A specially interested party may act as initiator.	Side-effects continue to flow from negotiating process.
In case of prolonged negotiations	Both sides lose.	In case of continuing hostilities, stronger party may win by force instead of negotiation.	Defensive side postpones loss, but redistribution may begin to look like normalization.	Interest in innovation may shift from one side to the other.	Side-effects nonetheless materialize and may be used to vindicate negotiations.
In case of *no* agreement	Interruption of customary arrangements.	*Either* continuation of fighting (or of abnormal relations) *or* subsiding of fighting (tacit truce).	*Either* status quo or implementation of threat by offensive side.	Continuation of status quo.	

As a sidelight on the types of objectives for negotiation, it is worth noting that domestic groups opposed to an innovation always picture it as a redistribution to the detriment of their own country. This happened with the various moves in European integration, where at one time the Germans were supposed to gain at the expense of the French, at another time the French or Italians at the expense of the Germans. Similarly, the nuclear test ban has been criticized by some Americans as resulting in military gains for the Soviet Union with no offsetting advantages for the United States.

SIDE–EFFECTS

The very process of negotiation can have important effects which do not concern agreement. These "side-effects" may be one of the reasons—or sometimes the only reason—why governments engage in diplomatic talks. Indeed, side-effects may provide the motive not only for going along with negotiations started by others but even for *initiating* negotiations. Proposals and speeches at the conference table, contacts with the opponent's diplomats, and the interest aroused among third parties may all contribute to various foreign-policy aims without leading to a settlement of the issues ostensibly discussed. For example, the negotiating process (or its simulation) can launch propaganda, produce intelligence, or modify political attitudes of nonparticipants.

If Western governments are engaged in negotiations where agreement appears highly unlikely or even undesirable, they frequently stress certain benefits from such side-effects. Of course, these side-effects may not materialize, or if they do, they may not meet the expectations of the parties that pursued them. Also, it is sometimes doubtful whether these alleged benefits are the real reason for negotiating or whether a government advances them to rationalize what it is doing out of habit or to conceal the fact that it clings to unrealistic hopes for a satisfactory agreement.

Side-effects are such an essential aspect of negotiation that they must be discussed more fully. Before going on, however, it may be worthwhile to scrutinize the five types of negotiation objectives as a group in the accompanying Table.

CHAPTER 4

NEGOTIATING FOR SIDE–EFFECTS

SIDE-EFFECTS—THAT IS, EFFECTS NOT CONCERNING AGREEMENT —may be an important part of the outcome, even if all parties negotiate primarily for the purpose of reaching agreement. They may arise either by accident or by design of one party or all parties involved. When diplomacy produces agreements only rarely—as between East and West—the objective of producing side-effects, in fact, often dominates. A type of side-effect that is frequently given as the main reason for negotiating is to keep in touch with the opponent.

MAINTAINING CONTACT

Secretary of State Dean Rusk was asked in a press conference on July 12, 1962, whether negotiations on Berlin had not reached a point where there was little to talk about, since the Soviets were willing to discuss only the diminution or elimination of the basic position of the Western powers. "No," the Secretary replied, "I think both sides still believe, as they have for some time, that maintaining contact on these issues is itself important, even though there has been no clear view as to how they might lead to a satisfactory solution." One of the leading exponents of this theme, that negotiating is of value apart from any agreement, is Walter Lippmann, who wrote in one of his columns:

The best reason for continuing to talk, though no agreement is in sight, is that by remaining in close diplomatic contact, Washington and Moscow have been able to prevent the dangerous situation in Berlin from getting out of control. . . . With no lasting settlement in sight, it is enormously important that Moscow and Washington be in such close contact that they cannot be dragged into war by local accidents and local misunderstandings. That is the reason why the talks as such, why continual meeting and talking as such, are a good thing.[1]

As Lippmann values East-West negotiations on Berlin, irrespective of agreement, so he values negotiations on disarmament. "It is so easy to write off as hopeless the coming disarmament conference," he noted in March, 1962, "that one may ask why the British, the Soviets, and we are taking the trouble to attend it. The reason is that nuclear war would be mutually suicidal, and that therefore the nuclear powers must keep in contact, must keep talking. . . ."[2] The view that negotiation helps to keep in contact was also expressed by President John F. Kennedy with regard to his Vienna talks with Khrushchev in 1961: "No new aims were stated in private that have not been stated in public on either side. The gap between us was not, in such a short period, materially reduced, but at least the channels of communication were opened more fully."[3]

There are two reasons why negotiation for the purpose of maintaining contact may be found desirable. First, the talks or conference may be seen as providing a forum for the exchange of views, either continuously or sporadically, on issues other than the ostensible topic of negotiation. Second, the meetings between the negotiators may be viewed as a *potential* channel for emergency communication and crisis bargaining.

Belief in providing a forum suggests that governments need the pretext of being engaged in some specific negotiation in order to communicate on other subjects. Where ordinary diplomatic relations are inadequate or nonexistent, it might be true that it is easier occasionally to improve contacts for some pretended negotiation than for general purposes. In journalistic accounts of diplomacy,

[1] *New York Herald Tribune*, June 5, 1962.
[2] *Ibid.*, March 8, 1962.
[3] President Kennedy's address to the nation, June 6, 1961.

however, the importance of this subterfuge tends to be overrated because a specific negotiation makes better news than an unfocused exchange of views.

Belief in keeping a potential channel open for communicating in an emergency has been stressed primarily for East-West negotiations. This line of reasoning tends to presume that governments of great powers behave like petulant persons, whose feelings might become so antagonistic that they would break off all contact unless pledged to reach agreement on some specific issue. On the contrary, although negotiations have often been broken off for tactical reasons, great powers do not stop communicating with each other purely out of pique. There is little evidence that ongoing negotiations are the prerequisite for communication in a crisis. One pertinent illustration is the settlement of the crisis about the Soviet missiles in Cuba in October, 1962. The emergency bargaining between Kennedy and Khrushchev took place without difficulty through diplomatic channels. The heads of the two major nuclear powers did not require negotiations on general and complete disarmament, on Berlin, or on a fisheries agreement "to keep in contact." To the extent that there were difficulties of communication, they resulted not from a lack of ongoing negotiations but from inadequate *technical* communication links.

The idea that ongoing negotiations might serve as emergency channels does not seem valid. A more supportable view is that a history of past negotiations establishes a *habit* of communicating, which may induce governments to keep in touch during emergencies. Such a habit is well ingrained between Moscow and Washington but lacking between Peking and Washington.

SUBSTITUTING FOR VIOLENT ACTION

According to a view which is fairly common in the West, the process of negotiation can be so gratifying to one's opponent or can entangle him so much in an obligation not to interrupt it that he will desist from some violent action he might have otherwise taken. Negotiating becomes an alternative activity in itself, one that distracts the opponent from offensive or otherwise undesirable moves.

What remains unexplained in this view is why the mere process of negotiation should provide a substitute for mischief. Is your opponent misled to wait for gains at the conference table, although you neither intend to let him win nor expect to find a mutually rewarding solution? Is the activity of negotiating with you politically or emotionally so rewarding to your opponent that he will be soothed and will desist from pressing his claims by force? Or, would your refusal to negotiate infuriate your opponent more than your refusal to accede to his demands?

Speaking about the Berlin crisis, Senator Mansfield said in June, 1961: "In early 1959, a military showdown appeared imminent to me. . . . It was forestalled by an almost continuous round of sub-summit and summit conferences and visitings back and forth. . . ."[4] But then in the summer of 1961, according to Walter Lippmann, "General de Gaulle imposed a veto on negotiations. Not long after that veto there took place the action of August 13 to raise the wall in Berlin. In all likelihood, had the West been allowed to explore the problem of negotiating, the action of August 13 would not have taken place, at least during the explorations."[5] Similarly, Lippmann and others have suggested that owing to the Rusk-Gromyko negotiations after August 31, 1961, Khrushchev removed his December 31, 1961, deadline for signing a separate German peace treaty.

Experience does not support the attribution of such beneficial effects to the mere process of negotiation (with no agreement in sight) and of disastrous consequences to its interruption. Would the Communists have found it unnecessary to build the Berlin wall if they had been allowed continuously "to explore the problem of negotiating" with the West? Perhaps the Soviet resumption of nuclear testing in 1961, in the midst of ongoing test-ban negotiations, can be explained as an exception to the rule that negotiating tends to serve as a substitute for violent action. But the removal of the December 31, 1961, deadline for the German peace treaty does not support such a rule either, because since 1958 there has been a long succession of Soviet deadlines, some more explicit, some vague, and they have always withered away, whether

---

[4] *Congressional Record,* June 14, 1961, p. 9598.

[5] "Refusal to Negotiate Cost the West Dearly," *Los Angeles Times,* Oct. 26, 1961.

there were exploratory talks, broken-up summit meetings, or no negotiations at all. And if we go farther back in history, the exceptions to such a rule are even more glaring: the Franco-British negotiations in Moscow in the summer of 1939 did not prevent Stalin's pact with Hitler, and the interruption of the Japanese-American negotiations on December 7, 1941, is well remembered.

While these many exceptions invalidate the flat rule that negotiation provides a substitute for violent action, they do not contradict a sound core of this idea. Being engaged in negotiation may keep a government from taking some action disadvantageous to the opponent, provided two conditions are met: (1) the government so restrained must deem it likely that if it took the action, the opponent would break off the negotiations; and (2) the government must value the avoidance of a break in negotiations—even when there is no agreement in sight—more highly than the action from which it desists. Both these conditions were met for the U.S. government during the moratorium on nuclear tests from 1959 to 1961. The U.S. government expected that its resumption of testing would lead to the threatened Soviet walk-out from the test-ban conference, and it considered such a rupture of the negotiations (for which it might be held responsible) more undesirable than a continued uninspected moratorium.

Similarly, in case of negotiations on a truce or some other normalization agreement, a party may be led to give up violence by the very fact that talks are taking place, provided, again, that (1) this party thinks violence would cause the opponent to break off the talks, and (2) that it considers continued talks more important or more profitable than trying to make gains through the use of force. This is what happened at the beginning of the Korean armistice negotiations. "In June, 1951, the Communist forces were falling back steadily, suffering grievously," wrote Admiral Joy, who was chief of the UN truce delegation. "Then Jakob Malik issued his truce feeler. As soon as armistice discussions began, United Nations Command ground forces slackened their offensive operations."[6]

A related side-effect is that ongoing negotiations may serve to

[6] C. Turner Joy, *How Communists Negotiate* (New York: Macmillan, 1955), p. 166.

communicate warnings against the use of force. In redistribution negotiations, the defensive side can try to convince the opponent that his use of force would meet with grave reprisals. This is expressed by the idea that "we must tell the Russians where we stand," to prevent them from miscalculating the consequences of pushing too far. Thus, the *process* of negotiation may serve to deter the opponent, not because it provides him with a substitute for his planned offensive, but because it relays a warning against the use of force.

This side-effect should not be confused with the tactic of promoting agreement by making the consequences of no-agreement seem more disadvantageous to one's opponent. In that tactic, one side wants an agreement and predicts all sorts of dire consequences if none should be reached, including perhaps the use of force. But in the case of deterrent warnings as a side-effect, the negotiating process is used to discourage an offensive move by predicting painful reprisals, while both sides may have little interest in, or hope for, an agreement.

INTELLIGENCE

The process of negotiation may be used to gather intelligence about an opponent. Sometimes the information thus obtained can be more important than the way in which the issues under discussion are settled. A government, by the way it negotiates, may reveal its long-term aims, expose differences with its allies or domestic conflicts, and divulge the point at which an offensive by the opponent would meet with resistance.

In redistribution negotiations, the offensive side may well be more interested in discovering this point of resistance than in making gains through an agreement. It may learn, from what the defensive side says or fails to say, that certain offensive moves are safe. This possibility provides a further reason for questioning the notion that redistribution negotiations help the defensive side by providing the offensive side with a substitute for violent action. Walter Lippmann, in the passage quoted previously, thought the Berlin wall would not have been erected "had the West been allowed [by De Gaulle] to explore the problem of negotiating."

But negotiations on Berlin took place on and off for a long time before the wall was built! It was perhaps not the temporary interruption in negotiations that induced the Russians to build the wall, but rather the Western emphasis on free access to *West* Berlin only, to the neglect of the rights for free circulation within *all* of Berlin.[7]

One can easily find other examples of redistribution negotiations that did not produce any agreement but had this side-effect of informing the offensive party how far it could safely advance. In 1935, Mussolini's talks with the British and the French prior to his attack on Abyssinia may have succeeded in reassuring him that the opposition of these powers to his military adventure would be weak. The British and French negotiators, in trying to find a peaceful settlement for Mussolini's demands, offered him half a loaf: the Hoare-Laval plan for a large zone of Abyssinia to be allocated exclusively to Italian economic development and in return for an Abyssinian corridor to the sea at the expense of some British and French possessions. Even though this proposal was criticized in the League of Nations and disavowed by the British cabinet, it might have made Mussolini's grab of the whole loaf look less dangerous, and it conditioned the British Parliament, the French public, and League members to the idea that substantial gains by Mussolini over Abyssinia would be tolerated by Great Britain and France.

Looking back at this episode, the British negotiator, Sir Samuel Hoare, felt he should have made a greater effort to convince

[7] Apart from this narrow focus of the Western negotiating position, additional signals from the West might have reassured the Russians that they could safely build the wall. In this connection, a statement by Senator Fulbright has often been cited. A few weeks before the wall went up, Fulbright is reported to have said on television that the closing of West Berlin as an escape hatch "might certainly be a negotiable point. . . . I mean we are not giving up very much because I believe that next week if they chose to close their borders they could, without violating any treaty. I don't understand why the East Germans don't close their border because they have a right to close it. So why is this a great concession?" (*New York Times,* Aug. 3, 1961). It is doubtful, however, whether this statement significantly encouraged the building of the wall, especially since Senator Fulbright said a few days later in the Senate that the right to move within all sectors of Berlin was not negotiable and that his television statement was meant to apply to travel restrictions between East Germany and all of Berlin (*Congressional Record,* Aug. 4, 1961, p. 13659).

public opinion at home of the merits of his plan: "How we and the French were only making recommendations at the express request of the League . . . , how much of the territory involved in the proposed change was unadministered and unpopulated desert, and finally how formidable were the risks to Europe of a complete break with Italy."[8] But if surrender of half the loaf had been made more acceptable to Britain, Mussolini would not have been deterred from taking the whole loaf! What was needed was a firmer indication that Mussolini would meet with resistance from Britain or at least with effective League of Nations sanctions. Such a course was made difficult by the fact that the French Premier, Pierre Laval, was so anxious not to antagonize Mussolini.

DECEPTION

A side-effect of negotiation which may be viewed as the converse of intelligence is deception. One must distinguish deception as a side-effect unrelated to agreement from deception as a technique for getting good terms in an agreement. The *technique* of deception is unavoidable in certain negotiating situations. Assume, for example, that your opponent offers you terms good enough so that you would rather accept them than be without an agreement. If you want your opponent to make you a still better offer, you may have to deceive him into believing that you would prefer having no agreement to accepting his offer.

But the deception to be discussed here has nothing to do with the terms of agreement. It is a side-effect of negotiation which may serve other foreign-policy objectives or military moves.

The talks of Japanese diplomats in Washington prior to the attack on Pearl Harbor are sometimes mentioned as an example of a negotiation for deception. But this interpretation is incorrect. These talks, while obviously not alluding to the specific attack, did not lull the American government into a false sense of security and were never intended to do so. On the contrary, they clearly were redistribution negotiations and as such provided warning of Japan's aggressive intentions. Given these Japanese demands and

[8] Viscount Templewood (Sir Samuel Hoare), *Nine Troubled Years* (London: Collins, 1954), p. 192.

the implied threats of force, an attack was indeed expected by the American government—although not against Pearl Harbor.[9]

An example of negotiation for deception can be found in the history of the Hungarian Revolution in 1956. Between October 31 and November 3, the new Hungarian government under Nagy negotiated with the Soviet ambassador about the withdrawal of Soviet troops and Hungary's wish to become neutral. Through these talks, the Soviets gained the necessary time for preparing their attack to crush the revolution and for setting up the Kádár puppet government. The Soviet ambassador kept promising to Nagy that the Russian troops would soon be withdrawn, and he tried to dissuade the Hungarian government from making appeals to the United Nations.[10]

Deception—as a side-effect of negotiations—may also have the opposite aim: instead of gaining time to prepare one's own use of force, such deception may have the purpose of diverting another country from the use of force until the opportunity for it has passed. This is what Secretary of State John Foster Dulles tried to do in the fall of 1956 when Britain and France threatened to use force against Egypt to reverse Nasser's nationalization of the Suez Canal. Dulles tried to put the British and French off by a rapid succession of new schemes, such as invoking the Constantinople Convention (which guarantees the international character of the Canal), summoning an international conference, establishing a new international board for the operation of the Canal, and forming a club of the Canal users. At first, Prime Minister Eden thought the Americans would support the use of force as a last resort: "Our Ambassador in Washington," Eden recalled in his memoirs, "assured us at this time that the Administration completely accepted the impossibility of leaving the control of the Suez Canal in the hands of a man like Nasser. Though they would strain every

[9] Robert J. C. Butow, *Tojo and the Coming of the War* (Princeton, N.J.: Princeton University Press, 1961), chap. ii; and Roberta Wohlstetter, *Pearl Harbor: Warning and Decision* (Stanford, Calif.: Stanford University Press, 1962), pp. 233–46, 263–77.

[10] Ferenc A. Váli, *Rift and Revolt in Hungary: Nationalism versus Communism* (Cambridge, Mass.: Harvard University Press, 1961), pp. 364, 368–69, 373–74; and Paul E. Zinner, *Revolution in Hungary* (New York: Columbia University Press, 1962), p. 325.

nerve to bring about a settlement by negotiation, they realized that in the last resort force might have to be used and they understood the necessity for the military precautions which we and the French were taking." However, Eden soon became worried that these prolonged negotiations with the Americans and with Nasser might deprive him of his principal bargaining power—the threat of force. "There was always a danger," he said in his memoirs, "that the passage of time and the multiplication of talk would weaken the resolve of [the powers negotiating with Nasser]. . . . The question was, how long we could pursue diplomatic methods and economic sanctions, which very likely would not succeed, before the possibility of military action slipped from our grasp."[11]

With the benefit of hindsight, it can now be argued that Dulles should not have tried to divert Britain and France from the use of force through deceptive negotiations but should have made it clear that the United States would oppose military action as long as the Canal was operated satisfactorily, while supporting a common Western position to reach a new arrangement with Egypt. But then, Dulles' delaying tactics might just as well have worked, leading to a situation for the Suez Canal much like the present, and without the unhappy episode of the Anglo-French attack, which—apart from being inadequate as a military operation—could scarcely have brought a long-term political solution.

PROPAGANDA

Propaganda—like intelligence and deception—can be either a technique for getting good terms of agreement or a side-effect of negotiation which serves other foreign-policy objectives. The former, propaganda as a bargaining technique, will be discussed later. The latter, propaganda as a side-effect, has three aspects. These may be termed: negotiating to have a sounding-board, negotiating to gain prestige, and negotiating to show rectitude like the Pharisee saying his prayers.

The *sounding-board* effect of negotiation occurs mainly at high-level conferences and summit meetings. Such conferences serve to

[11] Anthony Eden, *Full Circle* (Boston: Houghton Mifflin, 1960), pp. 497–98, 509.

publicize a government's views and policy goals, since national objectives presented in the form of conference proposals receive wide publicity and elicit serious discussions and evaluations within other governments. Policy aims that are put forward as negotiating proposals make a deeper impact on other countries than if they were simply promulgated at home as a government program. For example, the Soviet disarmament proposal for the abolition of foreign bases emphasizes Soviet objections to American bases more continuously and perhaps more effectively than earlier Soviet pronouncements that made the same point outside a negotiating context. By contrast, the position of the United States and other Western powers in favor of German reunification and/or self-determination in East Germany lacks impact precisely because it is not being reiterated as a negotiating proposal.

Some governments value negotiation for a different kind of propaganda effect, which might best be characterized as *publicity* or *prestige*. Like the junior politician who wants to be photographed talking with the President, these governments feel that their name and political standing are enhanced by attending international conferences or summit meetings, even though nothing of substance is decided. (If important decisions may be reached between the principal participants at a conference, participation by additional parties is no longer a matter of mere prestige but can actually serve to influence these decisions.) It has been speculated that Khrushchev's frequent demands for summit meetings in the late 1950s were partly motivated by his desire to enhance his political prestige. It seems a little curious that the leader of the second most powerful country in the world should have wished to gain international publicity and respect in this way—but it cannot be ruled out.

The main reason why being engaged in negotiation can serve propaganda purposes is that so many beneficial effects are attributed to it. Negotiation is thought to be desirable not only because it may prevent conflict by producing an agreement but, according to the views previously discussed, because the very process of negotiating is believed to help maintain contact and provide a substitute for violent action, even if no agreement is in sight. Given the prevalence of these views, governments are reluctant to refuse negotiation, no matter how unlikely or undesirable an agreement. They fear that such refusal would impair the good will of groups important to them—their own parliament, the public in allied countries, or other governments, for example.

These audiences may judge quite superficially in praising those willing to negotiate and censuring those who refuse. Outside groups may have only a vague notion as to what negotiating means and how it relates to the merits of the issue. Governments that negotiate in order to win public approval value the act of negotiating as the Pharisee values prayer. It is not the thoughts behind the prayer that matter, or the purpose pursued, or the deeds before and after—what counts is that the ceremony be performed with the proper gestures. If this becomes the only purpose of prolonged negotiations, ridiculous and corrupting consequences follow: the prayers can be performed by the prayer wheel! Some cynics maintain that conferences on general disarmament have reached such a state.

It is paradoxical that the view according to which the act of negotiating is in itself meritorious prevails particularly in a field where prolonged negotiations have been singularly unsuccessful— the field of *general* disarmament (as distinguished from more limited and specific disarmament issues). This paradox cannot be fully explained by the great value that is attached to the ostensible objectives of disarmament conferences, because anyone interested in these objectives must harbor some doubt whether this particular style of negotiation is the best road toward them, what with the dismal record of the past. Incidentally, the propaganda advantages of participating in disarmament conferences seem to be overrated both by the Soviet government and by policymakers in Great Britain and the United States. The French government seemed to lose little, or may even have gained some, prestige in the eyes of uncommitted countries and the Western public, by abstention from the fruitless Eighteen-Nation Disarmament Conference since 1962.

It would be wrong to maintain that the *principal* aim of Western governments in general-disarmament conferences is to make propaganda in the sense of wanting to appear good by engaging in a good activity, again like the Pharisee saying his prayers. But it seems undeniable that the Pharisaic aspect receives considerable attention by Western policymakers. A symptom of this is the frequent reversal of roles between the United States and the Soviet Union in gleefully pressing the other side to resume negotiations on disarmament precisely when the opponent is unprepared or disinclined to do so.

Even persons strongly in favor of negotiations on general disarmament have come to the conclusion that the governments engaged in the comprehensive disarmament conferences neither expect nor seek agreement but are trying to put the other side in the wrong. As John Strachey wrote:

> How can we avoid the lamentable conclusion that these offers and counter-offers for treaties of general and complete disarmament are never meant to be taken seriously as schemes which might actually be implemented? It is not the mistakes, prejudices or "mistimings" of this or that negotiator or statesman which are at the root of the repeated failure. It is that the negotiators and statesmen have no belief in what they are perhaps inevitably doing. They are playing the game of political warfare, busily putting each other in the wrong before the bar of world opinion. We are not witnessing, as Mr. Noel-Baker seems to imply, a high drama in which each act has, it is true, so far ended in failure, but which might at any moment open a new era for humanity. We are not witnessing a Greek tragedy but an international farce.[12]

IMPACT ON THIRD PARTIES

In August, 1939, while Molotov directed open negotiations with the French and British on a mutual-assistance treaty against German attack, he secretly negotiated a non-aggression pact with the Germans. The Soviets may never have intended that their negotiations with the Anglo-French delegation should lead to an agreement, but they surely could use these negotiations to improve their bargaining position with Hitler. They continued the talks with the French and British up to the day Ribbentrop arrived in Moscow

[12] John Strachey, *On the Prevention of War* (London: Macmillan, 1962), p. 162. This evaluation of disarmament negotiations has been carried further by John W. Spanier and Joseph L. Nogee, *The Politics of Disarmament: A Study in Soviet-American Gamesmanship* (New York: Praeger, 1962), who maintain that these negotiations *solely* serve propaganda purposes but that this is nevertheless a recognized function worth pursuing.

to sign the pact with Stalin and Molotov. This was undoubtedly one of the most dramatic triangular situations in modern history, where contrary negotiations were carried on simultaneously, one of them resulting in an important agreement and the other one affecting the terms of this agreement, although in itself it settled nothing.

To what extent were the three parties aware of this triangle? The Germans did fear that their proposals might strengthen Stalin's hand in his negotiations with the Western powers. On May 22, 1939, the German ambassador in Moscow reported to Berlin: "We must be extremely cautious in this field as long as it is not certain that possible proposals from our side will not be used by the Kremlin only to exert pressure on England and France." And a few days later, the German Foreign Office wrote back: "We are of the opinion here that the English-Russian combination certainly will not be easy to prevent."[13] The British, on the other hand, had no knowledge of the secret Nazi-Soviet talks and were only vaguely suspicious. As late as July 20, the British negotiator in Moscow, William Strang, reported to London, that while a break in the fruitless negotiations might drive the Soviet Union into isolation or a deal with Hitler, to continue negotiations, "although producing no immediate concrete results, would still probably worry Hitler. Russia would also be less likely to remain neutral or be on the wrong side in the case of war."[14] (The Western idea that the process of negotiation will discourage unfriendly action!) Completing the third side of this triangle, Göring sent a certain Herr Wohltat to London in July, allegedly with Hitler's knowledge. However, the British did not exploit this dubious emissary to put pressure on Stalin. We can only speculate, of course, whether doing so would have raised Stalin's fears that the British might connive at a German attack against him and thus have induced Stalin to conclude the mutual-assistance treaty with the Western powers.

Ongoing negotiations between two powers that belong to op-

[13] U.S. Department of State, *Nazi-Soviet Relations, 1939–1941* (Washington, D.C., 1948), pp. 8, 9.
[14] E. L. Woodward and R. Butler (eds.), *Documents on British Foreign Policy 1919–1939* (Third Series, Vol. VI [London: H.M.S.O., 1953]), p. 426.

posing alliances can have an impact on other allies who feel left out. Even though there is no agreement, the very fact that negotiations take place may be enough to stir up fears among some allies that a "deal" might be made at their expense. After De Gaulle opposed Britain's entry into the Common Market in January, 1963, mentioning the close link between Great Britain and the United States as one of his reasons, there was some apprehension in Washington that the French government might start separate negotiations with the Russians.

These fears, at least for the time being, did not come true. In fact, critics of Washington's diplomacy suggested that the shoe might fit the other foot. For example, Governor Nelson A. Rockefeller argued that "before engaging in hints about the possibility of separate French deals with the Soviets, we should recall that it was the present administration which set the precedent." Rockefeller reminded the public that in 1961 the U.S. government "negotiated with the Soviets over Berlin against the wishes of France and against the better judgment of the Federal Republic of Germany. The administration then strongly implied that it was ready to enter into arrangements which would involve recognition of Communist Eastern Germany in some form, and thus to weaken our long-standing commitment to German unification."[15]

At about the same time, Dean Acheson spoke even more explicitly of what he considered to be the deleterious side-effects on European allies from the American-Soviet negotiations on Berlin:

Since the disastrous Camp David meeting Germans have been disturbed over our constant negotiations with the Russians under Russian threats. Fruitless as they have been, with no real concessions made, they seem to Germans to edge toward increasing recognition of the East German regime, they kept German politics continuously upset and moved German sympathy toward General de Gaulle's support of German ambitions. . . . Our flirtation with Moscow, like many which have no serious purpose, has succeeded only in embittering more legitimate relationships.[16]

[15] Nelson A. Rockefeller, in a statement released to the press in Chicago, Feb. 9, 1963.

[16] Dean Acheson, in a speech at the University of California, Berkeley, March 13, 1963.

It would transcend the scope of this study to go into other problems of al-

Negotiating for some desired side-effect may have undesirable secondary consequences. By negotiating for Pharisaic propaganda, a government may make limited agreements less likely. By negotiating so as to offer the opponent a substitute for violent action, a government may reveal to the opponent how far he can safely advance. And negotiating to maintain contact may make allies distrustful.

---

liances, such as the excluded third party, shifting two-party alliances in a power triangle, etc. See George Liska, *Nations in Alliance: The Limits of Interdependence* (Baltimore, Md.: Johns Hopkins Press, 1962), for a recent treatment of this topic.

CHAPTER 5

THE CONTINUAL THREEFOLD CHOICE

THE OUTCOME OF NEGOTIATION, AS STATED PREVIOUSLY, MAY range from total disagreement to complete agreement, with varying mixtures of ambiguity and specificity in the eventual settlement. Moreover, there are many side-effects of the negotiating process that have nothing to do with an agreement between the negotiating parties but concern relations with third parties, international publicity, attitudes toward the use of force, or other matters. If one pursued all these heterogeneous effects, the process of negotiation would blend into the whole field of international relations like a seamless web. It is necessary, though, to keep some of these ramifications in mind when focusing on the central question as to how the negotiation process leads to the particular terms of an agreement.

What determines the arrangement of common and conflicting interests which emerges at the end of negotiations? How do diplomats personally affect the results, the gains and losses in the settlement? What is the effect of various tactics on the terms of the bargain that is struck?

A rudimentary system of analysis will serve to describe the effect of the negotiating process upon the terms of agreement if, step by step, certain complications and refinements are added so as to make this system conform more closely to reality. The rudimentary system subsumes all the negotiator's decisions under three basic choices: (1) to accept agreement at the terms he expects the opponent would settle for (the "available" terms), (2) to discontinue negotiations without agreement and with no intention of resuming them, and (3) to try to improve the "available" terms through further bargaining. Not only can the negotiator's decisions be subsumed under these three basic choices, but most of his actions can be understood as being designed to influence the opponent in *his* threefold choice. The threefold choice is implicitly exercised by each party throughout the negotiations, although explicitly the negotiators may face it only at certain junctures.

For brevity, the first of the three options can be summed up as *to choose the available terms.* This means to choose agreement at the terms that have been offered by, or seem to be immediately acceptable to, the other party (or parties).

In multilateral negotiations, it is true, a government often does not have the option of agreeing to the terms offered by, or acceptable to, the other parties, because the other parties disagree among themselves. Thus this government can no longer choose agreement by yielding to the terms of the opponent (as it theoretically always can in bilateral negotiations); it can only make choices that render agreement most likely (abstain, vote with the majority, buy off a recalcitrant party, etc.).

In bilateral negotiations the "available terms" can be described more simply. If a government is negotiating an agreement that is to be cast in the form of a treaty, the terms available at any particular time consist of the articles already agreed to, articles offered by the opponent, plus those terms for articles not yet discussed that the government expects its opponent would be ready to grant. Usually, the available terms are not spelled out during the early phases of negotiations. To the extent that the decision-makers consciously face the option of *choosing the available terms,* they must know— or at least believe that they can estimate—all these terms. Of course, if they decide to choose these terms, this does not mean that they will actually obtain agreement; it merely means that they expect to do so by accepting what they believe to be the terms for which the opponent is ready to settle.

The second option can be designated as *to choose no-agreement.* It means stopping negotiations and giving up the effort to settle with the other party for an explicit new arrangement. This choice still permits the government to use unilateral measures and tacit bargaining for improving the situation at issue, although it is distinct from the tactic of interrupting negotiation with the intention of inducing the opponent to soften his terms. A government which interrupts negotiation wants to put pressure on the opponent and may continue to bargain by other means, in the hope of resuming negotiation under better conditions.[1] But a government which *chooses no-agreement* discontinues all efforts to get an agreement. (However, even this move is not always final: sometimes the opponent can re-initiate negotiation by offering new incentives or by creating new pressures.)

The third option, to engage in *further bargaining,* covers not only a further confrontation of explicit proposals at the conference table but also any other moves by the government for the purpose of strengthening its own negotiating position and weakening that of the opponent. A choice to engage in *further bargaining* usually means more than just a postponement of the choice between available terms and no-agreement; it is a decision to make additional efforts for improving the available terms. If *further bargaining* is not accompanied by such efforts, it represents an interruption of negotiation with a passive attitude. That is, it becomes merely a waiting period during which the choice between available terms and no-agreement is held in abeyance, perhaps in the hope that extraneous new developments might help to change the opponent's mind.

If you are the negotiator, how do you choose among these three options? You will compare the probable gains and losses from agreement at available terms with the estimated consequences of no-agreement. Then you will estimate whether further bargaining is likely to lead to an improvement over the better of these first two options, while allowing for the risks and costs of further bargaining. Assume you have chosen to engage in further bargaining so as to improve the terms for agreement, in preference to either of the other two options of no-agreement and agreement at

---

[1] To repeat, "negotiation" in this book is defined as a process in which explicit proposals are put forward ostensibly for the purpose of reaching agreement on an exchange or on the realization of a common interest where conflicting interests are present.

presently available terms. In this case, your objective is to make your opponent choose agreement at the terms you will make available to him, which implies that *he* will have to reject no-agreement and give up further bargaining.

Before this interaction can be analyzed further, some concepts that play a central role in bargaining must be defined so as to give them a more precise meaning than their common usage.

WARNINGS, THREATS, BLUFFS, AND COMMITMENTS

Warnings, threats (whether bluffs or not), and commitments are moves made by a party for the purpose of changing the opponent's expectations and consequently influencing his choices. If you issue a warning or a threat, you try to alter your opponent's expectations about *his* gains or losses that would result from certain choices he can take; if you make a commitment, you try to alter your opponent's expectations about *your* future conduct, by changing your own incentives.

Warnings and *threats* thus belong to the same category, but they differ from one another. In both the warning and the threat, the menacing party tries to dissuade its opponent from making a certain move or from refusing to comply with a demand. To warn or to threaten means to predict to the opponent (or to those who might influence him) that he would suffer a certain loss if he did not comply. The difference between a warning and a threat lies in the role played by the warning or threatening party in the causation of the predicted loss.

On the one hand, the party that warns points out to the opponent *natural* consequences that are likely to follow from his noncompliance. These consequences flow from the laws of nature, economic or technical developments, or because other parties, as well as the warner himself, simply pursue their own interests. More precisely, to the extent that the warner's own actions contribute to the opponent's loss, these actions must be in the warner's interest for other reasons than that they cause a loss to the opponent. In fact, the actions would have been in the warner's interest even if the warning had never been made.

The party that threatens, on the other hand, asserts that it will make a special effort so as to cause the opponent to suffer the predicted loss should he fail to comply. In contrast to the warning, the threatener's course of action that results in the opponent's loss is not, by itself, in the threatener's interest. Indeed, this course of action may be costly for the threatener—perhaps even more costly than the loss is for the opponent. If the threat had not been made, or if the opponent was not to be forced to comply, it would never be worthwhile for the threatener to take this course of action. Given the fact that the threat has been made and has failed to compel the opponent, it may or may not be worthwhile for the threatening party to take this course of action.[2]

In the warning, the prediction of the opponent's loss is an act of bargaining, but the action which causes the opponent's loss after he has made the unwanted move is independent of the bargaining; the action would take place whether or not it inflicted a loss on the opponent. In a threat, however, both the prediction of the loss and the act of causing it are bargaining moves; the threatener causes the loss *only because* he has made the threat and does not want to turn out to be a bluffer, or because he wants to enforce compliance since he failed to obtain compliance by threatening.

Why are some warnings and threats ineffective? Your opponent may not heed your warning or not give in to your threat for three reasons: he may expect that it will be less costly to absorb the losses you predicted than to meet your demand; he may decide that these losses will be less harmful than the damage done to his bargaining reputation by giving in (this will be explored farther on); or, finally, he may not believe that your warning will come true or that you will carry out your threat. Disbelief in a warning is different from disbelief in a threat. The former is a question of factual belief: Is the warner's prediction correct or not? The

[2] The distinction here between threat and warning closely parallels that employed by Schelling (*The Strategy of Conflict*, pp. 123 ff.). Schelling emphasizes the extent to which carrying out a threat is undesirable to the threatener. "The distinctive character of a threat is that one asserts that he will do, in a contingency, what he would manifestly prefer not to do, if the contingency occurred, the contingency being governed by the second party's behavior." With a change of emphasis, however, a threatener is here defined as one who asserts he would, in a specified contingency, take some action which in itself is of insufficient interest to him, *perhaps* even costly, and whose only purpose was to inflict a loss on the opponent or force him to comply.

latter depends on the anticipated motivation of the threatener: Will the threatener, after his opponent fails to comply, be sufficiently motivated to inflict the predicted damage upon the opponent? If not, the threat will have turned out to be a *bluff*.

Whether or not the threat is a bluff can be decided only after it has been challenged by the opponent's noncompliance; before that, the threatener may still change his mind. What matters to the threatened party is not so much the attitude of the threatener at the time the threat is made but whether the threatener will have the capability and motivation to inflict the damage after he has been challenged. The threatened party, however, should not entirely ignore the question of whether the threatener, when he makes his threat, means it to be a bluff. Because if the threatener does not intend to carry out his threat even at the time he makes it, he will be particularly reluctant to have it challenged lest his bluff be called. The opponent who senses this reluctance can exploit it: he can pressure the threatener into buying him off to avoid an outright challenge.

In international negotiations warnings are far more frequent than threats. For example, in the test-ban negotiations, whichever side happened to be pushing for agreement (initially the Soviet Union and later the United States) issued repeated warnings about the spread of nuclear weapons to additional countries and the fallout hazard from continued testing. But these undesirable effects were presented as inevitable consequences of continued testing. Neither side ever threatened deliberately to make things worse should the opponent fail to come to an agreement. The United States did not threaten to turn over independent nuclear capabilities to its allies, nor did the Soviet Union threaten to do so for China. The President's prediction in the spring of 1962 that the United States would resume atmospheric testing unless the Soviet Union soon agreed to a treaty was perhaps intermediate between a warning and a threat.

Particularly rare are explicit threats, in distinction to hinted or implicit ones. Among the few examples of threats that can be found (conforming to the definition), most were implicit and turned out to be bluffs. For instance, when it became evident that the French Parliament would be reluctant to ratify the treaty for

the European Defense Community (EDC), Secretary of State
Dulles announced (December 14, 1953) that failure to bring
the EDC into being "would compel an agonizing reappraisal of
basic United States policy," thus hinting that American forces
might be withdrawn from Europe. When the French Parliament
finally rejected the EDC, no such reappraisal took place.[3] Another
example of a bluff, though less publicized, was the veiled threat
made by desperate British negotiators in 1958 that economic reprisals might be taken if the Common Market countries failed to
agree to the enlarged free-trade area that would have joined the
six Common Market members with the seven other countries that
later formed their own European Free Trade Association (EFTA).
Such reprisals were never taken.

It is even more difficult to find examples of explicit threats that
were actually carried out than it is to find explicit threats that were
not challenged or, if challenged, turned out to be bluffs. An example of an explicit threat that has been carried out is Germany's
"Hallstein Doctrine," but this threat was not made for the purpose
of a single negotiation. According to the "Hallstein Doctrine" the
government in Bonn threatens to withdraw diplomatic recognition
from any country (except the Soviet Union) that extends full
recognition to East Germany. By 1963 the threat was challenged
twice and carried out on both occasions. In October, 1957, Yugoslavia recognized the Pankow regime, and within three days Bonn
broke diplomatic relations (though not consular contracts) with
Belgrade. In January, 1963, the same happened with regard to
Cuba. Breaking diplomatic relations with Yugoslavia was not in
Germany's interest in itself. Bonn did so only with great reluctance
and after a heated debate within the government. The move was
made to preserve the credibility of the threat, and as such was
entirely successful. (The break with Cuba was expected by both
sides, provoked by Havana, and not regretted by Bonn.)

Warnings and threats so defined stand apart from *commitments*.
A commitment is a move to convince one's opponent that one will
maintain one's current position or implement one's prediction by

[3] It might be argued that the subsequent creation of the West European Union
to some extent satisfied Dulles' condition so that his threat need not be carried
out.

making it more difficult for oneself not to do so. In other words, a commitment is linked to specific intentions that have been conveyed to the opponent. By making it costly for oneself not to live up to them, the commitment suggests to the opponent that the intentions are not only true when stated but are also unlikely to change as long as the commitment cannot be annulled. If someone says that he will not retreat, he may be making a true prediction or only be boasting, but after he has burned his bridges, his intention has turned into a necessity—at least until the bridges have been rebuilt.

Commitments may serve either to make it credible that threats will be carried out when challenged or to make it unlikely that a negotiating position will be changed. That is, there are *commitments to threats* regarding a future contingency and *commitments to positions* currently held. However, commitments in international politics—unlike equivalent pledges under domestic law or in a parlor game—are both vague and fluid, their binding power is hard to determine by both parties, and they are subject to change or annulment. A commitment may make it more likely that a threat will be carried out, but it does not make it certain. Besides, something may happen tomorrow that will cancel the commitment of today.

What does the binding power of a commitment consist of? One type of commitment is based on constitutional restrictions or the power of the legislative branch, whereby a government can "force" itself to carry out a threat or stick to a certain position. To cite just one example, in 1962 Congress attached to the Foreign Assistance Act an amendment prohibiting aid to countries that expropriate American-owned property and fail to take "appropriate steps" for compensation within six months. This provided U.S. negotiators with a commitment to the threat that foreign aid would be discontinued should American-owned property be expropriated without compensation satisfactory to the U.S. government.

In other commitments the binding power stems from the fact that the executive branch of the government is subject to the influence of domestic groups or to the control of the electorate and that these domestic forces want their government to honor its promises or to carry out its threats. That is, if the executive wants to stay in power, it cannot afford an appearance of being grossly inconsistent and untrustworthy. Hence, once a pledge has been made to uphold a certain position or a threat has been issued, it would be costly for the government to act contrary to these expressed intentions.

This type of commitment is ineffective, however, for negotiations where the domestic forces deem it more important that agreement be reached than that the government remain consistent. For example, in 1959 De Gaulle repeatedly stated in public that he would not negotiate with the FLN (the representatives of the Algerian rebels) until they had agreed to a cease-fire. This commitment was too weak to prevent him from starting formal negotiations a year later without a cease-fire.

A similar type of commitment consists of a treaty or a promise to a third party that would have to be broken if the first party retreated from its negotiating position. Such a commitment is illustrated by the British pledge to the other six members of EFTA that their trading position would not be jeopardized should England join the Common Market. (The reason England gave this pledge, however, was probably not to strengthen its negotiating position in Brussels but rather to hold EFTA together in the event that it could not join the Common Market. Indeed, as long as England's prospects for joining the Common Market looked good, this EFTA pledge proved to be a hindrance.)

The commitment of tying one's negotiating position to a pledge can be strengthened if this pledge is not restricted to a single ally and a single situation, but made to represent all one's pledges to allies. This is what President Kennedy did in his speech of July 25, 1961, on the Berlin crisis: "If we do not meet our commitments to Berlin, where will we later stand? If we are not true to our word there, all that we have achieved in collective security, which relies on these words, will mean nothing."

There is another type of commitment. As will be discussed later, a party may place its bargaining reputation at stake when making a threat or advancing a negotiating position.

Commitments are so fluid because their content is often unclear and the criteria on which they are based can be eroded. What, for example, is "just" compensation for expropriated property? Or what is "adequate" international inspection, a criterion to which the U.S. government is committed in disarmament negotiations because it implanted it as a firm goal in the public mind. If a party wishes to make its commitment more forceful, it can take steps to minimize the erosion of criteria. On the other hand, the opponent can try deliberately to confuse the criteria. For instance, early in the nuclear test-ban negotiations, the Soviet delegate Tsarapkin even tried to refute the requirement for U.S. Senate ratification, in the hope of eliminating the commitment of the American delegate to reject any terms that would fail to win a two-thirds majority in the Senate.[4]

INDUCING THE OPPONENT TO WANT AGREEMENT

As long as you are negotiating but continuing to reject both no-agreement and the available terms, you are in fact trying to make your opponent choose the terms that you will make available to him (not necessarily the terms you offer, but those at which you will be willing to settle). This means that, while you are engaged in *further bargaining,* you must make your opponent prefer agreement to no-agreement and (to clinch the deal) dissuade him from further bargaining on his own behalf.

The first consideration is how to induce your opponent to prefer agreement to no-agreement. The opponent must be made to believe that the estimated consequences of no-agreement are worse for him than the terms you are willing to grant. One way of doing this is to make terms available that are more attractive to your opponent. Naturally, you will first try to do this without cutting into your own gains. That is, to sweeten the terms for your opponent, you will search for areas where his and your interests are not competitive. You may discover inducements to make agreement more valuable to your opponent without hurting yourself significantly. Formulations that help the opponent domestically fall into this category. Sometimes you may eliminate from your proposed terms aspects that are objectionable to the opponent without being of great importance to yourself.

[4] Conference on the Discontinuance of Nuclear Weapon Tests, 10th Plenary Meeting, Nov. 19, 1958.

Where there are only competitive interests, so that the terms cannot be made more interesting to your opponent without becoming correspondingly less desirable for yourself, you may promise to compensate in some other negotiation. The need for such extraneous inducements is one of the reasons for tie-ins or package deals between two negotiations. Parliamentary logrolling illustrates this process, as does its counterpart in the United Nations, where one delegate may induce another to vote for his favored resolution by promising to vote for some resolution favored by his colleague.

Instead of pulling your opponent toward agreement by making the terms more attractive to him, you can also try to push him by making no-agreement appear increasingly disadvantageous to him. It is here that threats and warnings play a key role. Warnings, as defined here, are useful where the absence of an agreement may have some inherently undesirable consequences for your opponent (without a special effort on your part). These inherent disadvantages of not having an agreement are precisely the reason why at least one of the sides wishes to begin negotiations.

Where the inherent disadvantages are not enough to make an opponent prefer a certain agreement to no-agreement, a threat will be needed. In redistribution negotiations, the defensive side is content to leave things as they are and has no incentive to satisfy the opponent's demands, unless the opponent succeeds in making a grave enough and credible enough threat. One of the particular difficulties of innovation negotiations is to make no-agreement undesirable to the opponent if the gains from agreement do not provide a sufficient pull. To last for some time, innovations usually require a certain amount of mutual accommodation. A complex and continuing cooperative undertaking cannot thrive if the parties act in a strongly antagonistic way toward each other. Therefore threats have to be used with utmost restraint—the threat of force is normally unavailable for innovations. As mentioned before, an important leverage to push reluctant parties into an innovation agreement is the prospect of exclusion.

Edward Heath, the chief British negotiator for England's entry into the European Communities, was in an unenviable position in 1962. He could not make agreement more attractive to the Six member countries without jeopardizing support at home, and he could not make no-agreement more undesirable to the Six without hurting his effort to be accepted as a loyal member. And since Britain was the excluded party, he could not use the threat of exclusion. Given the fact that France, the most powerful member of the European Communities, felt it would lose more by British membership than it would gain (in particular that it might lose its leading role in Europe), the British could not prevent France from choosing no-agreement in preference to agreement.

Both warnings and threats may be used to deter the opponent from choosing no-agreement, but both have to be supported. A variety of political, economic, or military preparations can make warnings more serious and threats, if carried out, more costly to the opponent. In addition, commitments serve to make threats credible. The opponent, in turn, can improve his prospects under no-agreement through various counteractions, so that he is less pressured to accept agreement at available terms. Such counteractions probably helped to settle the 1961–62 phase of the Berlin negotiations in favor of the West. Allied military preparations and contingency planning in the summer of 1961—in particular the strengthening of America's conventional forces in Europe—improved the means for coping with the threatened blockade. This made it less likely that the Communist threat would be carried out and less disastrous if it was. Hence the Western powers could more confidently challenge the threat and choose no-agreement instead of accepting Khrushchev's terms.

DISSUADING THE OPPONENT FROM FURTHER BARGAINING

The interaction of your threefold choice with that of your opponent must now be explored further. As has been said, it is not enough to make your opponent dislike no-agreement more than agreement at your present terms, for he is not forced to choose between these two options. He can choose to engage in further bargaining in the hope that you will soften your terms. His hope is not unreasonable, because he knows—or he thinks he knows— that you would rather have an agreement than not, even if you have to soften your terms, provided you do not have to soften them too much. But what is "too much"? If no-agreement looks sufficiently bad to you, you might be prepared to go a long way to avoid it by accommodating the wishes of your opponent. The tables can be turned; your opponent can try to influence your choice between agreement and no-agreement much as you tried to influence his. Only when he sees no gain in this attempt, while still preferring agreement at available terms to no-agreement, will he accept the terms that you make available to him. Hence to dissuade your opponent from further bargaining becomes your objective.

The most important tactic for this purpose is to demonstrate to your opponent that your terms are unlikely to become more advantageous for him. This can be done most convincingly if you can show that no-agreement will always look better to you than an agreement for which you would have to reduce your terms. If your terms are reducible only in a single big step, such as giving up a voting majority in a proposed organization, then your minimum terms (i.e., the terms below which no-agreement would seem preferable to you) may still secure you significant gains. But if your terms can be reduced in small slices (such as monetary compensation or, in fact, any complex agreement), your opponent will try to push them down to the point where you just barely gain something by having an agreement as compared with not having one. Hence you will try to make him think that your minimum lies higher than it really does.

Your opponent may realize, however, that you will still prefer agreement if you have to lower your terms. Other techniques are therefore required to demonstrate to your opponent that your terms are unlikely to soften. A useful device is a commitment not to change your terms or a commitment not to accept the opponent's demands.

Apart from trying to convince your opponent that your terms are firm, you might dissuade him from further bargaining by making procrastination seem dangerous to him. In an acute crisis, the danger of postponing a settlement is a particularly compelling reason for accepting the offered terms. Khrushchev's sudden acquiescence in October, 1962, to the demand for withdrawal of his missiles from Cuba was probably largely motivated by the fear of sudden American action—such as an air-strike against the missile sites—that would have put him in a worse position. It seemed wiser to Khrushchev completely to drop his counterdemand for a withdrawal of American missiles in Turkey than to face the risks of further bargaining.

A related technique is to make the opponent fear that one's terms, far from moving closer to his wishes, might actually harden. That is, your opponent must get the idea that he would miss an opportunity should he fail to accept your offer.

In more slowly moving negotiations, there are pressures of a different kind that can be generated to make the opponent anxious for a quick settlement. During the Korean truce talks, continued American casualties from Chinese attacks and the uncertain fate of the American prisoners induced the UN negotiators to accept the Communist terms on many issues. Often, one side suffers far more from the postponement of an agreement than the other side. Such an asymmetry is one of the most cogent factors in pushing the side that is in a hurry toward its minimum position.

Lastly, the opponent might be induced to accept the available terms by the prospect that the negotiations will end at a certain date regardless of whether or not an agreement has been reached. This prospect may arise either because a deadline has been imposed by external circumstances or because the first party deliberately created a deadline or issued a threat of rupture. After the 1946 Paris Peace Conference, the final decisions on the peace treaties were made at a Council of Foreign Ministers meeting in New York. When Molotov refused to accept most recommendations of the Peace Conference, Secretary of State Byrnes warned him: "It is with the greatest reluctance, therefore, that I have come to the conclusion we will not be able to agree upon the treaties. Having become reconciled to this, I think we should agree to disagree. . . ." Molotov was impressed by the risk of rupture when Byrnes stood by his warning, and a few days later he gave in, accepting almost all the Paris recommendations.[5]

However, threats of rupture and deliberate deadlines are double-edged swords. The opponent can turn it against you if he thinks that you are bluffing or if he is better at brinkmanship by risking more readily than you the danger of winding up with no-agreement. Your opponent can doubly tempt you not to carry out your

[5] James F. Byrnes, *Speaking Frankly* (New York: Harper, 1947), pp. 152–54.

threat to interrupt or break off negotiations: first, he can let the deadline approach closer and closer, waiting for you to make concessions; and, second, he can let the deadline pass but offer to continue negotiations. He might even consent to the fiction of "stopping the clocks" in the conference room, should this reduce the commitment of your bargaining reputation to your threat of rupture.

These drawbacks of deliberately imposed deadlines were experienced by the French Premier Pierre Mendès-France when he negotiated the Indochina settlement at the Geneva conference in 1954. On June 17, Mendès-France said he would resign as Premier unless he could produce a satisfactory cease-fire before July 20. While the Russians and the Chinese, of course, did not care about Mendès-France's resignation as such, they might have feared that a successor government would put a greater military effort into Indochina or would support the ratification of the European Defense Community that the Russians wanted to prevent. As the deadline approached, the French delegation clearly did make some last-minute concessions, and in the end the conference continued past the deadline by one day, with the "clocks stopped," so that no one expected Mendès-France to resign. It is somewhat doubtful whether Mendès-France's threat of rupture helped or hindered the French cause; but some observers feel that without the threat the conference would have ended only a few weeks later at terms slightly better for the West.

The threat of rupture can be highly effective if the negotiator is in the process of departing, in such a way that he would have no excuse at all for staying unless his opponent called him back by offering a concession. Here the negotiator is no longer saying, "I am going to leave." He is demonstrating, "I am leaving." This technique has numerous examples in diplomatic history. The ambassador of Louis XIV to Charles II, after negotiating at length over the price at which his king would buy Dunkirk from England, finally boarded a ship ready to sail for Denmark when Charles II sent for him and offered the final concession that closed the deal.[6] At the Berlin Conference in 1878, according to one account, Dis-

[6] G. Estrades, Comte de, *Lettres, Mémoires et Négociations* (London: J. Nourse, 1743), I, 377.

raeli forced Bismarck and the Russians to give in on a significant British demand by ordering a train that would have taken him back to London.[7]

De Gaulle reports that during his negotiations in Moscow in December, 1944, he also used this technique successfully. Stalin tried to obtain French recognition for the Communist Lublin Committee as the Government of Poland, before agreeing to a Franco-Russian Security Pact in which De Gaulle was interested. But De Gaulle did not want the pact at this price and succeeded in convincing Stalin of his determination by getting ready to leave Moscow. The negotiations had remained deadlocked for some days, when De Gaulle got up one evening at the end of a large dinner party and announced to Stalin and the astonished Molotov that he was returning home. He called for his Foreign Minister Bidault to follow him to the French Embassy, leaving only some junior members of the French delegation behind. These officials reported to De Gaulle, after a long meeting with Stalin and Molotov, that the Russians would now be ready to sign the pact in exchange for a quite adulterated version of recognition of the Lublin Committee. De Gaulle, however, still refused. Consequently Stalin soon dropped all demands for recognition of Lublin, and the Franco-Russian pact was finally signed.[8]

HEDGING AGAINST FAILURE

If a party engages in further bargaining, for the purpose of obtaining better terms, it is taking certain risks. It runs the risk that the outcome might deteriorate: the opponent might either stiffen his terms or might suddenly choose no-agreement while the first party would have preferred agreement even at the opponent's original terms. In other situations, the improved terms resulting from continued negotiation might not be worth the loss incurred by delaying agreement. As said previously, it is precisely these

---

[7] A. N. Cummings, "The Secret History of the Treaty of Berlin," *Nineteenth Century Review* (July, 1905), pp. 86–88. This account is disputed, however, by W. N. Medlicott, *The Congress of Berlin and After* (London: Methuen, 1938).

[8] Charles de Gaulle, *Salvation, 1944–1946* (*War Memoirs* [London: Weidenfeld and Nicolson, 1959]), pp. 78–81. The only concession De Gaulle made was to announce a few days later that a French officer had been sent to Lublin.

risks that your opponent exploits when he tries to dissuade you from further bargaining and make you accept his position. Agreement occurs at that delicate point, when both you and your opponent decide to settle for the available terms rather than incur the costs and risks of trying to do better.

Other risks result from the very process of negotiation. Two of the negotiator's principal instruments—commitments and threats —have the peculiar characteristic of hurting the party which uses them if they fail to achieve their purpose. A crucial instrument for the offensive party in redistribution negotiations is the threat to hurt the opponent should he choose no-agreement (such as Khrushchev's implied threat of a Berlin blockade). If such a threat fails to make the opponent comply, the threatener is forced to choose between two evils: either he accepts the onus of being a bluffer, or he carries out the threat—an act that may do him no good at that point and may actually harm him. If a threat to break off negotiations at a certain date fails to make the opponent soften his terms, this will put before the threatener an equally undesirable choice: either he continues negotiations and thereby admits to being a bluffer, or he winds up with no-agreement where he would have preferred an agreement.

Similarly with commitments. Your commitment to carry out a threat may convince your opponent that he should take your threat seriously, but by its very nature it will make *not* carrying out the threat more costly should you prefer to do so after your opponent fails to comply. Your commitment to a negotiating position, if it fails to persuade your opponent to accept your terms, will hurt you when you want to make a concession later to avoid winding up with no-agreement. Likewise, your commitment to a deadline will aggravate your dilemma when your opponent lets the deadline pass without moving closer to your position.

These risks, in part, account for the fact that threats are usually vague and used sparingly and that commitments frequently are kept ambiguous. Where the opponent's reaction remains somewhat unpredictable, governments want to hedge against failure of their negotiating tactics. Yet, this very hedging makes threats and commitments less convincing.

CHAPTER 6

THE BARGAINING REPUTATION

THE WAY IN WHICH A GOVERNMENT NEGOTIATES AND THE CONditions under which it accepts or rejects an agreement have an important bearing on its bargaining strength in the future. In every diplomatic confrontation, governments are trying not only to affect the terms of agreement under negotiation but also to protect or improve their strength in future negotiations. What they have in mind can best be explained as a *reputation*. A government acquires a reputation much as an individual does. On the basis of its performance in past negotiations, others will impute to it a diplomatic style, certain motives and objectives, attitudes toward the use of force, a degree of political will, and other attributes of power. Bargaining strength depends not so much on what these attributes really are as on what others believe them to be. Hence the importance of this reputation.

In Chapter 4, a number of effects from negotiation were discussed that do not concern agreement, such as propaganda, maintenance of contact, or substitutes for violence. These side-effects are peripheral to the bargaining process proper and may be found in conferences where neither party seeks or expects an agreement. A negotiator's reputation, however, *does* concern agreement. It is shaped by the way in which he has reached agreements in the past, and it affects his power to influence agreements in the future.

The influence of the bargaining reputation can easily be explained in the context of two opponents trying to influence each other's threefold choice between agreement at the opponent's terms, no-agreement, and further bargaining. If you are the negotiator, you know that your opponent's threefold choice will be governed in part by his anticipations of your reactions. He bases these anticipations on his image of you, concerning such attributes as your attitude toward risk-taking, your tendency to bluff, your evaluation of your own strength and his, your tendency to hold fast to a position, and so forth. Naturally, your opponent will assume a certain continuity in these attributes and base his estimates of them partly on your performance in previous negotiations. Knowing this, you will act in every negotiation not only so as to obtain a favorable outcome at that time but also so as to preserve or improve your negotiating strength in the future. The fact that these two considerations frequently conflict adds an important complication to the negotiating process.

The influence of the bargaining reputation can be paraphrased in the language of game theory: an international negotiation is never a self-contained "game" but is a phase vaguely related to a never-ending "super-game." Although each phase yields its own payoffs, the tactics used in it affect the opponent's calculations in subsequent phases and hence influence subsequent payoffs. The "super-game" comes to an end only under exceptional circumstances: a government whose existence is at stake and which expects no continuity with its successor may contemplate the losing situation (but not the winning one!) as the end of the "super-game."

However, a bargaining reputation is not permanent. It changes because governments do not behave the same way in every negotiation and memories are frequently short. Also, a particular reputation is often confined to a specific subject; what a government does in political conferences may not impress its opponents in commercial conferences.

IS HE A BLUFFER?

Whether or not your opponent imputes to you a tendency to bluff is one of the most important factors in a bargaining reputation. There are several ways of making your threats more credible. One way, as has been shown, is through commitments. Another way is to cultivate a reputation of not being a bluffer. A third way exploits the fact (to be dealt with later) that governments are organizations composed of human beings, who may carry out their threats because they tend to act in anger, impulsively, or out of feelings of revenge and spitefulness.

A reputation for not bluffing works much like a commitment: it creates a vested interest in being consistent. If your opponent takes you up on your threat, the disadvantage of carrying it out will be outweighed by the long-term damage to your reputation from not carrying it out. Your opponent, knowing this, may not challenge your threat. A reputation of carrying out one's threat can be acquired by a nation with a purely expediential orientation; it does not require feelings of honor or a moral conviction. It *pays* not to become known as a bluffer, in order to preserve one's capacity for making credible threats.

Diplomatic history records relatively few instances of clear, explicit threats that turned out to be a bluff (although explicit threats that were carried out are even rarer). Far more frequent are explicit agreements that have clearly been broken by one side. This is paradoxical, because it would seem to be as disadvantageous for a government to be known for violating agreements as for bluffing in negotiations. After all, not to carry out a threat might even be construed as a concession and used as an argument for demanding counter-concessions, but the same cannot be said about violating an agreement. And while occasional bluffs that have been called may damage the bargaining reputation, they will not ruin it. Those who are threatened next time cannot know for sure that they are facing another bluff.

This extraordinary reluctance of modern governments to have their bluffs called in an unequivocal fashion forces them to hedge by keeping threats vague. In contrast to threats for military deterrence, threats in diplomatic negotiations are usually vague whenever two conditions are met: the threatening government harbors some doubts as to whether the opponent will comply, and it anticipates that it would be reluctant to carry out the threat. Vagueness may be obtained in three ways: the threatener may not state categorically that he would inflict the reprisals on the opponent in case of noncompliance, he may not spell out what constitutes non-compliance, or he may fail to predict what the reprisals would consist of. Obviously, the vagueness will not go undetected by the opponent, who will accordingly be less impressed.

A curious example of clear-cut bluffing was Khrushchev's failure for over four years ever to carry out his repeated threats that he would sign a separate peace treaty with East Germany within a given time period unless the Western powers agreed to withdraw at least partially from West Berlin. The threat was first made in November, 1958, with a six-month time limit; then the time limit was extended by days, weeks, and months. After the Western powers had called the bluff of Khrushchev's first time limit, he put forward another one-year limit in June, 1959, and only a few days later extended it to a year and a half. A year later, in May, 1960, Khrushchev said the question would be negotiated "in six or eight months." This more veiled threat, again, proved to be a bluff. And on June 15, 1961, upon returning from the Vienna meeting with President Kennedy, he indicated again that the peace treaty would be signed within six months: "We ask everyone to understand us correctly: the conclusion of a peace treaty with Germany cannot be postponed any longer. A peaceful settlement in Europe must be attained this year."

The Berlin negotiations, like all redistribution negotiations, did require a threat by the offensive side to make no-agreement unde-sirable for the defensive side. Khrushchev's separate peace treaty, however, was only the first stage of such a threat. The cutting edge came with the second stage, the prediction that the East German regime would then interfere with Western access in Berlin. Having made the first stage so explicit, Khrushchev needed only to hint at the second stage and leave it to the West to fathom all its horrible implications. Initially, this tactic seemed to have several advantages. A peace treaty could be presented as normalization rather than redistribution, it was wholly in Khrushchev's power to sign it, and unlikely to provoke the West into major counteraction. Hence the first stage was credible. The second stage, for its part, was a safe threat to make. Its implementation was theoretically up to the East German Communists, and should it not be carried out—for fear of Western reprisals—Khrushchev would not be unequivocally proved a bluffer.

Soviet diplomacy, however, overplayed the two-stage threat tactic until it boomeranged. Naturally, an explicit threat with a deadline that can be carried out with impunity (hence a credible threat) must be carried out after the opponent challenges it. Otherwise the threatener becomes tinged with the reputation of being a flagrant bluffer. Since so many deadlines have passed without the East German peace treaty being signed, the Western powers and the world at large are less likely to take seriously similar threats of Khrushchev in the future. It is not so much that the credibility of Soviet threats decreased among Western decision-makers and their advisers—though this may be one effect. What counts more is the impact upon intra-allied and domestic decision-making in the West. Those who might consider it wise to heed a similar Soviet threat in the future would be hard put to justify this against those who will advise ignoring it. The proponents of a harder line might win the domestic debate, since there is little justification for giving in to threats by a proved bluffer.

When it comes to warnings or threats to break off negotiations, the Russians have been more successful in maintaining a reputation of credibility. Their past actions demonstrate that they have no inhibition against breaking up a conference. In fact, they often give the appearance of being ready to walk out any time, often without explicit advance warning. American and British diplomats, however, rarely break up an international conference. This puts them at a certain disadvantage in dealing with Soviet negotiators, since they feel under constant pressure of this latent or explicit threat of rupture. Thus during the unpoliced moratorium on nuclear testing, the U.S. government was unwilling to resume testing for fear that the Russians would discontinue the marathon talks (which could have led to criticism of the United States as having "caused" this break). Yet, after the sudden *Soviet* resumption of testing, the talks continued, and they continued also after American testing was then resumed.

The abruptness with which De Gaulle terminated the negotiations on Britain's entry into the Common Market in January, 1963, may in part have been motivated by his knowledge that it pays to be known as a man who suddenly breaks off negotiations. In 1958, he acted in a similar way when he abruptly stopped the prolonged negotiations with Great Britain and other European nations for an enlarged free-trade area. (This wider free-trade area might have dissolved the Common Market which was then just beginning to be formed.) Those who negotiate with De Gaulle know that in prolonged negotiations, rather than inching toward better terms, they may suddenly wind up with no-agreement.

Governments generally try to maintain a reputation for refusing negotiation under an explicit threat. This, of course, helps to deter threats, particularly those by the offensive side in redistribution negotiations. On this count, too, De Gaulle's bargaining reputation seems to be stronger than that, say, of the British or American government. In America and Great Britain the view that negotiation may serve as a substitute for violent action often takes precedence over the maxim that one should not negotiate under an explicit threat. Since 1961, De Gaulle has been opposed to negotiating on the Soviet demand regarding West Berlin. As his Foreign Minister Couve de Murville put it in December, 1961, at the time when the other two major Western powers were rather active in such talks: "As far as the methods [for dealing with the Berlin crisis] are concerned, we have never accepted the idea that it was possible to negotiate under a threat, even if this is the supreme threat, that of atomic destruction."[1]

DOES HE AVOID TESTS OF STRENGTH?

Between long-term antagonists, negotiation over issues of military or political importance always has a twofold effect on their balance of strength. First, the settlement reached may change attributes of power, such as the distribution of territory, the deployment of forces, or political influence. Second, the way in which the settlement has been reached may change the interplay of mutual expectations between the antagonists so as to alter their deterrents or incentives for future actions against each other. The way in which your antagonist has negotiated may lead you to revise your image of your opponent's view of the balance of forces

[1] *Journal Officiel de la République Française* (Sénat), Dec. 5, 1961, p. 2296.

and of his attitude toward the use of force. You will base your future actions against your opponent on this revised image of *his* views of your mutual power relationship.

One of the main indictments against British and French appeasement of Hitler has been that it encouraged the German dictator to increasingly bolder offensive action, because it suggested that the Western powers either felt themselves inferior in military strength or were simply unwilling to use force. On August 22, 1939, when Hitler was about to launch World War II, he reassured his commanders-in-chief: "Our enemies are little worms; I saw them at Munich."[2]

In the Cuban crisis in 1962, Khrushchev's sudden withdrawal of his missiles made it clear that he was unwilling to risk a show of strength in an area where he had local inferiority. He thereby indicated that he felt himself strategically inferior (certainly without enough superiority convincingly to threaten nuclear war) and hence did not want to initiate a local counteraction elsewhere (e.g., a blockade of Berlin) which could lead to a local war and eventual American strategic attack. Khrushchev therefore demonstrated that he doubts neither America's determination nor its superiority in strategic weapons.

The conflict concerning the Quemoy Islands also illustrates the importance of maintaining a reputation of strength. Since the mid-1950s the suggestion has been made that the United States induce the Chinese Nationalists to abandon these islands at a time when the Chinese Communists are not pressing to get them. The idea here is that, although the islands are of little value by themselves and hard to hold, their surrender under pressure would create a reputation of admitted weakness.

IS HE FIRM?

In the interplay of your threefold choice with that of your opponent, you want him to believe that he might just as well accept

[2] Quoted by Chester Wilmot, *The Struggle for Europe* (London: Collins, 1952), p. 21. For a recent study of the Munich conference and its after-effects see Keith Eubank, *Munich* (Norman, Okla.: University of Oklahoma Press, 1963).

your terms since they will not become more advantageous for him.
His expectations as to whether or not your position will remain
firm depends partly on his image of your customary behavior. If
you have a reputation of asking for less and less, until a long,
declining sequence of your demands has been rejected, your opponent will expect that he might gain through prolonged negotiations, and he will be reluctant to accept your terms. Your
opponent's expectations, however, are affected not only by your
reputation of firmness in the past but also by your interest in your
future reputation. That is, you may appear unlikely to give in, not
only out of habit since this is the way you have been acting in the
past, but also out of calculation since giving in would spoil your
reputation in future negotiations. The more you can convince your
opponent that giving in would spoil your bargaining strength in
the future, the more will he conclude that it is in your interest
to have no-agreement rather than to soften your terms; even
though for this particular instance in isolation, softened terms
would still be better for you than no agreement at all. What this
means is that the involvement of your bargaining reputation can
serve as a commitment to your negotiation position; and the more
you enjoy a reputation of always remaining firm, the more convincing is this commitment to the opponent.

This kind of commitment can be strengthened with a self-ful-
filling prophecy. A party may predict that if it gave in at the
present issue, it would "have to" give in over similar issues in
future negotiations. The "have to" here refers to an internal or-
ganizational rigidity rather than to external pressures. By linking
the present issue with certain future ones, the government tries to
convince the opponent that it cannot yield, since its domestic
decision-making process would then force it to yield again on those
future issues. The government is in fact arguing that it is so
attached to precedents that it cannot yield on the first issue without
yielding on the analogous second issue.

Accusing the opponent of "salami tactics" helps the defensive
side in redistribution negotiations to deny small concessions. Even
the smallest diminution of the status quo becomes part and parcel
of a process, a slice out of many. The defensive side commits itself
to the full integrity of its position by construing the surrender of

any slice as capitulation to the slicing process. Of course, this view need not be invented only for the sake of making a commitment. The offensive side might indeed want to turn the smallest victory into a series of advances. In addition, by giving in on the small issue, the defensive side might violate a guaranty to one of its allies and thereby undermine allied confidence in other guaranties and treaties.

Related here is the role of principles in the defense of a position. A government which demonstrates that it maintains a position for the sake of the principle involved indicates that it is not so much interested in the intrinsic value of that position but in the preservation of its reputation of being consistent. This interest in consistency need not be feigned, because in future negotiations the same principles might again serve to defend a position. Moreover, there is also an internal requirement for consistency in most governments, stemming from the bureaucratic need for a continuity of rules as well as from the difficulty of changing official doctrines and adapting national ideologies.

Though a reputation of firmness may discourage your opponent from trying to whittle down your position, it may also discourage him from entering negotiations at all and perhaps prompt him to create a *fait accompli* instead. Likewise, a commitment to principles may anchor your position to firm ground, but it may also keep you out of any region where the opponent would become interested in seeking agreement. This is illustrated by the Allied commitment in World War II to the principle of demanding unconditional surrender of all enemy powers. In the Italian campaign, the principle of unconditional surrender made it harder to extract Italy from German control, and in the Far East it worked against American and British interests by prolonging the war against Japan and permitting the Russians to make great gains with their last-minute intervention.[3]

The interaction of expectations is an essential feature of negotiation. The reason why your commitment to principles and your reputation of firmness help you is that they make your opponent expect that he cannot get better terms. Once he is sure that you are

[3] See Paul Kecskemeti, *Strategic Surrender* (Stanford, Calif.: Stanford University Press, 1958), especially pp. 228–30.

irrevocably committed, he will accept your terms, provided he finds them preferable to no-agreement and provided the loss to *his* bargaining reputation from accepting them does not outweigh his gains from agreement. However, your opponent need not remain passive toward these commitments and principles of yours that get in the way of his making further gains. There are techniques to loosen commitments.

In redistribution negotiations, for example, the offensive side may promise that it will not engage in "salami tactics"; it may suggest that it is making the notorious "last territorial demand," after which there will be no further conflicts. In this way Khrushchev hinted that after the solution of the Berlin crisis a general peaceful settlement of all conflicts in Europe would easily be found. Sukarno similarly reduced the resistance to his demands for West New Guinea in 1962 by declaring that he had no further territorial ambitions. Alas, after the *Anschluss* comes *Sudetenland:* less than a year after Sukarno had incorporated West New Guinea, he tried to interfere with North Borneo's merger with Malaya and so extend his dominance over this neighboring territory.

Commitments based on the attachment to principles can also be weakened by formulating the demands so that they seem to leave the principles untouched, carving out only the substance as it were. Khrushchev's promise, that West Berlin's political and economic system would be left undisturbed if his proposal for a "free city" was accepted, was designed to circumvent the commitment of the Western powers to the principle of not turning over territory to Communism. The Dutch surrender of West New Guinea to Indonesia was made easier by preserving the principle of Papuan self-determination to which the Dutch were committed. The principle was maintained because Sukarno pledged himself to hold a plebiscite in New Guinea six years later. But the Dutch must have recognized full well that elections so many years after the *Anschluss,* if held at all, would probably not be free enough to offer self-determination in substance.

As Thomas Schelling pointed out, secrecy in negotiations can be used to reduce the involvement of bargaining reputations and to eliminate those commitments whose binding power depends on public knowledge.[4] But secrecy cannot protect or suspend one's bargaining reputation entirely. For one thing, your opponent will know what happened, and *his* view of your reputation may be the most important one. In addition, the results usually become public even though the process of reacing the settlement may be kept secret.

Secrecy itself can throw negotiators under suspicion. If the public or nonparticipating governments sense an undercover bargain, a sequel unconnected with the agreement actually reached in secrecy may impair the bargaining reputation, whereas completely open negotiations could have proved the sequel to be purely coincidental. After the Cuban crisis in 1962, the American withdrawal of missiles from Turkey and Italy created such suspicions. Khrushchev's original demand for the withdrawal of American missiles in Turkey in exchange for the withdrawal of his missiles from Cuba was rejected by the United States. Accepting it would have seriously impaired the American bargaining reputation and American guaranties toward allies: it would have implied that Khrushchev could have forced an American retreat merely by canceling an advance of his own. Unfortunately, however, the United States waited only three months after the Cuban crisis to announce the withdrawal of its missiles from both Turkey and Italy for the reason that these weapons had become obsolete. Since part of the negotiations between Khrushchev and Kennedy during the Cuban crisis were kept secret, the suspicion could arise that this latter withdrawal was agreed to during these negotiations.

What happens in the reverse case, where the committed party itself wants to loosen its commitment? A party that wishes to facilitate agreement by offering its opponent a certain concession has every interest that this should not appear as a violation of its principles. It will try to make the situation appear unique and isolated, so that the concession stands all by itself and does not suggest repetition in similar contexts.

[4] *The Strategy of Conflict*, pp. 29–30.

CHAPTER 7

RULES OF ACCOMMODATION

IN NEGOTATIONS BETWEEN FRIENDLY COUNTRIES, THERE IS A SET of rules whose violation would almost invariably terminate the friendly relationship, at least temporarily. For example, unambiguous lies must be avoided, explicit promises have to be kept, invective is never to be used, explicit threats must not be issued, agreements in principle must not be blatantly violated when it comes to the execution of details, and mutual understandings must not be deliberately misconstrued later on. In addition to these hard rules, there are soft rules that cannot be violated repeatedly without eroding the friendly relationship. For instance, the opponent's domestic difficulties should not be exploited in public, debts of gratitude should be honored (e.g., a concession acknowledged as such must be returned when the opportunity arises), motives should not be impugned, and the discourse ought to be reasonable in the sense that questions are answered, arguments are to the point, facts are not grossly distorted, repetition is minimized, and technical discussions are kept on a factual level.

The parties, by adhering to these rules of conduct, may facilitate accommodation in two ways. On the one hand, they may make the negotiating process more efficient in the sense of increasing the chances for agreement on the immediate issues. On the other hand, rule-conforming conduct may reduce hostility between governments and perhaps stimulate friendly feelings between the leaders or between influential officials of each nation. These improved attitudes, in turn, will help to minimize conflict and make future agreements more likely.

Some rules of accommodation are observed even between bitter enemies whose relationship approaches a "zero-sum" conflict, as it is called in game theory. (In such a conflict, what one side gains in strength, security, or economic and political advantages, the other side loses.) Although any gain to one's deadly foe constitutes *ipso facto* a loss to oneself, in reality this loss is often outweighed by other considerations which stop the conflict short of "zero-sum." If this is the case for both sides, the prerequisite common interest for negotiation exists. And given a common interest in an agreement, both sides must also have an interest in methods that can help to bring agreement about. This explains the tacit or explicit understandings between bitter antagonists on rules to facilitate the negotiating process.

The less the hostility, however, the wider the scope of negotiating conduct that the rules can affect and the more infrequent their violation. Among friendly nations, the incentive to disregard a certain rule for the sake of a short-term gain is usually outweighed by the desire to preserve good relations.

Because of this interdependence, a change in foreign relations from hostility to friendship (or vice versa) is normally accompanied by a change in negotiating style. Often it is hard to say which is the cause and which the effect. Indeed, statesmen have tried—sometimes with success—to bring about friendlier relations by practicing an accommodating style unilaterally.

Khrushchev must have had this in mind when he maintained that the Soviet Union had been generous in recent negotiations with Iran. "It was on the Soviet government's initiative," he reported in one of his speeches, "that the Soviet-Iranian agreement was concluded, settling border issues. That agreement put an end to disputes 100 to 150 years old, and the border was redefined mostly at the expense of Soviet territory. Ours is a great country and our territory is vast. *We decided that we did not have to be closefisted, that we should rather yield some ground, but win friends.* This, as the saying goes, is better than having an extra kopek in one's pocket."[1]

The same idea, on a much grander scale, guided Franklin D. Roosevelt in his conduct of American relations with the Soviet Union. In 1942, he told William C. Bullitt, the former American ambassador in Moscow: "I have just a hunch that Stalin doesn't want anything but security for his country, and I think that if I give him everything that I possibly can and ask nothing from him in return, *noblesse oblige,* he won't try to annex anything and will work for a world of democracy and peace."[2] The failure of this approach was one of the most tragic setbacks in the history of American diplomacy.

There are less disappointing cases, however, where deep-rooted hostilities between nations did disappear when a tradition of accommodating negotiations became established. American-British relations went through such a transformation at the end of the nineteenth century, with a marked turning point in 1897 when Great Britain accepted President Grover Cleveland's request to submit her boundary dispute with Venezuela to arbitration. Although the British Foreign Secretary, Lord Salisbury, was first taken aback by the American request and its peremptory tone, he was induced to be cautious by some developments against British interests in other areas, and fifteen months later he decided to make a conciliatory move by proposing a general arbitration treaty between Great Britain and the United States, and by accepting most of the American conditions for arbitration with Venezuela. As it turned out, the British-American treaty was not ratified by the U.S. Senate, and the concessions in accepting arbitration of the dispute with Venezuela did not hurt British interests, since nearly all the contested territory was awarded to British Guiana. Nonetheless, Salisbury's concessions were followed by a lasting Anglo-American *rapprochement.*

The improvement in Franco-German relations after World

[1] Speech given Feb. 24, 1959. Italics added. N. S. Khrushchev, *World without Arms, World without Wars,* Book 1 (Moscow, 1959), p. 141.

[2] William C. Bullitt, "How We Won the War and Lost the Peace," *Life,* Aug. 30, 1948.

War II was facilitated by the accommodating negotiating style of both Paris and Bonn. This style was particularly important for reaching a settlement on the protracted conflict about the Saar, which had obstructed the consolidation of the new friendship between France and Germany for years.[3]

Another reason for the observance of rules of accommodation, in addition to the idea that they may lead to friendlier relations on a bilateral basis, is the expectation that other nations will reciprocate the negotiating *style*. That is, the rules establish a mutually useful form of conduct, rather than serving as an expression of good will. Each government knows that it will always be engaged in negotiation, and it may expect that its own negotiating methods will be reflected in those of its opponents. Hence governments may adopt those methods which they would like to see adopted generally. This is the equivalent in diplomacy of Kant's categorical imperative in ethics.

However, while those who observe rules of accommodation would obviously prefer the opponent to reciprocate, this is not always felt to be mandatory. Some rules are expected to produce beneficial results even if the opponent ignores them; others require reciprocation only in the long run. (As mentioned, unilateral generosity may be a means of overcoming old antagonisms.) At any rate, to some negotiators the efficacy of the rules seems secondary because they follow them as the conventionally correct behavior, in keeping with the proprieties. Breaking the rules—rather than being simply inexpedient—would appear to be unseemly, a breach of decorum, or even immoral.

Thus a negotiator may adhere to rules of accommodation for any of three reasons. First, in some situations he may think that rule-conforming behavior is expedient, either because it enhances friendly relations with another country or because it makes other countries reciprocate and thus facilitates agreement. Second, in other situations, he does not hope for such results but adheres to certain rules merely because he thinks that others feel it is proper to do so, and he is afraid to shock domestic critics or governments of third countries by breaking the rules. Third, he observes some

[3] For a thorough study see Jacques Freymond, *The Saar Conflict, 1945–1955* (New York: Praeger, 1960).

rules regardless of external circumstances because he himself would consider it unseemly or immoral to violate them. The second reason, the desire not to shock others, is particularly cogent if the negotiations can be affected by a mediator who might turn against the party that violates the rules.

Normally, negotiators do not separate these three reasons clearly. Western statesmen and diplomats, in particular, are usually motivated by a mixture of expediential calculations and moral convictions when following an accommodating negotiation style. If the adherence to certain rules is questioned at all, it is the expediential calculation which is usually stressed in private discussions within the government, while the moral justification might be emphasized in public. Very often, a rule is followed without questioning. And even if an expediential explanation is given, it may well have been invented to justify in a hard-boiled way what is obscurely but strongly felt to be the "proper" thing to do.

Some rules of accommodation can now be examined in greater detail. In many cases, incidents when these rules were *not* being observed make the better illustration, since such exceptions demarcate the customary conduct. Besides, it must be stressed that most of these rules are not universally accepted. Although some are fully shared by Communist and Western negotiators (even though there may be many breaches in their observance), a greater number are considered valid only by Westerners or by Americans alone. Discussing the rules is not equivalent to saying that all of them actually serve the purposes they are supposed to serve: they do not necessarily facilitate agreement, engender good will, or enhance any other interests of the governments adhering to them. On the contrary, some rules make negotiation more difficult; far from facilitating agreement, they create additional conflicts or lead to protracted debates.

Some of the rules of accommodation that are being observed in negotiations—or that, according to Western views, *ought* to be observed—are related to, or part of, public international law. They can be deduced from international conventions regarding diplomatic immunities and representation and from the legal doctrines about treaty-making, equality of states, and the pacific settlement of international disputes.

NEVER KILL A NEGOTIATOR

The most elementary rule of accommodation is that the opponent's representatives should not be physically harmed. In fact, the inviolability of the messenger who has been sent by a neighboring state, a rebellious province, or a feuding rival might be said to mark the beginning of international diplomacy. In spite of repeated violations during antiquity and the Middle Ages, this principle became firmly established and was gradually expanded into the modern code of diplomatic immunities.

If political authorities do not have diplomatic relations with each other—as in the case of a rebellion or war—the authorized envoy may be given a promise of safe conduct to assure him that the rule of inviolability applies despite his contestable diplomatic status. The emissary would be risking his life without such a guaranty, and, what might be worse for both parties, the negotiations might never get started. One would expect that no government would want to discredit its promises of safe conduct by imprisoning or executing negotiators to whom it gave assurances, since this could deprive it of negotiating channels at some future occasion when it might badly need them.

People have such short memories, however, when it comes to violations of international norms, that twentieth-century dictators are no more likely than ancient kings to be deterred from killing or imprisoning envoys whom they promised safety—and they have used this trick repeatedly. In March, 1945, for example, the political police of the Soviet Union invited the Polish Underground to send a delegation to Moscow to discuss the formation of a united Polish government in accordance with the Yalta agreement. The delegation had received a written guaranty of personal safety. It was made up of fifteen people headed by General Okulicki, and it included eleven leaders representing the major political parties in Poland. None of them returned from the meeting. Not until two months later did Molotov admit that these men were being held in Russia. In June, after Stalin denied that the Polish leaders had ever been invited to Moscow, they were tried and most of them sentenced to long terms of imprisonment.[4]

[4] See Winston S. Churchill, *Triumph and Tragedy,* pp. 497–501.

Eleven years later the same government repeated this performance. During the Hungarian Revolution, the Soviet Military Command in Hungary invited General Maléter (who had just become Minister of Defense) and other delegates of the revolutionary Hungarian government to complete certain technical details of an agreement for the withdrawal of Soviet troops. This invitation turned out to be a trap for the arrest of Maléter and his delegation by the Soviet security police.[5] Later, these Hungarian leaders were killed.

Moise Tshombe, the secessionist leader of the Congo's Katanga province, twice found out how twentieth-century diplomats—much like the ambassadors in antiquity—risk imprisonment if they displease the opponent while they are negotiating. In April, 1961, Tshombe attended a conference with officials from the central Congolese government in Coquilhatville and was arrested when he threatened to leave because of disagreement. He was not released until two months later, after having agreed to integrate his provincial army into the military organization of the central government. A year later, Tshombe again went to confer with the central government, with more explicit guaranties of safe conduct than before. When he wanted to leave for his provincial capital, after several days of fruitless negotiations, his plane was blocked by trucks of the central government. This time the United Nations, which had underwritten the guaranty to Tshombe, interceded more vigorously, and the secessionist leader was able to depart several hours later.

[5] United Nations, General Assembly, *Report of the Special Committee on the Problem of Hungary* (New York, 1957), p. 9. A similar violation of a promise of safe conduct, though not directly connected with a negotiation, was the abduction of Imre Nagy when he left the Yugoslav embassy in Budapest, where he had sought refuge. Kádár, as President of the Soviet-installed Hungarian government, had assured the Yugoslavs in writing that the Hungarian government did not desire to apply any sanctions against Nagy. As may be recalled, after this abduction Nagy was imprisoned in Rumania and later executed. The Yugoslav government condemned the Hungarian action as "a flagrant breach of the agreement reached" and as being completely contrary to the generally accepted practices of international law (*ibid.*, pp. 10–11).

AVOID DISPUTES ABOUT STATUS

Many of the long-established diplomatic customs serve to avoid disputes about the status of negotiating parties. Examples are the neutral meeting ground for conferences, the rotating chairmanship, and the use of alphabetic order to seat delegates in multilateral conferences or to arrange signatures on a treaty. The rule about the neutral meeting ground, however, is often ignored: the head of a smaller state usually travels to the capital of the larger state; and even among big powers exceptions are sometimes made, such as President Roosevelt's trip to Yalta to meet with Stalin, or the selection of New York as the site of the United Nations headquarters. It remained for De Gaulle to seek out a dispute about status, instead of avoiding it, when, after President Kennedy's funeral, he refused to meet President Lyndon B. Johnson anywhere but on French soil.

To a large extent, rules to avoid disputes about status have become like social conventions, whose violation would be a breach of etiquette. But unlike some conventions that have become useless, these rules do facilitate negotiations. This can be seen from the prolonged quarrels which arose before the rules were established or in cases where they failed to apply. Avoiding disputes about status permits the parties to concentrate their negotiations on those other issues for which the conference presumably was convened.

The negotiations at Münster and Osnabrück, which terminated the Thirty Years War, were slowed down during the whole first year by disputes about precedence and the admission of delegates. Incidentally, two conference sites were chosen to avoid arguments about status, Münster being a Catholic city and Osnabrück a Protestant one. In 1815 the Congress of Vienna finally regulated many aspects of diplomatic precedence. Since then, conflicts of this sort are normally confined to conferences where one side promotes a would-be participant whom the other side does not recognize as representing a legitimate government. For example, at the 1959 Foreign Ministers' Conference, the Western powers objected to the participation of an East German delegate.

A simple solution to end disputes about status, such as arise concerning the order of signatures, is often available to one of the major negotiating parties. One of the senior powers present can simply make it clear that it does not care a bit about the order of signatures and treat it as a joking matter. As a result, the order automatically loses its importance. This is what President Harry Truman and Prime Minister Clement Attlee did at the end of the Potsdam Conference. Truman recalled in his memoirs:

> The draft of the communiqué was finally approved, but now the Soviet delegation raised the question of who should sign first. At the previous two conferences of the Big Three, they pointed out, the Prime Minister or the President had been first to sign the communiqué. According to the procedure of rotation, Stalin said he felt that his signature should come first on the Potsdam document. "You can sign any time you want to," I said. "I don't care who signs first." Attlee remarked that he was in favor of alphabetical preference. "That way," he said jokingly, "I would score over Marshal Zhukhov."[6]

No efficient rules have yet been developed to select a common language for international conferences. The resulting disputes are usually solved by arranging for various unnecessary translations. In the European Communities, for instance, all four languages of the member states were accepted as official ones, although informal records are mostly kept in French and German only, and in oral exchanges French predominates.

ADHERE TO AGREED AGENDA

Agreement on the agenda has two implications. First, it means that prior to, or at the beginning of, a conference the parties agree on the subjects they will discuss. (Consent to the official title for a conference can also imply an agreement to discuss a certain topic.) Second, the agreed agenda constitutes a procedural agreement as to the *sequence* in which the subjects will be negotiated. Both of these implications affect the outcome of negotiations: the subjects that are discussed obviously determine the issues that may be settled, and the particular sequence in which separable issues are negotiated may favor one side and handicap the other. At first glance, therefore, it seems obvious that negotiators should argue

[6] Harry S Truman, *Memoirs,* I, 410.

about the agenda or the title of a conference. Upon more careful examination, however, disputes about the agenda make sense only if one assumes that the parties either feel somehow bound by agreeing to an agenda or wish to exploit the fact that the opponent is thus constrained. But why, and to what extent, do parties feel bound by an agenda?

In part, negotiators may feel that they ought to adhere to an agreed agenda because this is simply a special case of the general precept that agreements ought to be kept. Western negotiators, in particular, might think it "improper" to ignore an agreed agenda or might fear that they would make a bad impression at home and among allies. In part, negotiators may have a more expediential reason in mind: that adherence to an agenda will expedite negotiation and increase the chances for agreement. Some examples ought to be inspected to see whether this expediential reason is valid.

At the beginning of the nuclear test-ban conference in 1958, East and West argued about the agenda for the first ten meetings. The Soviet Union tried to push an agenda according to which nuclear testing would first be prohibited and a control system discussed afterwards. As the Soviet delegate put it neatly in the third meeting: "The work of the Conference should start with the conclusion of an agreement." In the tenth meeting, both East and West argued that the agenda proposed by the other side was not "impartial," since it confined the discussion to the type of treaty favored by the other side. The deadlock about the agenda was finally broken in an informal meeting, when both sides agreed, at the suggestion of the American delegate, to deal with the topics proposed by each side in alternating two-day periods. In the future course of this prolonged conference, even this arrangement was quietly abandoned, and each side brought up proposals or discussed issues raised by the opponent as it pleased. Thus, while both sides quickly agreed on the expedient of a rotating chairmanship, it took them over ten meetings to decide on *rotating agenda*.

In the surprise-attack conference of the same year, East and West repeated this procedure. Considerable struggle was also reflected in the official title for this conference: "Conference of Experts for the Study of Possible Measures Which Might Be Helpful in Preventing Surprise Attack and for the Preparation of a Report Thereon to Governments." This elegant phrase was largely the accomplishment of the American delegation, which feared that a less qualified title might somehow constrain its freedom of decision in the conference, much like an agreement on an agenda.

Disagreement on the agenda has become so common in East-West disarmament conferences that the rotating agenda has lately almost acquired the quality of a diplomatic convention. The following illustration shows how meticulously the equality of two conflicting agendas may be preserved. As much importance is attached to the geometry of the competing agenda items on the page as sovereigns formerly attributed to the arrangement of their signatures on a treaty. A United Nations document of the Eighteen-Nation Disarmament Conference in 1962 records the agreement to disagree on the agenda by stating that the United States and the Soviet Union, as the two Co-chairmen of the meeting:

recommend that next priority in the Committee of the Whole should be given to concurrent consideration of proposals on:

Measures to prevent further dissemination of nuclear weapons.	Reduction of the possibility of war by accident, miscalculation, or failure of communications.

The Co-chairmen recommend that one of these two topics be presented by one of the Co-chairmen, and the other be presented by the other Co-chairman, at the first meeting of the Committee of the Whole held to discuss them. Thereafter, the two topics could be discussed at alternate meetings.[7]

Disputes about the title of a conference are not confined to East-West meetings. In the negotiations on an enlarged free-trade area that would have combined the six Common Market countries with the "Outer Seven," the Six suggested that the subject of the negotiations be defined as "European Economic Association" instead of as "European Free Trade Area," so as to support their own position in favor of a looser association between their customs union and other European states.[8]

[7] Conference of the Eighteen-Nation Committee on Disarmament, ENDC/C. 1/9, May 25, 1962, Committee of the Whole.

[8] A memorandum outlining the position of the Six on these negotiations contains the following passage: "With regard to the term 'Free Trade Area' used

Two questions must be raised about the traditional views of negotiators regarding the agenda and the title of a conference. First, we may wonder why it takes diplomats so long till they abandon their attempt to agree on an agenda (or on an official title), when it turns out that this effort merely delays substantive negotiations. In fact, if both sides are under strong time pressure, negotiations can proceed without title or agenda. Imagine that during the Cuban crisis in 1962 President Kennedy had first proposed a name for his negotiations with Khrushchev, such as "Discussions about the Removal of Offensive Soviet Missiles from Cuba," and that Khrushchev had then argued that their joint enterprise should be entitled "Conference about Possible Measures Which Might Be Helpful in Reducing Tension in the Caribbean and in Turkey," at which point Kennedy would then have made a counter-proposal for another title, and so forth.

The second question is why negotiators expect to be constrained by the agenda to which they agree. Experience shows that agreed items on the agenda are often not followed closely, and objections by a party that the opponent fails to adhere to the agenda seem of little consequence. Even if the negotiators should be concerned about public opinion, there are many ways to depart from an agenda without admitting it or without seeming to violate the agreement implied by it. For example, a negotiator might declare, after he has perfunctorily dealt with the topic favored by the opponent, that this first item on the agenda had now been sufficiently discussed, and then simply pass on to *his* favorite topic.

The rule that an agreed agenda should be observed or that there should be an agreed agenda to begin with sometimes impedes negotiations more than it facilitates them—certainly in East-West conferences. If, on the contrary, there was a rule giving each party complete freedom to ignore an agenda as soon as it felt handicapped, negotiations might move to substantive issues more ex-

hitherto to describe the Treaty under negotiation, it should be pointed out that, from the point of view of doctrine, the term 'free trade' evokes a specific economic system. In view of the content of this Treaty as now envisaged, this term does not seem to be very appropriate and should be changed. The Community suggests that the title 'European Economic Association' should be adopted" (Great Britain, *Negotiations for a European Free Trade Area*, Cmnd. 641 [London: H.M.S.O., 1959], pp. 97–98).

peditiously. There would be less need to quarrel about the agenda, since the agreed items would constitute nothing but a tentative preview of the order in which issues might be taken up. Such an optional agenda was actually adopted by the Eighteen-Nation Disarmament Conference in July, 1962. To the list of items to be discussed the following disclaimer was added: "Nothing contained herein is intended to preclude any delegation from raising and discussing any subject or proposal in any plenary session. . . ."[9]

Questioning the wisdom of the rule that an agreed agenda must be adhered to is not the same as denying that, if adhered to, an agenda can be influential. To the extent that an agenda is, in fact, being followed, its particular ordering of issues affects opportunities for tie-ins. Also, agreeing to put a topic on the agenda signifies consent that the topic is a subject of negotiation. Conversely, barring a certain issue from the agenda may help to reassure third parties that their interests will not be tampered with on this issue. (These aspects of an *observed* agenda are dealt with in Chapter 11.)

HONOR PARTIAL AGREEMENTS

Any but the most simple agreement has to be negotiated piecemeal, since all points obviously cannot be settled at once. Treaties, in particular, are negotiated article by article. (Sometimes a number of issues may be tied together, in the sense that a party makes its acceptance of an article dependent on the opponent's acceptance of another article.) While it is understood that the parties are not bound by their acceptance of individual articles in the way they are bound by the conclusion of a final agreement, each party expects that its opponent will generally preserve agreed parts as the building blocks for the over-all agreement. The very fact that the parties laboriously negotiate with each other to settle their issues point by point constitutes an implied promise that yesterday's work will not be destroyed tomorrow by reopening these partial agreements.

The rule that partial agreement should be preserved has clearly an expediential character. It facilitates negotiation. In contrast to rules regarding the precedence of parties or the agenda, reciproca-

[9] ENDC/1/Add. 3, July 24, 1962, p. 1.

tion is not essential here, because it is feasible to preserve partial agreement even if the opponent fails to do so. In the long run, however, the side which always preserved partial agreement would be handicapped, since only the opponent could exploit his hindsight or new information indicating previously accepted terms to be undesirable.

Western negotiators are generally more reluctant to reopen component parts of an agreement than their Communist adversaries. They seem to feel that it is not only inexpedient but somewhat improper to go back on agreed articles. In the first year of the nuclear test-ban conference, 1959, the United States and the United Kingdom decided they had to ask for a revision of some of the conclusions in the so-called Experts' Report (which formed the scientific basis for the original detection system) because new seismic research invalidated them. This demand for revision—strongly resisted by the Soviet Union—was presented with considerable embarrassment by the Western powers.

On the other hand, as the test-ban conference met again in the spring of 1961, after the new Administration in Washington had formulated its position, the Soviet Union withdrew its agreement to a single administrator for the detection system and later, in effect, canceled all the agreed articles by objecting to any inspection system within its territory. By wiping the slate clean of all agreed points after three years of negotiation, the Soviet Union could begin anew with a much harder position late in 1962 and offer the "concession" to accept three inspections on its territory plus a number of seismic detection stations much smaller than the one originally agreed to. By becoming known for withdrawing partial agreements, a government can improve its bargaining strength, since it acquires the reputation of easily stiffening its terms. This, as noted previously, might spur its opponent to accept its terms more quickly in the future, for fear of missing an opportunity.

Similar to the rule that partial agreement should be preserved is the notion that a completed agreement should not be annulled before it becomes effective or just before it has been signed. At the height of the Berlin crisis in 1961, the American government refused to sign an otherwise completed aviation agreement with the Soviet Union, in order to express its determination on Berlin and its general opposition to Soviet pressures.[10] A certain amount of opposition to this step within the U.S. government stemmed precisely from the feeling that it was improper to violate the rule regarding the preservation of partial or nearly completed agreements.

In the Eighteen-Nation Disarmament Conference in 1962, the Soviet Union withdrew its consent from an agreement that had reached an even more formal stage of completion. On May 29, the Soviet delegate Zorin objected to the "Declaration against War Propaganda," which he had approved the week before and which had originally been put on the agenda at his insistence. This sudden reversal might have been caused by ideological objections in Moscow or perhaps by Chinese remonstrations. Zorin's justification was curious: he referred to an article written by West German Defense Minister Strauss, a book by Edward Teller, the landing of American troops in Thailand, plus some other events of the recent week, as necessitating a complete revision of this agreement that was supposed to contribute toward general and complete disarmament. Zorin in his zeal to expunge this rather vacuous agreement went so far as to delete all references to it from the official conference records—an Orwellian move which the American delegate managed to set straight.

Similar to the reneging of partial agreements is the withdrawal of an accepted offer. In Western diplomacy, this is considered to be highly improper. It is viewed not just as a breach of promise but also as a retrogression retarding the negotiation process.

Nonetheless, in the East-West disarmament negotiations of 1955, the United States withdrew an offer after the Soviet Union appeared to accept it. This was an unimaginative reaction to the the sudden discovery that an inadequately prepared Western proposal might become the subject of detailed negotiations. Naturally, such clumsiness caused considerable public embarrassment. What happened was that the Western powers had put forward a pro-

[10] The agreement, which provided for reciprocal air services, had been initialed on August 21, 1961, and on the same day the State Department announced that this was "not an appropriate time" for going through with the agreement "in view of the international situation, for which the United States is not responsible" (*New York Times*, Aug. 22, 1961).

posal providing for the total prohibition of nuclear weapons after the constitution of an effective control organ and after major reductions in conventional forces. Then, on May 10, 1955, the Soviet Union made a proposal which accepted the general principles of this Western position but added certain provisions of its own (such as an early cessation of nuclear testing and the liquidation of foreign bases). Four months later (September 6, 1955), the U.S. delegate Harold Stassen declared that the United States was now placing a "reservation" upon all its previous substantive positions. Only after he had committed this unnecessarily cautious withdrawal did he hazard a timid move forward: "In placing this reservation," he said, "may I make it perfectly clear that we are not withdrawing any of these positions, we are not disavowing any of them. But we are indicating clearly that we do not now reaffirm them, that we turn our attention upon the central factor of the inspection and control methods. . . ." Stassen could of course have protected his position without withdrawing the American offer, by focusing on the inspection issue. The course of disarmament negotiations would probably not have been much different had the United States stood by the Western offer. The two positions would have been no closer than they were from 1961 onward, when both sides had accepted "general and complete disarmament" as their goal.

MAINTAIN FLEXIBILITY

In the West, the rule that one should be flexible in negotiations assumes a moral value. The question of whether it is expedient to be flexible is suppressed by the conviction that it would clearly be improper to be *inflexible*. Those who advocate this rule as a way of facilitating agreement would grant that in prolonged negotiations or in case of a serious conflict both sides have to evince some flexibility for negotiations to succeed. But in the short run, or to settle minor difficulties, they do not consider reciprocity as essential.

In 1961, when the Soviets were actively exerting pressure against West Berlin, Senator Mansfield said: "The responsibility which we have . . . and which the Soviet Union has, is not merely to reassert positions already assumed and which are obviously irreconcilable. The responsibility is to seek to determine whether or not there is a third way on Berlin. . . ." Similarly, a *New York Times* editorial a few months later maintained: ". . . neither Moscow nor Germany nor the Western allies can expect to win all their points. There has to be some give as well as take."[11]

The rule that there must be "give and take" has become a crippling cliché, owing to its nebulous content and because of indiscriminate claims that it is universally valid. If flexibility is deemed to be so essential, it seems appropriate to examine what it means and how it affects negotiations. A government might show flexibility by: (1) formulating its position in an indeterminate fashion, (2) offering the opponent several *specific* alternatives, (3) expressing its willingness to consider *any* alternatives proposed by the opponent, and/or (4) changing its position in response to the opponent's demands. There is yet a greater degree of flexibility. A government might not only keep its own position changeable and show openmindedness toward the opponent's proposals, but it may abandon having a position at all. Rather than being a sign of modesty, this may result from a lack of conviction or the absence of ideas on the issue under negotiation. In multilateral negotiations, smaller powers often do not care as long as their interests appear unaffected. They might even exploit their lack of a position to incur the favor of a more committed party with which they can align themselves. Similarly, in innovation negotiations, some participants may simply choose to examine what the initiating party has to propose and go along with any arrangement that does not discriminate against them.

It may be argued that negotiation is a creative process: the less attached parties are to a certain position, the more receptive they will be to the discovery of new solutions. Walter Lippmann possibly had this in mind when he wrote about the Berlin negotiations in 1961: "Someone has to begin to negotiate to begin to find out precisely what the negotiation is about. It is a mirage to expect the four Western Powers to guess correctly in advance just what Khrushchev will ask and just what he will concede, and to have an

[11] *Congressional Record,* June 14, 1961, p. 9598; *New York Times,* Oct. 18, 1961.

agreed 'position' on every guess."[12] Flexibility to the degree of not having a position at all, however, seems a trifle too passive for the defensive side in redistribution negotiations, especially if the offensive side clearly knows what "the negotiation is about"—which the Russians seemed to do in their Berlin crisis in 1961.

Related to the rule of flexibility is the precept that ultimatums should be avoided. (An ultimatum may be defined as an offer or a demand that is presented as being unchangeable and is coupled with the prediction that negotiations will cease if it is rejected.) Ultimatums are, of course, the antithesis of flexibility and may lead to the rupture of negotiations. In the West, they are often considered to be both improper and dangerous. Only in defense of vital interests or against some extremely aggressive move are they in keeping with the proprieties; for example, the British ultimatum to Hitler in September, 1939. And in such situations the ultimatum is usually not meant as a move in negotiation but as a preliminary step to going to war. When war seems justified, the ultimatum as a ritual preceding it seems entirely proper. In all other situations, governments do not admit to issuing an ultimatum. Indeed, if the opponent complains of having been given an ultimatum, most governments—even Communist ones—will ardently deny such a charge. This shows how deeply ingrained is the view that issuing ultimatums shows one to the world as wicked and reckless.

RECIPROCATE CONCESSIONS

A standard recommendation for facilitating agreement is that parties should make concessions.[13] The rule that a concession by the opponent ought to be reciprocated with a concession by oneself combines the virtue of flexibility with the norm of reciprocity.

If one pauses to analyze the meaning of this rule, however, it is remarkable that it enjoys such wide and unqualified support in the West. It is often accepted as a moral precept that takes precedence

---

[12] *New York Herald Tribune,* Dec. 19, 1961.

[13] A "concession" may be defined as a revision of a negotiating position so that it will come closer to the opponent's wishes; and a "compromise" may be classed as a way of reaching agreement through concessions by *both* sides. Frequently, the point where the two revised negotiating positions coincide, rather than the process of reaching this point, is referred to as "the compromise."

over the question whether or not the morality of the substance of one's position would be impaired by a concession. According to this view, it is more important to negotiate "properly," by reciprocating concessions, than to maintain a "proper" negotiating position. To put it differently, not to reciprocate concessions may be regarded as unfair, without examining the fairness of either side's initial position from which the concessions would have to be subtracted.

Curiously, although concessions ought to be reciprocated, it is neither mandatory nor even proper to reciprocate the *withdrawal* of concessions. In 1961–62, when the Soviet Union canceled all its concessions of 1959 and 1960 on the nuclear test-ban treaty, the Western powers did not respond by withdrawing concessions of their own. To have done so might well have been considered objectionable by important segments of public opinion. (Also, the Western negotiators felt that they derived a propagandistic advantage from being able to blame the Soviet Union for having withdrawn its concessions.)

RETURN FAVORS

A negotiator has an incentive to grant his opponent an advantage gratuitously if he knows that he will build up a long-term credit on which he can draw later. In other words, he may find it worthwhile to let his opponent make certain gains, even without being compelled to do so in order to secure his desired terms of agreement and without getting anything in return *at that time.*

The rule that favors should be returned tends to generate feelings of friendliness in the long run. But perhaps more important, it can greatly facilitate negotiations in the short run. Under this rule each party to an agreement need not always come out with a net gain, since the balance sheet of gains and losses does not have to be closed with every single settlement. If one party should incur a net loss in order to reach agreement, it can trust that the other parties will repay it in later negotiations.

American negotiators have learned that their Communist opponents, by and large, do not observe the rule of repaying debts of gratitude. Many diplomats who have had experience with Communists have even come to believe that gratuitous concessions by the West would be taken as a sign of weakness, not as something entitling the generous negotiator to a credit. However, this view conflicts with the idea, discussed before, that an accommodating negotiating style might gradually lead to friendlier relations. There is no simple answer to this puzzle. Only cautious probing can show whether gratuitous concessions will merely be exploited or whether they will lead to a long-term improvement in the opponent's attitudes.

During the World War II alliance with Russia, the experience was surely disappointing, even with negotiations on such issues as Lend-Lease, where America was offering to help the Russian war effort. In December, 1944, General John R. Deane, who led Lend-Lease negotiations in Moscow, wrote a bitter letter to his superior, General George C. Marshall. He warned Marshall that the Russians "simply cannot understand giving without taking, and as a result even our giving is viewed with suspicion. Gratitude cannot be banked in the Soviet Union. Each transaction is complete in itself without regard to past favors. The party of the second part is either a shrewd trader to be admired or a sucker to be despised."[14]

REFRAIN FROM FLAGRANT LIES

No one would argue that a general who leads his army into battle should eschew disguise, deception, and dissimulation. If he succeeds in misleading his adversary, he will be called great rather than dishonest. Diplomats, however, are expected to observe certain rules of sincerity. Like other rules of accommodation, these are meant to facilitate negotiation or enhance good relations in the long run. They play an important role among friendly nations, by making communication more reliable and by engendering a relationship of trust. But their content is rather vague; what would be condemned as a lie in one situation may be a shrewd tactic in another.

[14] U.S. Department of State, *Foreign Relations of the United States: The Conferences at Malta and Yalta 1945* (Washington, 1955), p. 448.

Outright lies are a serious breach of decorum, even in negotiations between hostile nations. A brazen lie may cause as strong a sense of grievance as an offensive act. This seems to have been reflected by the tenor of President Kennedy's speech on October 22, 1962, which announced the blockade against the Soviet missile buildup in Cuba. The President related how the Soviets had made two "false" statements by pretending that their armaments in Cuba were only defensive, and then he exclaimed: "Neither the United States of America nor the World Community of Nations can tolerate deliberate deception and offensive threats on the part of any nation. . . ." The lie is just as bad as the offensive missiles!

The rule that negotiators should be truthful may be interpreted more broadly, not only as prohibiting outright lies, but as requiring that no important facts be withheld. Walter Lippmann criticized the President after his speech on the Cuba crisis for not having lived up to the broader rule of truthfulness in his meeting with Gromyko a few days earlier. The President should not have "suspended diplomacy," Lippmann argued, by withholding from Gromyko the fact that he already possessed evidence as to the offensive character of the Soviet missile buildup:

If [diplomacy] had not been suspended, the President would have shown Mr. Gromyko the pictures, and told him privately about the policy which in a few days he intended to announce publicly. This would have made it more likely that Moscow would order the ships not to push on to Cuba. But if such diplomatic action did not change the orders, if Mr. Khrushchev persisted in spite of it, the President's public speech would have been stronger.[15]

Telling the full truth—according to this argument—would have had one of two advantages: it would either (1) have induced the Soviets to retreat before the open confrontation with the blockade or (2) have made the President's speech more effective. Lippmann ignores two other possibilities: (3) that the Soviet Union might have taken the initiative politically—for instance in the United Nations—to undermine Latin American support and divide public opinion and (4) that Khrushchev might have committed himself

[15] *New York Herald Tribune,* Oct. 25, 1962.

to threats of reprisals, which would have made the crisis more dangerous.[16]

That to withhold important facts from the opponent suspends diplomacy—as Lippmann argued in the foregoing passage—may reflect a view of international negotiation which is fairly common among Americans. Harold Nicolson, in his widely read book on diplomacy, goes even further; he lays down the rule of truthfulness in its broadest possible meaning:

By [truthfulness] is meant, not merely abstention from conscious misstatements, but scrupulous care to avoid the suggestion of the false or the suppression of the true. A good diplomatist should be at pains not to leave any incorrect impressions whatsoever upon the minds of those with whom he negotiates. . . . Even if we judge negotiation by its lowest standards, it is evident that the correction of inaccurate information increases present credit and fortifies future confidence. Nor should the negotiator for one moment allow himself to agree with Machiavelli that the dishonesty of others justifies any dishonesty in oneself.[17]

Nicolson generously extends the applicability of this rule "to those who have to deal with the subtleties of the Oriental mind." He approvingly quotes the advice of a British diplomat with "long experience in the Far and Middle East" that you should not waste time "in trying to discover what is at the back of an Oriental's mind" but should make quite certain that the latter "is left in no doubt whatsoever in regard to what is at the back of *your* mind."[18]

---

[16] Later on, Walter Lippmann discovered this himself: "The American intention was to react sharply, but for a limited aim. . . . Had this intention become known before it was announced . . . , there was a probability that the Soviet Government would take the initiative either by proclaiming defiantly the presence of the missiles or by denouncing the proposed quarantine as an act of 'piracy.' Had that denunciation been made before the quarantine was proclaimed and enforced, both Moscow and Washington would have been committed to a collision course" (from an address delivered in Paris, *The Atlantic Community* [March, 1963], pp. 39–40).

[17] Harold Nicolson, *Diplomacy* (London: Oxford University Press, 1960), pp. 110–11.

[18] *Ibid.*, p. 111. This racial segregation of negotiators into subtle and truthful ones—a quaintly old-fashioned touch like a yellow leaf from Rudyard Kipling —was repeated as late as 1961 in an article Nicolson wrote for *Foreign Affairs* (Oct., 1961), p. 45.

Much of this has no relation to facts. A diplomat who could leave no incorrect impression whatsoever upon the mind of his opponent and had to reveal all that was back of his mind would no more be negotiating than, say, a businessman who not only posted his minimum prices but also revealed all his cost calculations and whether he expected to sell more cheaply tomorrow.

Now, among close allies it might be argued that important objectives and intentions should not be concealed from one's partner. The "special relationship" between the United States and Great Britain means, among other things, that London and Washington should keep each other fully informed about their intentions (a practice that was possibly breached by both sides in the negotiations that led up to the Suez crisis of 1956). Efforts have been made to extend this practice to other Atlantic allies. Sometimes, close allies oblige themselves explicitly to such an exchange of information: for example, France and Germany in their Treaty of Cooperation of January, 1963.

The rule against concealing one's major objectives has its counterpart in the rule that negotiators should not impugn the opponent's motives. If it is improper to harbor ulterior motives in negotiations, it is even more so to accuse your opponent of just that.

The question of motives is justifiably touchy in negotiations among friendly nations, where the assumed compatibility of major objectives provides the principal basis for agreement. However, if domestic opinion-makers attribute hidden motives to the negotiating position of their own government, the diplomats of other governments may no longer be reluctant to allude to these motives. During the negotiations for a larger European free-trade area in 1957–58 between the six Common Market countries and seven other European nations, British newspapers openly mentioned the one-sided advantages that this arrangement would have secured for the United Kingdom, and official British statements even alluded to the objective of holding up European integration.[19] As a result, however, the negotiators of the Six often impugned British

---

[19] Miriam Camps, *The Free Trade Area Negotiations* (Occasional Paper No. 2 [London: Political and Economic Planning, 1959]), p. 33; and Karl Kaiser, *EWG und Freihandelszone*, pp. 111–12, 115–21.

motives in private meetings. And in retrospect this was also done publicly, by De Gaulle in his press conference of January 14, 1963, when he said that Great Britain applied for membership in the Common Market:

after refusing earlier to participate in the community that was being built, and after then having created a free trade area with six other states, and finally—I can say this, the negotiations conducted for so long on this subject can be recalled—after having put some pressure on the Six in order to prevent the application of the Common Market from ever getting started.

In East-West negotiations, particularly on disarmament, the impugning of motives takes up a large amount of time and fills page after page in the verbatim records. There are protestations from the Western side of the sincerity of its objectives, accusations from the Soviets that the West harbors hidden motives, complaints from the West for having had its motives impugned, assurances from the Western delegates that they—in contrast to their opponent—would not want to question Soviet motives, new Soviet impugnations, and occasionally a cautious questioning of Soviet motives by the West.

When the nuclear test-ban conference was only in its third meeting in 1958, the U.S. delegate James Wadsworth declared: "I came to Geneva, fully convinced that the Soviet delegation would come here in good faith to negotiate, and I must say that it gives me quite a shock to find this continued misunderstanding of motives and impugnment of motives." Fifty-three meetings later, speaking about the Soviet delegate Tsarapkin, he said: "I fully believe in his sincerity, I fully believe in the wrongness of his position. He has every right, of course, to believe that our position is wrong. He has no right to question our sincerity." Another one hundred and seventy-six meetings later this protestation by the U.S. delegate continues: "But, Mr. Tsarapkin, you are now doing something which I deeply regret, particularly in view of our excellent associations during approximately two years. I beg you to refrain from impugning the motives of my country. I beg you to understand that we mean what we say. I beg you to inform your Government that we sincerely wish to see a test-ban treaty con-

cluded on terms which are acceptable to all three of us." Mr.
Tsarapkin remains undaunted. Seventy-two meetings later he
accuses the West: "You do not want agreement; you know that
unless there is agreement on questions of control . . . , there will
be no treaty; and if there is no treaty, you will feel splendid, you
will be able to continue carrying out nuclear weapon tests, alleging
that you have not succeeded in reaching agreement with the Soviet
Union on questions of control. That is the simple outline of what
you are obviously striving to obtain from our negotiations."[20]

Evidently, such an exchange of words about each other's motives
does not enlighten either side about the issues ostensibly under
negotiation or about the opponent's position, even if the exchange
is conducted in the conciliatory Western fashion of crediting the
opponent with sincerity. The rule not to impugn motives, provided
it is observed by both sides, certainly helps to expedite negotiations.

NEGOTIATE IN GOOD FAITH

To blame the opponent for not "negotiating in good faith" is a
grave accusation. Most governments concede that they cannot reveal
all the pertinent facts when negotiating, and some would occasionally admit—at least in domestic discussions—that they have hidden
motives. But none would ever accept the charge that it was not
"negotiating in good faith." Although this canon is compelling, it
allows for several distinct or even conflicting interpretations. At
least four different meanings might be given to this rule. "Negotiating in good faith" may mean:

1. To make it highly probable that agreement will be reached.
This means concretely that a party has to lower its terms whenever
the probability of reaching an agreement falls below the desired
level. Evidently, if a party is "negotiating in good faith" according
to this criterion, the opponent should not know it; otherwise he
would have an incentive to make agreement unlikely until his terms
were met.

[20] Conference on the Discontinuance of Nuclear Weapon Tests, 3d Plenary
Meeting, Nov. 4, 1958, p. 17; 56th Plenary Meeting, Feb. 17, 1959, p. 31;
232d Plenary Meeting, July 21, 1960, pp. 19–20; 304th Plenary Meeting,
May 10, 1961, p. 28.

Another difficulty with this criterion is that the likelihood of agreement on any given terms depends on the pressures and counter-pressures exerted. Hence a party whose terms were unlikely to be accepted could meet this criterion of "negotiating in good faith" not only by lowering its terms but, paradoxically, also by putting more pressure on the opponent so as to make agreement likely. For example, when Stalin negotiated with Finland in October, 1939, for the transfer of some Finnish territory to Russia, he came to realize that his demands precluded agreement. Then he sent the Red Army against Finland, and after some three months of fighting, the Finnish government (which had continued to negotiate with Moscow) accepted a Soviet proposal that demanded more territory than Stalin's original position. Now, according to the above criterion, Stalin was not "negotiating in good faith" in October, for he made unacceptable demands; but he was "negotiating in good faith" in March, after Red Army pressure made even greater demands acceptable.

2. Not to maintain a position which one feels sure will preclude agreement. For instance, General de Gaulle's position in 1959 that military disengagement in Europe would have to "cover a zone which is as near to the Urals as it is to the Atlantic" was certainly expected by him to preclude agreement. (This may have been a more effective way to counter Communist disengagement proposals than to refuse disengagement in principle.) [21]

According to a more stringent variant of this second criterion, a government should not make even *initial* proposals which it knows to be "unacceptable" to the opponent. This means that not only the position ultimately held but also the first proposals have to be such that there is at least a possibility of the opponent agreeing to

---

[21] De Gaulle announced this position in a press conference on March 25, 1959: "As regards turning Germany into a neutralized territory, this 'extrication' or 'disengagement' in itself says nothing to us which is of value. For if disarmament does not cover a zone which is as near to the Urals as it is to the Atlantic, how will France be protected . . . ? Certainly we are supporters of the control and limitation of all weapons of war." (Quoted in E. Hinterhoff, *Disengagement* [London: Stephens, 1959], p. 268.)

Spanier and Nogee (*The Politics of Disarmament*) maintain that in the postwar disarmament negotiations, neither side ever "negotiated in good faith" (according to this second criterion), because they always included a "joker" in their proposals to make sure they would be rejected.

them. The American government has felt curiously ambivalent toward this rule. On the one hand, it has shown great reluctance in the negotiations on Berlin to make some counter-demands regarding the Wall or self-determination for East Germany, because such demands would have been "unacceptable." On the other hand, it has maintained and vigorously defended a position on general and complete disarmament since 1961 which it clearly knows to be totally unacceptable to the Soviet Union.

3. To want an agreement of the type that is being negotiated and to be eager to have one's terms accepted. In other words, not being determined always to prevent an agreement even when terms are favorable. For example, until 1955 the Russians did not seem to want an Austrian State Treaty even if their terms on reparations and on the definition of German assets had been accepted.

4. To follow certain rules of accommodation while negotiating. Thus if a government violates the rule that concessions must be reciprocated, it may be criticized for not "negotiating in good faith."

The question is often debated whether this or that government really "wishes to negotiate" or is only pretending. Again, the meaning of this phrase "wishing to negotiate" is not clear. Usually, it seems to mean the same as "negotiating in good faith" according to the second or third criterion.

One reason why governments frequently fail to show "good faith" (according to the second or third criterion) is that they pursue Pharisaic propaganda effects. They want to appear good by being engaged in negotiation but do not wish to reach an agreement on the disputed issue.

U.S. legislation on labor-management negotiations throws an interesting sidelight on the difficulty of defining "good faith." The National Labor Relations Act of 1947 (Taft-Hartley Act) imposes on labor and management the obligation to bargain collectively. The act specifies that this obligation means that the employer and the representative of the employees must "meet at reasonable times and confer in good faith with respect to wages," etc., but that it "does not compel either party to agree to a proposal or require the making of a concession."[22] In the earlier Wagner Act, the corre-

[22] 61 Stat. 142 (1947), Sec. 8 (d).

sponding provision went further, requiring the parties to "bargain collectively in a good faith effort to reach an agreement." The question as to what the Taft-Hartley Act required as a test of "good faith" came up in a case before the U.S. Supreme Court, which decided "that the act does not encourage a party to engage in marathon discussions at the expense of frank statements and support of his position . . ." but that the National Labor Relations Board could not "compel concessions or otherwise sit in judgment upon the substantive terms of . . . agreements."[23]

AVOID EMOTIONALISM AND RUDENESS

In his enumeration of the qualities of the "ideal diplomatist," Harold Nicolson includes the quality of calm: "Not only must the negotiator avoid displaying irritation when confronted by the stupidity, dishonesty, brutality, or conceit of those with whom it is his unpleasant duty to negotiate; but he must eschew all personal animosities, or personal predilections, all enthusiasms, prejudices, vanities, exaggerations, dramatizations, and moral indignations."[24]

With this kind of advice, the exceptions are always more interesting than the rule. Sometimes, stiff upper lip notwithstanding, the negotiator should indeed display irritation, to stop his opponent from repeating the same argument or from impugning his motives. At other times he must indulge in dramatization to strengthen his commitments or to focus the discussion on the issue he prefers. And sometimes he must show moral indignation, lest his moral conviction seem doubtful to the opponent.

Although most Western diplomats would not practice Nicolson's precept of complete emotional calm, they do observe the rule that strong emotions should rarely be displayed, and they always adhere to certain conventions of politeness. According to these conventions, invective is to be avoided, the opponent is to be addressed respectfully and may not be interrupted while he has the floor in a formal session, nor should one walk out while he makes his presen-

[23] National Labor Relations Board vs. American National Insurance Co., 343 U.S. 395 (May, 1952), 72 *Supreme Court Reporter*, p. 829. See also Archibald Cox, "The Duty to Bargain in Good Faith," *Harvard Law Review*, LXXI (June, 1958), 1401–33.

[24] *Diplomacy*, p. 116.

tation, arrive deliberately late for an agreed meeting, and so forth. Between allied or friendly nations, almost any breach of these rules of etiquette provokes a deterioration of the relationship.

Yet, it is not obvious why a violation of such conventions should endanger friendly relations between countries. It cannot be explained as offending the "national honor" (except, perhaps, in case of a direct insult to the chief of state), since Western diplomats regularly expose themselves to rudeness in negotiations with the East without involving their "national honor." Nor can it be explained as an impairment of the negotiator's personal relations, since Western diplomats are quite adept at receiving expressions of hostility from the opponent's delegate without ever considering them as a sign of *personal* animosity. Indeed, in East-West negotiations, this distinction between official rudeness and good relations on the personal level is practiced all the time. The significance of rudeness in negotiations between friendly nations must result from something else. Rudeness acts as a signal, it suggests to the aggrieved government that the government of the other party is shifting to a more hostile policy. Not the invective as such, but the expectation of future unfriendly acts provokes the crisis.

In addition to the rules of politeness, friendly countries are expected to refrain from making *explicit* threats and, with certain exceptions, to abstain from intervention in the opponent's domestic affairs. It is interesting to note that these rules may take precedence over the rule of truthfulness. While it is taboo between friendly nations to make threats explicit, threats can be used provided they are disguised as warnings.

An incident between the United States and Canada early in 1963 illustrates that the rule of noninterference in domestic affairs may take precedence over the rule of truthfulness. During a debate in the Canadian Parliament on the question of whether Canada should accept nuclear weapons under U.S. control, Prime Minister Diefenbaker referred to confidential negotiations between Ottawa and Washington on this subject. The U.S. government found that these negotiations were misrepresented by the Prime Minister's statement and issued a correction (State Department release of January 30, 1963). A week later Diefenbaker's government fell. Subsequently, the American government was blamed more for its violation of the noninterference rule than the Canadian Prime Minister was criticized for his lack of truthfulness concerning confidential negotiations.

Communist negotiators do not adhere to the rule that rudeness must always be avoided. But their rudeness is not a wild outburst of emotion or coarse pugilism. No Communist diplomat has ever engaged in a fist-fight at an international conference (unlike some parliamentarians, both Communist and non-Communist, in Rome, Tokyo, and other Western-type parliaments). And Khrushchev's infamous shoe in the United Nations was used as a gavel, not as a cudgel to hit an antagonist.[25]

According to Bolshevik thought, as Nathan Leites explained in his book on the subject, "it pays to be rude." Rudeness as a technique of negotiation has its rationale as well as less conscious motivations but is not an expression of anger. It may serve as a counter-offensive to discourage the enemy, it may be a defense against inner temptations to reveal one's weaknesses (which would mean begging the enemy to desist), or it may reassure oneself that one is not succumbing to the temptation of entertaining good feelings toward the enemy or of imputing such feelings to him.[26] "If my words are disagreeable to some," Khrushchev explained in the UN General Assembly, "this means that I have achieved my aim —this is what I wanted!"[27]

Western diplomats, on the other hand, generally believe that calm, politeness, and respectfulness help to reduce feelings of hostility and hence facilitate agreement. They observe these rules not merely because they feel that rudeness is unseemly but also because they think that it is inexpedient. They remain polite, even while the opponent insults them. At the Korean armistice nego-

[25] "Diplomatic suppleness was shown," reported Adzhubei about this incident. When "Comrade N. S. Khrushchev . . . took off a shoe and began to pound with it on the desk," he "posed the shoe in such a fashion (in front of our delegation sat the delegation of Fascist Spain) that the tip of the shoe was almost set against the neck of the Fascist minister of foreign affairs, but not fully so." A subtle suppleness! (Quoted in *S'ezd KPSS. Stenogr. otchet* [22d Congress of the Communist Party], II, 473–74.)

[26] Nathan Leites, *A Study of Bolshevism* (Glencoe, Ill.: The Free Press, 1953), pp. 34–42.

[27] N. S. Khrushchev, *Ovneshnei politike Sovetskogo Soiuza* (Moscow, 1961), II, 474.

tiations, the Communists never referred to the Republic of Korea or the Nationalist Government of China by their official names, calling them instead "the Syngman Rhee clique" and "your puppet on Formosa." The United Nations delegates, however, faithfully used the official Communist titles, such as "Democratic People's Republic of Korea" when referring to North Korea, and "Democratic People's Republic of China" for Communist China.[28]

A related idea is that one should not push the opponent to the limit. If the last ounce is squeezed out of the opponent, he will show ill will when it comes to carrying out the agreement.' A little generosity may be handsomely rewarded by friendlier relations in the long run. As Khrushchev put it (in the speech quoted at the beginning of this chapter), this "is better than having an extra kopek in one's pocket." For Communist negotiators, however, such an attitude is rather exceptional (or modern?).

EXPEDITE AND RATIONALIZE NEGOTIATION PROCESS

Part of the negotiating process consists of an exchange of words at a conference table. As discussed, there are rules of accommodation that can make this exchange more efficient and encourage friendlier attitudes. Thus, rules against invective or against the impugnation of motives serve to eliminate hostile talk (and such talk rarely helps a party to obtain better terms or to reach agreement more quickly). However, other aspects of diplomatic rhetoric that are just as inefficient usually remain strangely exempt from any rules.

This discrepancy is particularly stark in East-West negotiations. On the one hand, elementary rules of politeness may well be observed, and a pretense; at least, is being made of maintaining flexibility, adhering to the agreed agenda, and reciprocating concessions. But on the other hand, there are no rules against repetition, illogical reasoning, unanswered questions, irrelevant arguments, and pointless speeches. While Western diplomats indulge in such activity less than their Communist colleagues, neither side condemns this behavior as improper or inexpedient. Indeed, not only the participating diplomats, but the public at large have become so

[28] William H. Vatcher, *Panmunjom* (New York: Praeger, 1958), p. 209.

used to the inefficiency and pointlessness of the exchange of words in East-West conferences that this wasted motion is no longer questioned. On the contrary, instead of promoting rules against it —as rules have been promoted against, say, inflexibility or invective—diplomats perform these verbal rituals out of habit. If there are any conventions concerning the verbal exchange, they tend to promote these purposeless rituals rather than curb them.

The lack of rules to expedite and rationalize the verbal exchange is all the more bizarre in that these lengthy speeches and unresponsive arguments have little impact on the central purposes of negotiation. They affect the outcome only marginally, if at all. Their main effect is to prolong the process of negotiation. In most cases, they also fail to have a propaganda effect outside of the conference. For the repetitious speeches are heard and read by nobody but the delegates of the other side, and sometimes not even by them.

It is easy enough to imagine the existence of rules to rationalize the talk at the conference table. Much as negotiators are not supposed to out-lie each other, there could be a rule that they should not try to out-argue each other. (After all, a display of rhetorical arguments is not an efficient way of changing the opponent's position.) Much as diplomats are supposed to refrain from invective, there might be a rule that they ought to refrain from repetition. And much as the delegates are expected to show some flexibility, one could conceive of a rule that they should be responsive to questions.

There is a method, however, which sometimes helps to avoid the more irrational and inefficient aspects of the verbal exchange at the conference table. This is the *informal meeting,* where speeches are ordinarily dispensed with, questions are more likely to be answered, and repetition is reduced. Thus, as far as the conduct of the debate is concerned, "informal" negotiations paradoxically are governed by more sensible rules than "formal" ones.

THE COMMUNITY SPIRIT

Nations closely linked in a common effort sometimes develop a highly accommodating negotiating style, which resembles the decision-making process within an intra-governmental committee rather than the usual mode of bargaining between governments. The cooperation between the United States and Great Britain during World War II was conducted in this fashion, particularly on the highest level between Roosevelt and Churchill. More recently, the advocates of closer integration in the European Communities have been promoting such an accommodating style. In the negotiations among the six member states and within the Community organs, the participants are reminded regularly to act in accordance with the "community spirit," *l'esprit communautaire* as it is called in Brussels.

Back in 1950, when Jean Monnet chaired the negotiations for the formation of the Coal and Steel Community, he first taught his co-negotiators to see their task in the "community spirit." He wanted them to focus on the common interest, rather than on trades between conflicting interests, and to maximize the advantages of their joint undertaking, rather than to exchange separate gains and losses with each other. He discouraged compromises in which a party would barter a concession on one issue against some advantage on an entirely different issue. He felt logrolling or heterogeneous package deals would not be conducive to a constructive, joint effort in behalf of the common objectives. Monnet conducted the initial meetings, where the principles of the Coal and Steel Community were first discussed, without any verbatim records. The negotiators were not allowed to hold anyone else to his opinions or statements from earlier meetings. This facilitated the formation of a common view, based on a single conception of the joint undertaking, rather than on bartered compromises. Thus, in this setting a procedure proved fruitful which was the exact opposite of the rule that partial agreements should be adhered to.[29]

Of course, not all negotiations in the history of European integration were conducted in this harmonious fashion. One of the most jarring departures from the *esprit communautaire* was De Gaulle's sudden and unilateral decision to veto Britain's application

[29] Robert Schuman called these negotiations "a new type of a conference," not the usual form of negotiation in which opposing national interests were being defended. "On allait construire une oeuvre commune, à six" (Robert Schuman, "Origines et Élaboration du 'Plan Schuman,'" *Les Cahiers de Bruges* [Dec., 1953], pp. 266–84).

for membership in the Common Market. Walter Hallstein, the president of the Common Market Commission, criticized this decision in his report to the European Parliament, not so much for its substance (although he seemed to disagree with that, too), but for the way in which it was imposed upon the other five member states:

> The manner in which one member Government took and communicated its decision to interrupt the negotiations [with Great Britain] is not in harmony with the duties imposed by the Community. The results of an interruption affect the Community as a whole, not just one Member State. . . . The opening of the negotiations was decided unanimously. . . . In these circumstances one might at the very least have expected that the question of the future of the negotiations, if it had to be raised, would have been discussed fully and frankly amongst the members of the Community. . . . The life of our Community depends on everyone looking upon and treating Community matters as matters of real joint responsibility.[30]

A negotiating style in the "community spirit" is a necessary, but not a sufficient, condition for a successful integration of independent nations. Other conditions must, of course, be met, such as the formation of interest groups that cut across national boundaries, the absence of strongly conflicting objectives, and the existence of specific functions that are important to the member states and can be delegated to a supra-national level. A common external enemy also encourages integration.

What helps to preserve the "community spirit" is the interest of each partner in reciprocation. When nations are engaged in a long-term common effort, each government needs the future collaboration of its partners and remains dependent on their good will. This makes it possible to regard an act of generosity today as establishing a credit for tomorrow. And it makes it safe for negotiators to accept an agreement in principle—provided all partners have the same understanding of it—and to leave the details to the experts or technicians. The "community spirit" permits the negotiators to dispense with some of the more rigid

[30] European Economic Community, Commission, "Statement on the Negotiations Concerning Great Britain's Accession . . . by Walter Hallstein," Strasbourg, Feb. 5, 1963.

rules of accommodation that may seem necessary between less friendly nations, such as the pettifogging concern about agendas, the objections to a revision of partial agreements, the one-to-one reciprocation of concessions, and the stickling equality of negotiating languages. Instead, there is a strong emphasis on the common objectives, there are no important hidden motives, and the discourse is free from the wasted verbiage to which the world has become so accustomed in East-West conferences or in the United Nations General Assembly.

CHAPTER 8

DOMESTIC AFFAIRS

IT WOULD BE A MISTAKE TO VIEW THE PARTIES IN INTERNATIONAL negotiations as if they were unitary decision-makers. Domestic politics, bureaucratic idiosyncrasies, and personal motivations all influence their objectives and negotiating tactics. Governments are complex organizations, staffed by officials who compete and disagree and who must in fact negotiate among themselves to formulate the national interest in any conflict with external opponents. Indeed, individual officials as well as whole branches within the government may pursue private interests unrelated to, or sometimes even opposed to, the national interest. Each party will seek to exploit these domestic constraints of the other side and try to take advantage of any dissensions it may detect within the other party's government. However, the fact that governments are not unitary decision-makers does not necessarily benefit the opponent. The diversity of forces at work within a country can lead to greater initial demands and more rigid commitments than if a party were all of one mind.

The interplay of personalities and parochial interests is more apparent in Western governments than in Communist regimes. It is particularly significant in the United States government, whose large size and federal structure permit many forces to impinge on the conduct of foreign affairs. The government's approach to negotiation is the product of diverse personal motives, bureaucratic preferences of different departments, and various public pressures.

This interaction can be traced through debates among government officials, inter-office memoranda, committee meetings, cabinet sessions, and discussions with congressional leaders. It is a process in which news media and the wider public participate in various degrees.

MESSENGERS, DELEGATES, AND SUMMITRY

The diplomat who faces his opponent over the green baize sometimes acts only as a messenger. His powers may be so restricted that he can merely deliver prepared statements, outline positions as prescribed by his government, and receive communications from the opponent. At the other extreme is the negotiator who can make all decisions by himself; that is, while in face-to-face contact with the opponent, he can accept new proposals from the other side, develop counter-proposals on the spot, and conclude agreements or break off negotiations at his own discretion. Negotiators with such wide powers appear only at summit meetings (except for conferences on issues so minor that delegates may be given full freedom). And even "at the summit" the chiefs of government from democratic countries are usually limited in the decisions they can take by themselves.

Soviet diplomats are often constrained to act as mere messengers. This was especially true under Stalin. The narrow instructions of Soviet negotiators handicap Western delegates. Such limitations render the assessment of hard and soft spots in Soviet positions difficult, since all aspects are defended with equal vehemence until new instructions from Moscow permit a sudden concession. This difficulty is compounded by the fact that in Moscow, foreign policy is made in almost complete secrecy.

However, in the Stalin era Soviet diplomats themselves were handicapped by their narrowly limited powers of decision. Since they were unable to explore new developments at their own discretion and were not expected to contribute suggestions for new departures, they were less interested than Western diplomats in exploring the tactical weaknesses of the opponent. Also, they were less capable of engaging in debate and fencing with arguments, since they felt constrained to keep repeating the same line pre-

pared for them in Moscow. Partly because of their narrow instructions and partly for other reasons, Soviet diplomats were
unable to develop the more intimate, personal relations with the
delegate from the other side that would have given them a deeper
understanding of the opponent's position. Nonetheless, Soviet
diplomats may have preferred to receive such rigid instructions.
Knowing what their government wanted of them may have given
them a feeling of safety. They were not expected to explore that
treacherous border area where the opponent must be both con-
tradicted and catered to, both attacked and seduced.

In recent years, some Soviet diplomats have acted less like
messengers, and occasionally they have even developed personal
relations with a Western opponent. But on the whole they still
show less initiative and independence than Western diplomats of
comparable rank.

Although the messenger-type diplomat may be designated "chief
negotiator," he plays only a minor role in negotiation. He acts as
the end of a transmission belt for communications that have been
determined in his foreign office or by his chief of government, and
he may collect some intelligence about the opponent which he will
simply send back home. But his risk calculations, changing expectations, and personal feelings scarcely enter into the decision-
making process.

More interesting is the role of the delegate who does have
some powers of decision and who is given a wider latitude in
influencing his home government. Traditionally, such a diplomat
is still subject to guidance from his foreign minister or chief of
government. But he is one of the important independent actors in
international negotiation; he is not just performing a predetermined
service-function like a translator or a coding clerk.

The limited authority of a delegate serves to some extent as a
commitment. It is not a definitive commitment, of course, since
new instructions can break it. Nonetheless, if you are negotiating
with a delegate with limited authority, you realize that his instructions represent a certain barrier whose penetration would cost you
time and require that you exert additional pressure. Hence your
realization that you have pushed your opponent's delegate to the
limit of his instructions may dissuade you from further bargain-

ing and cause you to accept the available terms. It is precisely for this reason that your opponent's delegate may want you to be aware of his instructions and may try to convince you that it would be very cumbersome to change them. But you will seek your own information to ferret out what chances there are within your opponent's government for a change in instructions. If you are knowledgeable about the internal forces within your opponent's government, you will seek to encourage those forces that favor a revised position more advantageous to you.

To be negotiating with a delegate whose authority is narrowly limited can be a frustrating experience. When you realize that the opponent's delegate is allowed only to hold to his initial position, you may feel as if you were talking to a phonograph. It will seem futile to argue with such a delegate, the only hope is that he will properly communicate your message to his government. But in the absence of any response, you might be tempted to start experimenting with your own position, particularly if you have a strong preference for agreement. A revised version of your own position might at least produce a new response from the opponent's government and perhaps lead to new instructions to its delegate. The danger here is that you might increasingly adapt your position to that of the opponent, so as to entice a response, but fail to obtain compensating changes in his rigid instructions. To avoid both this danger and the frustration of talking to the messenger instead of to the master, diplomats often first try to ascertain whether the opponent's delegate has any authority to change his position. If not, they may refuse to become drawn into negotiations.

Yet, there are also disadvantages and pitfalls in the other extreme, where the representatives on both sides are of such senior rank that they have full authority. This raises the question of *summit diplomacy*. In the 1950s, summit meetings between East and West were a lively issue. An East-West summit meeting was first advocated by Winston Churchill in 1950, when he was still leader of the opposition. After Stalin's death, in May, 1953, Prime Minister Churchill renewed his call for a conference "on the highest level . . . not overhung by a ponderous or rigid agenda, or led into mazes or jungles of technical details, zealously contested by hordes of experts and officials drawn up in vast, cumbrous array. The Conference should be confined to the smallest number of powers . . . [and] meet with a measure of informality and still greater measure of privacy and seclusion."[1] Later in the decade, it was Khrushchev who seized the initiative in pressing for summit meetings, with the British government generally willing to go along, but the United States showing considerable reluctance.[2]

The main consideration in summit meetings (as sometimes in other types of conferences) may be the side-effects of negotiation. One reason for the American coolness toward top-level meetings was the feeling that Khrushchev wanted them primarily for propaganda purposes. The propaganda effect can be twofold. First, summits are particularly suited as "sounding boards": any policies that the participants advocate will be endowed with world-wide prominence because the news media devote such central attention to a summit conference. The summit serves like a huge megaphone for national programs on foreign policy. Second, as mentioned before, some leaders may wish to attend summits to enhance their prestige. This, too, may have been an objective for Khrushchev during the 1950s, since he was still in the process of gathering all the reins of power in his own hands.

Another important side-effect of summit negotiation is to establish or to maintain contact between the chiefs of government. According to President Kennedy, this was the primary purpose of his Vienna talks with Khrushchev in 1961. The idea here is that a face-to-face meeting will give statesmen a better understanding of each other's intentions and will strengthen the habit of communicating with one another whenever matters of conflict arise.

Less controversial and less dramatic are summit meetings between friendly powers. They fit more easily into the larger context of intimate diplomatic relations, and the broader basis of common interests facilitates the conduct of negotiations at the summit. Indeed, if friendly powers wish to collaborate extensively and in diverse fields, summit diplomacy plays a key role. Negotiation on a lower level will often reach an impasse finally, because each delegate is in charge of only a narrow sector of the over-all national in-

[1] *Hansard*, 515 H.C. Debate 5 s, col. 897 (May 11, 1953).
[2] For an account of this debate about summitry, see Coral Bell, *Negotiating from Strength: A Study in Politics* (New York: Knopf, 1963).

terest and cannot make trades or package deals encompassing several sectors. Who but the Prime Minister or the President can trade a tariff concession against a military advantage or a clause in a political agreement against a clause in a financial compact?

Summit meetings, in a way, are characterized by the coalescence of several processes that remain separate in other types of negotiation. The chiefs of government formulate their own proposals, put forward supporting arguments, receive information from the opponent, weigh the opponent's proposals, develop their counter-arguments, and decide whether to modify or to maintain their position. The exchange of proposals and counter-proposals and the modification of positions all take place within a few hours—or a few days at the most. Normally, different people are in charge of different phases of this process and considerable time may lapse between one move and the next. Because of this coalescence, summit diplocacy can be more efficient, in terms of the ground covered at a conference, than lower-level negotiation. But for the same reason, summit meetings are also moments of crisis, where great opportunities might be exploited or missed, and where a wrong step can cause a national disaster. As Dean Rusk put it: "The direct confrontation of the chiefs of government of the great powers involves an extra tension because the court of last resort is in session."[3]

Americans have their own historical reasons for distrusting summit diplomacy. There is the memory of President Wilson's fatal experience at the Paris Peace Conference, which dramatizes the fact that in the United States foreign policy cannot be made by the executive alone. There are other Constitutional reasons why the President finds it particularly difficult to attend international conferences. In Dean Rusk's words, negotiation at the summit "diverts time and energy from exactly the point at which we can spare it least."[4] The President can ill afford the time for the extensive preparations that negotiation usually requires, and the vast machinery of the United State government is not centralized enough fully to serve the President at a distant conference site and in situations changing by the hour. As a result, the most fatal

---

[3] Dean Rusk, "The President," *Foreign Affairs* (April, 1960), p. 365.
[4] *Ibid.*, p. 361.

decisions are not only taken at the spur of the moment—which is inevitable in fast-moving negotiation—but often with the advice of people who had to master the detailed issues in as hurried a fashion as the President himself.

It is true that with modern communications it may now be easier than in the days of Yalta and Potsdam to draw on the skills and expertise of the State Department and Defense Department— if the President wishes to do so. In the past the President had to rely on a few men who traveled with him and who may have had a quite limited knowledge of the issues at stake or took a rather special point of view. Thus the summit added to the influence of the special Presidential adviser who was neither elected nor appointed by Congress. It offered the occasion when a Colonel House, a Harry Hopkins, a Presidential speechwriter, or the President's press secretary were called upon to make history. Nonetheless, today any summit conference in which the American President participates is accompanied by enormous publicity so that momentary propaganda effects will inevitably be of major concern. This may not only divert attention from the more important issues, but it may put the Russians at an advantage since they know how to be more callous about public opinion.

PAROCHIAL BUREAUCRATS

Negotiators are sometimes diverted from serving the interest of their government by loyalties to a department or a service, as distinct from the government as a whole. Most international negotiations affect several government departments. In the American government, for example, tariff negotiations are the concern of the Commerce, Treasury, and State Departments, and at times the Department of Agriculture; disarmament negotiations involve the Disarmament Agency, the Defense Department, and the AEC; and in the Berlin negotiations, the State and Defense Departments are drawn in.

Usually the various government departments derive different practical implications from agreed national objectives and have conflicting domestic interests to defend. In fact, in democratic countries, the continuous bargaining that normally takes place between different parts of the government is the principal way in which the national interest becomes formulated.[5] For officials involved in negotiations, the national interest is therefore not a given constant but is something that has to be discussed in each case and frequently revised as the situation evolves.

But there is more to this than different conceptions of national objectives or different syntheses of conflicting domestic interests. Sometimes, government departments favor a certain course in negotiations in order to increase their own power or to get a larger share of the budget.

In the American government, owing to its federal structure and large size, the interests of departments and various offices intrude into the conduct of international negotiations more strongly than, say, in the French or the British government. How a parochial concern with bureaucratic power disabled the U.S. government in the pursuit of its foreign policy objectives is illustrated by Philip Mosely's account of the wartime negotiations on the zonal boundaries for Germany. During 1943–44, representatives of the United States, Great Britain, and the Soviet Union met in the European Advisory Committee in London to settle a number of postwar arrangements for Europe, in particular the zonal boundaries in Germany. The American delegation to the Committee was to receive instructions from an interdepartmental group in Washington. However, the State Department representatives in this group were unable to convince their colleagues from the War Department of the importance of settling with the Soviet Union and Great Britain the postwar arrangements for Germany. Owing to the War Department's opposition—which perhaps stemmed from the desire to reserve complete freedom of action for its occupation troops—there was no American position on how the zonal boundaries with the Soviet occupation forces in Germany should be drawn, and no specific provisions for access to Berlin were prepared. In the end, the agreed upon zones for Germany were based entirely upon a British proposal (which had originated with recommendations

[5] Charles E. Lindblom, "The Science of 'Muddling Through,'" *Public Administration Review*, XIX (Spring, 1959), 74–88. For a comparison of the British, American, and Soviet systems for coordinating the conduct of foreign policy among different departments, see Joseph Frankel, *The Making of Foreign Policy* (London: Oxford University Press, 1963), pp. 33–35.

from the British Chiefs of Staff). The only concern of the War Department was that detailed arrangements be made with the British, so that the American forces would have free access to their zone through the British zone.[6]

The interdepartmental coordination of a negotiating position can be rather cumbersome. It may bring forth a prolonged exchange of memoranda and require repeated conferences and consultations. Points that cannot be reconciled will have to be sumbitted to the President for a decision. The fact that an appeal to higher authority is possible marks the difference between bargaining *within* a government and international negotiation. Sometimes the chief negotiator and his team may spend more energy and time arguing with government officials back home, in order to have the positions of other departments changed or overruled, than in trying to change the opponent's position. Occasionally though, the sluggishness of interdepartmental coordination may serve the negotiator like a commitment: the fact that it is so difficult to change an agreed position within his government provides the negotiator with an extra incentive to resist the opponent's pressures for concessions.

The difficulty of intra-governmental coordination also helps to explain why a minimum position (distinct from the terms offered to the opponent) can be rarely maintained by a government whose departments enjoy a certain independence—as in Washington. For if such a minimum existed, the negotiator would soon be urged to fall back on it by those branches within the government that are anxious to conclude an agreement but consider the particular terms less important. Precisely for this reason, other branches within the government, for which the particular terms *are* important, will not agree to a minimum position to begin with.

[6] Philip E. Mosely, "The Occupation of Germany: New Light on How the Zones Were Drawn," *Foreign Affairs* (July, 1950), pp. 580–604. According to Mosely's account, the War Department held that the determination of the future zones of occupation "was a 'military matter' which would be decided 'at the proper time' and 'at the military level' " (pp. 587–88). Llewellyn Woodward, in the official British history of World War II, reports that Eden complained to Stettinius, that the Americans were not keeping to the directives given to the European Advisory Commission at the Moscow Conference. "Mr. Stettinius agreed that the War Department was largely responsible for the American attitude" (*British Foreign Policy in the Second World War* [London: H.M.S.O., 1962], p. 477).

DOMESTIC PRESSURE GROUPS AND SECRET DIPLOMACY

Domestic forces may desire to influence international negotiations for either of two reasons: a concern about foreign policy, or private interests. Domestic groups that are concerned about foreign policy hold their own views regarding the national welfare or regarding international issues and have their own convictions as to how principles like freedom and justice ought to be pursued in practice. This is exemplified by the groups worried about disarmament negotiations, both those in favor of reaching agreements by conceding more to the Russians and those favoring greater caution and firmness—the "peace groups" and the advocates of military strength. Other examples are the involvement of the German population in the Berlin negotiations and the interest in European integration shown by the younger generation in Western Europe.

Then there are the private-interest groups whose members are concerned with the effects of an agreement on their *personal* welfare, as distinct from holding a certain view of the *national* interest. Tariff negotiations and commercial agreements make characteristic battlegrounds for such private interests. The negotiations for the American-Japanese peace treaty mobilized both foreign-policy interests (particularly on the question of Communist China's relation to Japan) and the private interests of the West Coast fishing industry.[7]

Occasionally, the opponent can encourage these private interests to fight for his cause. Proposing to swap duty reductions in tariff negotiations has this effect. Exporting industries in the United States, for example, may become the advocates of American tariff reductions requested by European countries, if such American reductions have been made the condition for lower tariffs in Europe. In a sense, there is an alliance in tariff negotiations between private interest groups in each of the countries involved. However, these groups rarely go so far as to join forces to oppose an agreement that their governments wish to negotiate. Before World

[7] For an account of how the fishing industry influenced the course and outcome of these negotiations, see Bernard C. Cohen, *The Political Process in Foreign Policy: The Making of the Japanese Peace Settlement* (Princeton, N.J.: Princeton University Press, 1957), pp. 253–77.

War I and in the 1920s, some writers speculated about a conspiracy of the "munition makers" in sabotaging disarmament conferences. A parallel would be if industries threatened by imports conspired to prevent agreements for tariff reductions; say, the French farmer ganging up with the American textile and bicycle manufacturers to wreck a GATT conference! Such stories, of course, are usually apocryphal.

Ethnic, historical, and ideological sympathies sometimes lead domestic groups to try to influence international negotiations, as illustrated by the concern of Americans of Polish descent for the impact of the Yalta and Potsdam Conferences on Poland and the involvement of American Zionists in U.S. policies toward Israel and the Middle East.[8] Such groups represent neither private interest nor a particular view of the national interest. They express an attachment to the cause of a foreign country or a foreign population.

Governments often feel handicapped in the pursuit of national objectives if domestic interest groups become involved in their negotiations. Citizens in favor of a "hard position" will criticize any concessions to the opponent, those who want an agreement will criticize the government's "inflexibility," but neither group may take an over-all view of the prospects of getting an agreement at various terms and of the value of these terms to the nation as a whole as compared with no-agreement. For this reason, many writers and statesmen have favored *secret diplomacy*. Woodrow Wilson's phrase has been revised; nowadays it is said that governments should seek "open agreements secretly arrived at."

In the spring of 1963, U.S. Senator J. William Fulbright listened with some exasperation to Congressional hearings on the seemingly endless test-ban negotiations and offered this counsel to the Secretary of State: ". . . I rather disagree with the whole procedure you are following—that you try to get agreements of this kind in the open. I think they do not lend themselves to fruitful discussions, if everything the negotiators say has to be addressed

<hr>

[8] See H. Bradford Westerfield, *Foreign Policy and Party Politics* (New Haven: Yale University Press, 1958), for a discussion of the Zionist role in the American policy regarding the Palestine question, as well as for an excellent general account of the impact of domestic forces on American diplomacy from 1939 to 1950.

to the local constituency back home, rather than to the people participating in the meeting. . . . It seems to me you ought to be able to arrange for negotiations to be private, of course making whatever you conclude public."[9] Four months after Senator Fulbright had made this comment, the test-ban talks were indeed conducted in secrecy, when Averell Harriman and Viscount Hailsham concluded a treaty with Andrei Gromyko to ban all but underground tests.

Much has been written about the merits of secret versus open negotiation since the Wilsonian injunction against secret diplomacy. Although Harold Nicolson and other writers have done a service in debunking the strictures against secret bargaining,[10] both the advocates of secrecy and those of openness have gone too far in making such a clear-cut distinction between these two forms of diplomacy—one of them being the right way and the other one being wicked. Secrecy is a matter of degree.

Negotiations are often kept partly secret. The discussions between the diplomats may not be revealed, but enough about the basic demands and offers may become known to stimulate domestic pressures for changes in the government's position. At times, the mere fact that negotiations take place about a certain issue may be sufficient to lead to uneasiness and protests among certain groups and arouse impatient demands by others that an agreement be concluded. This kind of public reaction all depends on the way in which the news media report the semi-secret negotiations.

Some of the reporting on certain phases in the Berlin negotiations in 1962, for example, maintained a feeling of crisis and urgency among the public, although there was no apparent danger of a Soviet intervention at that time. Important newspapers, particularly the *New York Times,* tended to give prominence to every encounter between the Soviet ambassador and the Secretary of

[9] U.S. Senate, Committee on Foreign Relations, *Hearing: Test Ban Negotiations and Disarmament,* March 11, 1963 (Washington, 1963), pp. 23–24.

[10] Nicolson points out that President Wilson himself negotiated one of the most important agreements in utmost secrecy, less than a half year after promulgating in the first of his Fourteen Points that in the future there should be "open convenants of peace openly arrived at." At the end of the Versailles Conference, he shut himself up in his own study with Lloyd George and Clemenceau, excluding not only the press but all other powers from the crucial deliberations (*Diplomacy,* pp. 83–84).

State and to any similar secret discussions on which Berlin may
have been a topic, portraying each of these meetings as another
fruitless round in the Berlin negotiations. This stimulated the
public feeling that the situation was abnormal and ought to be
resolved by a new agreement; that is, the crisis atmosphere fed the
expectation that a satisfactory outcome would have to be different
from the status quo. To appreciate this influence of the news media,
one must recall that every time an ambassador meets with the
Secretary of State, issues are discussed which often remain unresolved. The public will remain unaware of all these "negotiations" that continue day after day without a "solution," unless the
news media convey the impression that a critical situation exists.

The distinction between open and secret negotiation should not
be confused with the distinction between *formal* and *informal*
negotiation. In informal negotiations, the deliberations are usually
secret, whereas a formal conference can be either open or secret.
What distinguishes informal negotiation is that the talking done
by the diplomats is more conversational, more an exchange of
questions and answers than a confrontation of prepared statements.
In informal negotiation, the diplomats normally have a tacit understanding that all positions taken are tentative; that is, they feel
they need not adhere to the rules that partial agreements ought to
be preserved and that concessions must not be withdrawn. But
sometimes a party does not share this understanding (or breaks
it) and may complain openly that the other party reversed a position put forward in an informal meeting. Another aspect of
informal negotiation is the importance of personal relations between the diplomats. In informal contacts, negotiators are more
likely to be influenced by feelings towards each other than in
formal conferences.

Secrecy (as distinguished from informality) has two major
effects in diplomacy. First, it keeps domestic groups ignorant of the
process of negotiation, thereby preventing them from exerting
pressures during successive phases of bargaining. Second, it leaves
third parties in the dark and thus reduces their influence.

The exclusion of the public may help to overcome domestic
opposition to concessions or threats before negotiations are completed. Once the agreement is signed, it tends to act as a *fait*

accompli, weakening dissent and mobilizing interest groups in support of it. Thus the requisite domestic consent (such as Senate ratification for the United States) may be obtained in the end, whereas the individual concessions would have been opposed. At other times, open negotiations get stuck in a rut where the parties feel compelled to follow a certain formal routine, although they all realize its inefficiency. This seems to have happened with most disarmament conferences. (Actually, many secret talks on disarmament have been just as unsuccessful as the open ones!) However, if all participating governments desire agreement and feel that open negotiation would not succeed, they are likely to collaborate in maintaining secrecy. Their collaboration will usually end as soon as one side thinks that it can gain by appealing to the public. This may be done by means of a "leak" to news media. Indeed, a leak about a secret conference often gets more attention than the daily reports from open meetings. No matter what preferences one might have regarding secret versus open diplomacy, one must realize that each party will try to move toward or press for that form of negotiation from which it expects the best results.

The second important effect of conducting negotiations in secret—provided secrecy can be maintained—is to keep governments of third parties in the dark. This is essential in triangular situations, when two parties want to make a deal at the expense of a third one. On other occasions, two parties may have a common interest in keeping their negotiations secret to prevent a third party from exploiting their differences. The parties will then have to maintain a precarious balance between their common interest in excluding the third party and their conflicting interest in using leaks and publicity in order to put pressure on the opponent. This is illustrated by the Sino-Soviet conflict, about which more and more is being revealed in both Moscow and Peking.

A sub-group *within* an alliance may negotiate in secret in order to confront the other partners with a finished agreement which it will be difficult to oppose. In international organizations such coalitions are constantly formed under various degrees of secrecy. For example, there are regular caucuses among members of the United Nations General Assembly. If an alliance is to maintain its cohesion, however, partners who negotiate secretly must be careful not to give the impression of "ganging up" on the others. In January, 1963, both Paris and Bonn had to reassure the other four partners in the Common Market that the Franco-German Treaty would not be used to form secret coalitions on issues relating to the Common Market.

Prior to the wartime conference at Teheran between Roosevelt, Churchill, and Stalin, there was to be an Anglo-American meeting at Cairo. President Roosevelt was anxious that the discussions between the American and British staffs in Cairo should not give Stalin the feeling that he was being excluded from important secret negotiations. He wrote to the Prime Minister: "In regard to Cairo, I have held all along, as I know you have, that it would be a terrible mistake if Uncle J. thought we had ganged up on him on military action. . . . It will not hurt you or me if Molotov and a Russian military representative are in Cairo too. They will not feel that they are being given the 'run around.' . . . Let us take them in on the high spots." Churchill did not care for this reference to "ganging up." He cabled back: "His Majesty's Government cannot abandon their rights to full and frank discussions with you and your officers about the vital business of our intermingled armies. A Soviet observer cannot possibly be admitted to the intimate conversations which our own Chiefs of Staff must have. . . ."[11]

THE EXECUTIVE, THE LEGISLATURE, AND THE PUBLIC

In all international conferences, negotiators are prone to argue that their government has made more concessions and bigger ones than the opponent. In part, they may do so out of habit, as one of the routine forms of speech-making at the conference table.

In part, negotiators emphasize their concessions in order to induce the opponent to make concessions of his own. This may be effective, on the one hand, when your opponent feels constrained by the rule that concessions ought to be reciprocated. On the other hand, if you are negotiating with a more hard-headed opponent, you magnify your own concessions for a different reason. Such an opponent will not think that he ought to make a concession in

[11] *Closing the Ring* (Boston: Houghton Mifflin, 1951), p. 319.

return, merely to follow the rule of reciprocation. But he might be convinced that you cannot give another inch before he concedes something, since you could not afford to create the impression back home (or with other powers) that you were constantly receding while he stood firm. That is, you magnify your concessions in order to create a commitment. This commitment stems from the fact that your domestic public or your legislators believe concessions ought to be reciprocated.

However, like most negotiating tactics, this method has to be used with moderation. The negotiator must be cautious not to magnify his concessions so much that his legislators and the domestic press will turn against him. Of course, the same domestic opposition groups may favor hard bargaining on one issue and soft bargaining on another, depending on their foreign-policy preferences. For example, the British Labour Party criticized the Macmillan government for having made too many concessions when it tried in 1962 to gain entry into the Common Market. But on the nuclear test ban, Labour often criticized the Conservative government for not conceding enough to obtain a treaty with the Soviet Union.

While the inspection system for underground tests was an issue (that is, before the partial ban of August, 1963), the American negotiators at the test-ban conference were criticized for the opposite reason. From 1958 through 1962, the United States revised its demands for underground detection several times, in ways that brought its position closer to Russia's. This helped the American delegation to maintain a common stand with the British (who were under domestic pressure to concede more), and it also won support for the Western position among the neutral participants at the disarmament conference. But this series of revisions—which appeared to be unilateral concessions—was less well received by some members of Congress. Senator Thomas J. Dodd, for example, made a critical speech in which he listed a large number of American concessions and argued: ". . . we have repeatedly shown ourselves willing to compromise and to go the 'extra mile.' By this time we have gone the 'extra mile' so many times over that we have virtually lost sight of our point of departure. We have made these concessions piecemeal, so that our position at any given moment has never been too different from our position 3 months previously. It is only by going back to the beginning and laying our concessions end to end that the terrifying scope of our retreat becomes apparent."[12] Similar criticism had been voiced earlier. In August, 1962, for instance, Governor Rockefeller and other Republican leaders complained that the United States was moving "steadily toward the Soviet position."

In response to these charges, the State Department Press Officer found it necessary to justify the U.S. negotiating tactics by arguing that the new proposals were based "not on concessions but on scientific findings."[13] And Senator Hubert Humphrey defended the revisions in the American position similarly:

. . . every time I pick up a paper . . . I read about the "concessions" that we are making, which has the effect with the public of saying, "What's the matter with the administration, this Government, this country of ours—conceding to the Russians?"

It would be like this. If you found that it required 100,000 units of penicillin to check pneumonia, and you had been giving 1 million units of penicillin . . . , I suppose then we should say the doctors are making a concession to pneumonia.[14]

The drawback of such explanations on the domestic scene is that the opponent can turn them to his advantage. If Washington says that the revised Western positions are based not on concessions but on new scientific findings, the Russians can use this to argue that they, on the contrary, *did* make concessions—not just adaptions to scientific requirements—and that it is time for the West finally to make sacrifices.

Yet, even the Russians sometimes have to steer between the Scylla of failing to magnify concessions while talking to the opponent and the Charybdis of appearing to concede too much while explaining a new position to domestic critics or allies. No doubt when Khrushchev withdrew his missiles from Cuba in 1962, he would have liked to press for "counter-concessions" in exchange. But back in Moscow, it was felt necessary to let the

[12] Speech on the Senate floor, Feb. 21, 1963, *Congressional Record*, pp. 5–6.
[13] *New York Times*, Aug. 10, 1962.
[14] U.S. Senate, Subcommittee of the Committee on Foreign Relations, *Hearings: Renewed Geneva Disarmament Negotiations*, July 25 and Aug. 2, 1962 (Washington, 1963), p. 47.

First Deputy Premier, A. N. Kosygin, describe the resolution of the Cuba crisis as follows: "Who gave in to whom in this situation? We consider that it was a concession from both sides, a concession to reason and peace. . . . On the basis of compromise and mutual concessions, the acuteness of the conflict has been eliminated. . . ."[15]

Different attitudes toward concessions of course constitute only one of the reasons why the executive branch of the government may come in conflict with the legislature or with other domestic forces. More important than this question of negotiating tactics, quite different views may prevail on the objectives of agreement and on whether agreement is to be preferred to no-agreement. In fact, these more basic preferences often determine the attitudes toward concessions. If the domestic public views no-agreement as a serious failure, so that it worries only about a breakdown of a conference while showing little interest in the possible terms, it will not object to concessions. In response to the public mood, therefore, the negotiator may feel forced to accept what he considers to be unsatisfactory terms.

Secretary of State James Byrnes found himself in this quandary at the first meeting of the Council of Foreign Ministers in September, 1945, where important peace settlements for Europe and the Far East were discussed. After a number of meetings, Molotov made it clear that the Soviets would not proceed with the conference unless France and China were excluded. "We were determined to yield no further," reported Byrnes of this impasse. "Yet we were reluctant to let the first test of the peace-making machinery result in complete breakdown. . . . The public at home did not have the clear view of Soviet ambitions that the President and I got at Potsdam. . . . The first meeting of the council would be a complete failure and I realized that the failure would be attributed to me." After Byrnes had refused to yield to Molotov's demands and the conference broke up, he was still worried about what he thought was a strong preference for an agreement among the American public. "With the break-up of

---

[15] Kosygin's speech at the Kremlin Palace in Moscow, Nov. 6, 1962 (Daily Report, Foreign Radio Broadcasts, *Foreign Broadcast Information Service* [Nov. 7, 1962], p. BB15).

the council I headed for the United States knowing I had to face criticism."[16]

John Foster Dulles, who accompanied Byrnes as a Republican adviser, takes credit for having encouraged Byrnes to maintain what he thought was such an unpopular stand. "Without my presence," Dulles wrote, "Secretary Byrnes could not have known that he could come home with what, superficially, was a total failure without being subject to criticism by the opposition."[17]

After this experience, Secretary Byrnes concluded "that hereafter people would have to be more fully informed if we were to maintain a firm position in international affairs with full public support."[18] During this early postwar period, other American officials felt themselves to be under similar pressure because they thought American public opinion forced them to avoid a conflict with Russia at all costs. In March, 1946, the American ambassador in Warsaw, Arthur Bliss Lane, recommended that the United States take a firmer stand against the suppression of non-Communist parties in Poland. He wrote to the State Department: ". . . it is essential for the Congress and for the American public to be informed regarding conditions in Poland, Yugoslavia, etc. Education of the public cannot take place overnight. . . . There will be attacks on us from the left-wing press and from some of the more radical labor elements to the effect that we are endeavoring to bring about hostilities with the Soviet Union."[19]

A chief of government who feels secure about public opinion can fortify his representatives against the temptation to please the public with quick agreements. When General de Gaulle sent his foreign minister to the San Francisco conference in 1945, his instructions included a specific warning against yielding to criticism in the press:

You will have to defend yourself not only against the pressure of those Powers who are in a hurry to consolidate a balance of power which is at the moment to their advantage *vis-à-vis* us, but also against the natural desire of our own negotiators—a desire to agree with their partners, and finish the job, so to speak. But I must insist that any such

[16] James F. Byrnes, *Speaking Frankly*, pp. 104, 107.

[17] John Foster Dulles, *War or Peace* (New York: Macmillan, 1950), p. 127.

[18] *Op. cit.*, p. 107.

[19] Arthur Bliss Lane, *I Saw Poland Betrayed* (New York: Bobbs-Merrill, 1948), p. 195.

action would prove to our detriment in the present period. This means you must on no account yield even if an outcry is raised in the press and in foreign broadcasts, or even French, which may try to force you to a decision. Since we have been reduced to our present situation our most successful moves have been those that have raised the most violent storms.[20]

Sometimes the senior negotiator himself may make a special effort to gain public support and to protect himself against domestic pressure that could adversely affect his conduct of negotiations. John Foster Dulles did this rather successfully when he was the chief American negotiator for the Japanese Peace Treaty.[21] At that time, Dulles had a specific objective in mind: he knew what kind of peace treaty he wanted, and he made sure—by paying considerable attention to Congressional and public opinion—that he would obtain the requisite consent from the Senate.

However, if the negotiators (or the decision-makers instructing them) fail to develop their own objectives and strategy, their attempt to marshal public support will be vitiated: it will become a way of seeking guidance *from the public*. The mass media, editorial writers, columnists, commentators, and spokesmen for interest groups will take the lead in determining what the country should want to bargain for and how it should go about doing it. So-called public opinion—that is, mainly the current views of the news media—will become the primary concern of the government's policy, and the objectives of gaining the support of "public opinion" will be used to conceal the lack of any more substantial foreign-policy objectives.

In intra-governmental discussions, officials may rationalize their personal preferences in favor of a certain negotiating position with arguments such as "public opinion wants us to . . ." or "public opinion would not permit us to. . . ." Perhaps these officials could not get away with their facile claims if their colleagues pressed them for the following three explanations: First, how they define "public opinion" (whether it is the view of a couple of newspaper editors, a Gallup poll on a particularly phrased question, or the verdict of a popular referendum). Second, how they

[20] General de Gaulle, *Salvation*, 1944–1946, Vol. II, *Documents*, p. 237 (from a letter to Georges Bidault, April 17, 1945).

[21] Bernard C. Cohen, *The Political Process in Foreign Policy*, pp. 133–42.

know that public opinion, thus defined, would react in the indicated way to the issue under discussion. And third, how they
came to the conclusion that public opinion should take precedence
over the judgment of officials whom the electorate put in charge
of foreign affairs and who ought to be better informed than the
public at large.[22]

There is another risk in trying to conduct negotiations so as to
please public opinion. The mood of the public may be genuinely
misjudged. As a result, a negotiator may be afraid to make concessions that not only would have benefited his country but also
would have been quite acceptable to the public. Conversely, he
may fail to pursue his objectives more aggressively, even though
his country would have supported him. Such an underestimate of
public support may have handicapped the American government
at the end of World War II and during the first few postwar years.
The editorial opinion of a few leading newspapers and some
prominent columnists may have misled the American decision-
makers into believing that the country would not support a firmer
stand against the Soviet take-over of Eastern Europe. A series of
opinion polls from that period show that the American public, as
distinct from the editorial opinion in the news media, would have
gone along with a slower demobilization after World War II,
thus providing the basis for a firmer foreign policy, and that
Congress was influenced by a vocal minority which wanted "to
bring the boys back home."[23]

All this is not to say that the views and attitudes of the electorate
are not important for the conduct of foreign relations. The electorate ought to support and participate in the basic value judg-
ments that have to be rendered, both explicitly and implicitly, in
foreign-policy decisions. And the people must approve of the
sacrifices they may have to make in support of a foreign policy.

[22] The difficulties of defining and measuring "public opinion" are of course
well known to experts. See, for example, Leonard S. Cottrell, Jr., and Sylvia
Eberhart, *American Opinion on World Affairs in the Atomic Age* (Princeton,
N.J.: Princeton University Press, 1948), chap. i, for a brief and judicious
discussion of these problems.
[23] Nancy Boardman Eddy, "Public Opinion and U.S. Foreign Policy 1937–
1956," unpublished paper of the Center for International Studies, M.I.T. (Cambridge, Mass., 1958).

CHAPTER 9

PERSONALITIES

LIKE ANY HUMAN BEINGS, OFFICIALS WHO PLAY A ROLE IN negotiations have their emotions, personal frailties, and quirks, whether they work in the lower echelons of the government or in its highest decision-making councils, whether they stay in the home capital or participate in a conference abroad. They are all influenced by their own sympathies or hostilities; they all respond to anger, impatience, and feelings of gratitude. They have personal ambitions which are rarely, if ever, identical with the interests of their country.

NEGOTIATOR OR MEDIATOR?

Agreement in itself, regardless of the terms, may become a measure of success for a diplomat. Although it is sometimes best for the national interest to terminate negotiations with no agreement, for the negotiator himself such an outcome is often tinged with failure. He will consider an agreement as his target unless he has been specifically instructed to avoid reaching one. It is the goal toward which his efforts and labors are dedicated. In the end, especially in protracted conferences, the reaching of a formal accord will assume importance for him independent of the terms of settlement.

This view of agreement as a measure of success affects not only the chief negotiator but also the members of his delegation. In many international conferences, junior officials and supporting staff members will have to work long into the night and over weekends to evaluate some new proposal from the other side, to revise a position, or to prepare a speech for the next session. If there is no agreement when the conference ends, all this work—the carefully calculated positions and the shrewdly drafted proposals— might seem to have been in vain. As for the chief negotiator himself, it takes a detached view to remain confident that the "failure" of his conference need not at all imply that *he* has failed, much as his reaching an agreement per se does not mean he has succeeded. Indeed, if the negotiator asks himself how history will come to judge his work—and which senior diplomat does not do so?—he must realize that diplomats are generally praised for the good agreements they concluded, not for the bad ones they avoided, since historians find it hard to reconstruct what the terms and consequences of such unborn accords might have been.

This attachment to agreement per se is not new to the nuclear era. From the days of Munich in 1938, Sir Samuel Hoare recalled that he had been "caught up in the toils of a critical negotiation," like Prime Minister Neville Chamberlain and Hoare's cabinet colleagues. "The longer it went on and the more serious the issue became, the more anxious I grew to see it succeed. This is almost always the course of negotiations. As they proceed, the parties concerned in them become increasingly obsessed with the need to prevent their final failure."[1]

It seems paradoxical that the *defensive* party in redistribution negotiations (as at Munich) should be "obsessed with the need to prevent their final failure." For what do "failure" and "success" mean? The defensive side may be successful even if such negotiations "fail," since it may have deterred the offensive side from carrying out its threat and thus preserved the status quo in peace. This has been the success of the "failure" of the Berlin negotiations between 1958 and 1963. If the negotiator is attached to agreement, he may believe that there will be a "solution" for almost any negotiation, meaning that a formal accord can be found to satisfy the basic objectives of both sides. However, as long as he is engaged in redistribution negotiations, such an accord is not possible (the

[1] *Nine Troubled Years*, p. 311.

opponent's objectives being incompatible with his own). Therefore, if he remains nonetheless dedicated to finding a "solution,"
this means one of two things: either he expects that the opponent
will change to more benign objectives (such as normalization), or
he will modify his own objectives and himself furnish the "solution" by accepting a deterioration of the status quo.

As a consequence of this bias in favor of agreement, the chief
negotiator (and his team) may prefer agreement to no-agreement
more than the interests of his government would indicate. Unless
he is a disciplined public servant, he may even act as a *mediator*
between his government and that of the opponent instead of as an
advocate of his own side. Should this go so far that the reaching of
an agreement becomes his dominant measure of success, he will
resemble a broker who obtains his commission only if the transaction is concluded, while the price at which his client buys is a
secondary matter.

A tendency to mediate impinges upon the course of negotiations
in various ways. One effect is that the negotiator will seek to obtain agreement by leaving out all the hard-core residual issues of
disagreement. Carried to the extreme, this leads to the pseudo-
agreements discussed before. Another effect is that the negotiator
will be strongly devoted to the rule of flexibility. He may from the
start present his government's position in a way suggesting that
he expects to split the difference. Or, the negotiator may tempt his
own government into making concessions by predicting that they
would bring about a desired counter-concession. Occasionally, he
may even use a *fait accompli* to force his government to agree; he
might, for instance, report that the opponent has already consented
to a certain compromise at an informal meeting. And if there is a
dispute within the government over a softer position and a harder
one, the mediating negotiator will invariably take advantage of it
by pushing the soft position.

Communist diplomats hardly permit themselves to slide into
such a mediating role. Unlike their Western opponents, they do not
reveal the slightest difference between their own position and that
of their government. In fact, they probably scarcely think of having
a position of their own but see their role only as that of an advocate.
In Western democracies, on the other hand, the politically active

citizen is accustomed to look critically at the policies of his government. Even after entering government service, therefore, he is able to maintain his own views on foreign affairs. In countries like the United States, this is encouraged by the fact that senior diplomats often move back and forth between government service, private life, and political activity in behalf of the domestic opposition. Such part-time diplomats may find it more natural occasionally to act as a mediator than to maintain an unwavering advocacy of all the positions that happened to have been formulated by the administration in power.

While a tendency to mediate may be stimulated by the broker's interest in his commission (i.e., the felt satisfaction and expected advantages of having one's negotiations "succeed"), it can usually be explained by less egotistical motives. More often than not, the efforts of Western diplomats to mediate between their own government and the opponent stem from the desire to further the common good. Westerners may seek to transcend their national interests by using their insight and wisdom in behalf of a larger unity, and in the knowledge that their own government has no monopoly of the truth. Indeed, West European unity and Western alliances could never have been forged had the diplomats on all sides not been able to identify themselves with these larger interests. And which larger interest is more noble and more important than that of world peace?

Yet there is a dilemma here. If the negotiator of the first party conscientiously tries to find merit on both sides of the dispute, while his opponent does not, who will fully bring out the merits of the first party's position? Can a negotiator switch back and forth, being an advocate on Monday and a mediator on Tuesday, or will the cause of his own side fail to get a fair hearing if he "transcends" his client so often?

In 1961, when the Soviet-provoked Berlin crisis was acute, Senator Mansfield viewed the Western position with a certain detachment, probably because he had a larger common good in mind: "The responsibility which we have," he said on the Senate floor, "and which the Soviet Union has, is not merely to reassert positions already assumed and which are obviously irreconcilable. The responsibility is to seek to determine whether or not there is a third way on Berlin which corresponds more accurately to the needs of Germany today, Europe today, and the world today—indeed, a third way which meets more fully the contemporary needs of both the Soviet Union and ourselves."[2] At a later occasion in the same year, Senator Mansfield further elaborated this picture of East-West symmetry as concerned the Berlin crisis: "There are German fears of the East. There are Polish, Czech and other fears of Germany. There are NATO fears of the Warsaw Pact forces and similar fears in reverse. There are capitalist fears of Communism and Communist fears of capitalism. . . ."[3] To the extent that Mansfield, as the Senate Majority Leader, spoke for the American government, or at least for the majority in Congress, the United States mediated against its own position. While the fears between East and West may be symmetrical, this kind of mediation surely is not. There is no comparable spokesman in the Soviet government who defends "a third way" on Berlin or who speaks sympathetically of West European fears of the East.

The verbatim records of East-West disarmament conferences provide many examples of the contrast between Communist and Western negotiators in the tendency to mediate between one's own position and that of the opponent. When the nuclear test-ban conference resumed in 1961, the American delegate Arthur Dean suggested, "We must all be willing to consider new approaches which differ . . . both from our previous positions and from our . . . desires. Obviously, adjustments will be necessary on each side in the future as they have been in the past." Tsarapkin, however, expressed the "hope that our partners will . . . accept the . . . proposals submitted by the Soviet Union on the points still at issue."[4]

Discussing the impasse on the inspection issue in disarmament negotiations, UN Ambassador Adlai Stevenson wrote: "With a modicum of common sense and the desire for progress it ought to be possible to break this impasse. . . . We in the West will have to scale our demands for inspection rights in accordance with the

[2] *Congressional Record*, June 14, 1961, p. 9598.
[3] Speech at the Virginia Education Association, Richmond, Va., Nov. 3, 1961.
[4] Conference on the Discontinuance of Nuclear Weapon Tests, 274th Plenary Meeting, March 21, 1961, pp. 32, 5 (provisional).

degree of disarmament we are seeking. The Communists will have to recognize that they must live on their own territory with inspectors. . . . If East and West come into the Geneva Conference determined to break out of the vicious circle of the spiraling technological arms race they have an unusual opportunity. . . ."[5] East and West appear here almost as if they were equally far apart from a reasonable middle.

At the Eighteen-Nation Disarmament Conference in 1962, it was the British Foreign Secretary—not one of the *neutral* delegates —who said: "We begin to see much in common between the American and Soviet plans. If we can work on this common ground, we should be able to produce a master plan. . . ." And the American delegate later took the same view: "What we must try to do, is devise a single over-all agreement which draws upon the best from each proposal." But Gromyko would never show such detachment toward the proposal of his own government and abandon it at the outset in favor of some common ground. He instead expressed the hope that the Disarmament Committee, "after impartially and carefully studying the draft treaty submitted today by the Soviet Government, will recognize the need to make it the basis of the Committee's work."[6]

Early in 1963, disagreement in the nuclear test-ban conference focused on the number of inspections, the Soviet Union offering two to three inspections to detect underground tests, while the United States and the United Kingdom asked for eight to ten— later seven. (This was before the conclusion of the partial treaty.) At that time, Dr. Jerome Wiesner, the President's Science Adviser, was reported to have said in a broadcast for the Voice of America: "I am sure that this is a gap which can be closed by continued negotiations and we hope that in the next few months we will see the gap closed."[7] At the same time at a reception in Moscow, however, the Soviet Foreign Minister Gromyko, in private conversation with diplomats, "appeared to define the Soviet offer of three on-site inspections as a final figure rather than as a negotiating

[5] *New York Times,* March 11; 1962, Magazine section.
[6] Eighteen-Nation Disarmament Conference, March 27, April 4, and March 15, 1962.
[7] As quoted by Senator Dodd, *Congressional Record,* Feb. 21, 1963, p. 2661. Cf. *New York Times,* Jan. 23, 1963.

position."[8] If American officials mediate between the United States and the Soviet position, while Russian officials defend the position of their government as final, who is left to defend the U.S. position?

PERSONAL FEARS AND AMBITIONS

Instead of this tendency to play mediator, the negotiator's personal ambition may lie in the opposite direction. He may want to prove himself a hard bargainer by clinging to his position more stubbornly than is either required by his instructions or warranted by any prospects that the opponent might yield first. If a junior diplomat does this, the delegate from the other side may see through it and hold fast until the stubborn official is overruled from above. But in the case of senior negotiators, the desire to prove oneself a hard bargainer contributes to the bargaining reputation of the government as a whole. This is particularly true for the head of a government. De Gaulle's reluctance to revise any position he has taken (with the exception of his positions on Algeria), endows French diplomacy in the early 1960s with a reputation of firmness —or rigidity.

From the point of view of the national interest, however, it is undesirable that negotiators become unwilling to make concessions for fear that this might damage their *personal* reputation. One drawback, in some situations, is that this personal stubbornness may prevent an agreement that would have been in the country's interest (although in other situations stubbornness may pay off). Another drawback, more subtle but often more important, is that government officials who are very reluctant to make any kind of concession will become overly cautious in preparing their initial negotiating positions. They will insist on entering each conference with very modest demands, or with no clear position at all, so that they will not have to give the appearance of conceding points to the enemy. Such officials will ardently defend the rule that one should not make "unacceptable demands." The tendency to make modest initial demands will be aggravated if the officials have no

[8] *New York Times* (according to a report by the Moscow correspondent), Jan. 22, 1963.

reason to fear criticism for their initial modesty but will be censored only for later concessions.

Reinforcing this fear of external criticism, negotiators sometimes have another motive for making only modest initial demands. This is the fairly common human predilection for "prophylactic pessimism": to avoid later disappointment, a person may start out with deliberately lowered expectations. But in negotiation, one's expectations have a potent effect on the outcome, even while the national objectives remain firm; and in the long run stunted expectations lead to stunted objectives. By indulging in "prophylactic pessimism," diplomats become less effective bargainers. John Foster Dulles' pessimism about obtaining self-determination for the Soviet zone of Germany may have been a case in point, particularly after Stalin's death, when the uprisings in the Soviet zone and the attitudes of the new leaders in the Kremlin would have warranted a less resigned diplomatic approach.

There are other fears which may cause negotiators to pursue objectives that do not coincide with those of their government. Some diplomats worry how their actions will look in the eyes of history. They compose their inter-office memoranda, position papers, and telegrams always with a view toward a future historian who might read these documents at the distant date when the government's archives will be opened. If they expect the judgment of history to condemn the current position of their government, they will support it only cautiously and with restraint. Of course, to serve the long-term interest of their country, diplomats *should* use their historical perspective and foresight in the formulation and conduct of foreign policy. Would that some of the officials in the German foreign office under Hitler had anticipated how their actions would be evaluated by the next generation! On the other hand, the ambition to appear wise to future historians may encourage throwing good capital after bad, in an obstinate effort to prove oneself right. Diplomats with such an attitude tend to cling to their predictions and objectives long after they should have abandoned them, as if the vindication of their personal judgment was part of the national interest.

MOODS AND MANNERS OF THINKING

There are many factors that determine at what point a government decides to accept the available terms instead of engaging in further bargaining. To begin with, the terms of agreement have to create a situation that seems preferable to no-agreement. Second, the expected gains from further bargaining must seem small or uncertain compared to its costs and risks. However, the final decision to accept certain terms often results not from gain-and-loss calculations but from purely personal moods and impulses of the negotiator.

Frequently, negotiators stop bargaining at a certain point and settle for the available terms simply because they feel *impatient*.

At the Potsdam Conference, Stalin and Churchill debated at length about the western frontier of Poland and the German territory that the Russians wanted to put under Polish administration. President Truman, although he took essentially the same position as Prime Minister Churchill, entered the debate only a few times. He was in favor of passing over the disputed issue to move ahead with the conference, which meant the outcome would be that the Poles kept all the East German territory that the Russians had turned over to their administration. "I was getting tired," he writes in his memoirs, "of sitting and listening to endless debate on matters that could not be settled at this conference yet took up precious time. I was anxious also to avoid any sharpening of the verbal clashes in view of the more immediate and urgent questions that needed to be settled. I was becoming very impatient, and on a number of occasions I felt like blowing the roof off the palace." Again, toward the end of the Potsdam Conference, Truman recalls in his memoirs, "prolonged and petty bickering continued on the final wording of the protocol. I was getting very impatient, as I had many times before in these sessions, with all the repetition and beating around the bush, but I restrained myself because I saw that we were very slowly making progress in the right direction."[9]

There are a variety of other personal feelings that can affect the outcome of negotiations. For example, a negotiator who has

[9] *Memoirs*, I, 369, 410.

struggled through a long conference to settle issues of great importance to him may experience a sudden feeling of *gratitude* when the opponent turns out to be more amenable than he expected. This may spur him to throw in a concession of his own, with the idea of handing out a reward for good behavior rather than as a tactic calculated as being necessary to reach agreement.

At the Yalta Conference, Roosevelt and Churchill objected to Stalin's claim for huge reparations from Germany. Since this issue had reached a deadlock, it was decided to refer it to a Reparations Commission in Moscow, but it seemed impossible to agree on directives to this commission. At the final meeting at Yalta, when these directives were being debated, Harry Hopkins wrote the following note to Roosevelt: "The Russians have given in so much at this conference that I don't think we should let them down. Let the British disagree if they want to—and continue their disagreement at Moscow. Simply say it is all referred to the Reparations Commission with the minutes to show the British disagree about any mention of the 10 billion." Roosevelt took that advice.[10]

As a negotiator acts out of personal gratitude, so he may make a concession to another diplomat because he feels sorry for him or wants to protect him against his superiors. Philip Mosely reports that in negotiations with Soviet representatives on Bulgaria's armistice (after World War II) he once argued successfully that he might be punished unless a particular provision, desired by the American government, was inserted into the treaty. "At the word 'punished,' a sympathetic gleam of understanding came into the eyes of my Soviet colleagues, and on the following day they agreed to insert the provision. . . ."[11]

Standards of equity, as we shall see, are usually quite indeterminate. To the extent that decision-makers wish to base a negotiating position on such standards, their personal views as to what is "fair" will determine the government's position. This is illustrated by an incident which took place early in the Eisenhower administration.

In April, 1953, when the Korean armistice negotiations were

[10] Robert E. Sherwood, *Roosevelt and Hopkins, An Intimate History* (New York: Harper, 1948), pp. 861–62.
[11] *The Kremlin and World Politics*, pp. 24–25.

still dragging on, Emmet John Hughes, the President's speech-writer, prepared a basic speech for the President. As he worked on it with other advisers, Secretary of State Dulles urged him to make it plain that American signature of a Korean armistice would be contingent on restoration of peace in Indochina. At the last editing session for this speech, Hughes later recorded, "We 'forgot' this suggestion, for it seemed outrageously illogical to insist upon such a condition while, simultaneously, excluding as irrelevant the matter of Nationalist China and Formosa."[12] It is a curious logic which permits a flat statement that a package deal between an armistice in Korea and the restoration of peace in Indochina would be "outrageously illogical," merely because the original proposal for the package deal leaves out some other disputed issue. Why was it more "logical" to negotiate the Korean armistice separately, only —as it turned out—to have to negotiate the peace in Indochina one year later, without, incidentally, including "the matter of Nationalist China" at that time?

This incident also illustrates another point: the haphazard influence that the Washington speechwriting process may have on the conduct of negotiations. When the President's speechwriters "forgot" to include a suggestion of the Secretary of State, because it seemed "illogical" to them, did they know whether or not the Secretary—who is responsible for the conduct of foreign policy—had some larger plan in mind? To let the President say in a speech that the conclusion of the Korean armistice would be contingent on the restoration of peace in Indochina could have served a number of different purposes. It might have expedited the Korean armistice negotiations, since the demand could have been dropped later to provide a face-saving formula for the Communists in exchange for their final and crucial concession on the prisoners-of-war issue. Or, this proposed package deal could have been the opening move for a larger arrangement in the Far East, which in the end need not necessarily have excluded "the matter of Nationalist China."

---

[12] Emmet John Hughes, *The Ordeal of Power: A Political Memoir of the Eisenhower Years* (New York: Atheneum, 1963), p. 112. Hughes writes that he did, however, report Dulles' view to Eisenhower, who indicated support for Hughes' decision.

It is part of the job of Presidential speechwriters to make the President's statements sound eloquent and to create a favorable impact on public opinion. However, this may give the experts on rhetoric considerable say in the conduct of diplomacy, since Presidential speeches usually affect ongoing negotiations. In addition, the chief negotiator himself may take a strong interest in his effect on public opinion. This leads to what might be called the "rhetorical way of thinking": how he sounds is of greater concern to the negotiator than how he bargains.

Particularly in formal conferences, a delegate may actually adapt his day-to-day tactics to suit his taste for rhetorical effects. He will pay a great deal of attention to the speeches he reads at the conference table, which he views not so much as communications designed to influence the opponent but as a means to obtain public support. He may not realize how little attention the public pays to the verbiage in a conference and how quickly his speeches are forgotten. Indeed, the preoccupation with the exchange of words may divert the negotiator from more important moves for influencing the opponent. If a conference is protracted, he may be forced to devote so much time to the debate that rhetorical achievements become more important to him than improvements in his negotiating position. Telegrams can be found in which a delegation asks its home government that it be permitted to offer a certain concession because "this would make the position of the delegation easier"—meaning that the concession would win a debating point.

The "rhetorical way of thinking" diverts negotiators from the essence of bargaining. Preoccupation with diplomatic routines or minor details will do the same. The negotiator may become engrossed in the phrasing of a press release, the wording of a preamble, or in other aspects of an agreement that will be outdated shortly after the ink is dry. Even senior decision-makers, when reviewing the conduct of negotiations, frequently focus on ephemeral details rather than on major policy choices. In reading the minutes of intra-governmental meetings, one is sometimes reminded of Parkinson's "Law of Triviality": The time spent on any one item is of inverse proportion to its importance. Parkinson illustrates this with his finance committee which spends two and a half minutes to decide the purchase of a ten-million-dollar reactor but deliberates for forty-five minutes on how to save three hundred dollars on a bicycle shed.[13]

In the Korean armistice, for example, the only important condition, apart from the exchange of prisoners, was the location of the cease-fire line. Yet, this line received far less attention than, say, the composition of the "neutral" inspection teams. These teams have never been of any significance and are now almost forgotten, whereas the armistice line still divides the Communist from the Western world.

Perhaps it is reassuring for a diplomat to become absorbed in small details and preoccupied with routines of procedure. He can comfortably take the larger context for granted, feel less responsible for the over-all outcome, and occupy himself with the rounding out and polishing of smaller points. He can ignore the unsettling questions of whether the opponent even wants an agreement and whether his own government ought not to prefer no-agreement. During the prolonged test-ban negotiations (with the exception of the initial phase and the 1963 negotiations leading to the partial treaty), the American side was frequently immersed in small details which often became obsolete soon after they were settled.

As able a negotiator as John Foster Dulles may have succumbed to excessive concentration on details in those ill-fated episodes of his career: the Suez and Hungarian crises. He kept proposing varied schemes and legal artifices to put off England and France from using force against Egypt; but in spite of what the CIA or other intelligence sources must have told him about the impending explosion, he failed to press Nasser into specific concessions that could have been used to extract a firm commitment from Britain and France not to use force. At the same time, being so preoccupied with legal details and United Nations schemes regarding Suez, he did not try to negotiate with the Soviet Union a compromise settlement for Hungary's freedom (for example, a neutral position similar to that of Finland or a position like Yugoslavia's). Although we cannot know how good the chances were for such a compromise, the Hungarian Revolution opened the way as almost

[13] Northcote Parkinson, *Parkinson's Law and Other Studies in Administration* (Boston: Houghton Mifflin, 1957), chap. iii.

no other development could have. Dulles' failure is not excused by the fact that he suddenly became ill the very day the Soviet military intervention turned into the open attack against Budapest. American bargaining with the Soviet Union would have had to begin several days or weeks before that date, that is, while Dulles was working out details of his innumerable schemes for Suez.

A negotiator may become diverted from the essential objectives and stint too much in his ends and means for still different reasons. He may be concerned with good workmanship and success only within the narrow limits of his career to the neglect of wider national interests. Because he sticks too much to his last, he may represent his country inadequately and cause a fragmentation of the national capabilities.

For example, a negotiator who is afraid to stray from the diplomatic profession may fail to ask his government to strengthen his bargaining position through military or economic measures. W. W. Rostow concluded that one of the reasons why the United States did not move more forcefully to maintain the independence of Eastern Europe in 1945–46 was that Secretary of State Byrnes viewed foreign affairs as an area for high-level personal negotiations and was reluctant to turn to the President to change the framework within which he operated. "Only the President could have altered the pace of demobilization or the basic attitude toward Moscow. And Byrnes was not in a mood to seek the President's help."[14]

The converse case is the *military* negotiator who fails to see merit in "political" objectives. Whereas the diplomat may ignore military strength as a means to bargain for his political ends, the negotiating soldier often refuses to consider political ends in his pursuit of military objectives.

In the decisive months in the spring of 1945, when Churchill was urging that Western military power be used in behalf of a more advantageous political bargain with the Russians, General Eisenhower cabled to President Truman: ". . . I do not quite understand why the Prime Minister has been so determined to intermingle political and military considerations in attempting to establish a

[14] W. W. Rostow, *The United States in the World Arena* (New York: Harper, 1960), p. 180.

procedure for the conduct of our own and Russian troops when a meeting takes place."[15]

Today, of course, it is widely recognized that it was a grave mistake for the United States at the end of World War II to be preoccupied with military objectives to the neglect of political aims. Nonetheless, the American military officer, when he finds himself in negotiations with the opponent, may still fail to see that military power must serve the over-all aims of foreign policy and that the distinction between military and political objectives is only a question of emphasis between means and ends, not a choice between two divergent goals. An illustration is provided by Admiral Joy, who served as chief of the United Nations delegation during the first phase of the Korean armistice conference. This illustration is all the more remarkable because Admiral Joy's book about this conference shows a keen understanding of the weaknesses of certain Western negotiating techniques in confrontation with a Communist opponent. But after one hundred and fifty pages of penetrating insight and useful advice, Joy's book lapses into the following error: "A military armistice agreement should be no more than an agreement between opposing commanders to stop the fighting. It should never be concerned with political questions."[16]

Another personality trait that can affect the course of negotiations is the reliance of some diplomats on their personal experience from the past, instead of on an analysis of the current situation. This trait is more common among older negotiators. With diplomats of senior rank it can, in fact, dominate the conduct of foreign policy. Rather than digging into day-by-day details, the gray-haired diplomat may make excessive use of analogies, of both the historical and the personal kind. This can be infuriating to junior officials, who may work long and hard to collect and interpret the relevant facts on an issue only to have them swept off the desk with a fifteen-

---

[15] Quoted in Truman's *Memoirs*, I, 215.

[16] *How Communists Negotiate*, p. 151. Joy made this assertion to support his argument that the UN insistence on the voluntary repatriation of prisoners was a mistake. Yet, even if it should have been a mistake, the reason would have been not that an armistice ought never to be concerned with political objectives, but that this particular political objective had overriding disadvantages.

year-old anecdote: "In 1946, when I dealt with Stalin, I faced the same situation . . . ," or "I know how Orientals negotiate; this is just like the situation I faced in Chungking when I was stationed there during the war. . . ." A defense against anecdotage which sometimes works wonders is to identify the reasoning involved— or the lack of reasoning: "That's a delightful anecdote, sir!"

More far-reaching in its implications than this anecdotage is the penchant for *historical* analogies, especially since the addiction to a specific analogy may be shared by many government officials. It is a difficult question where to draw the line between useful lessons from history and the making of inappropriate analogies.

Anthony Eden's policy against Egypt after Nasser's seizure of the Suez Canal was strongly influenced by analogies from the Hitler era. In Eden's widening disagreements with the United States, these analogies make a constant theme. For example, Eden records in his memoirs that, after receipt of "a disquieting message from Mr. Eisenhower" which took exception to the use of force against Egypt, he replied to the President in a message on which he "had spent much care":

. . . I think that the divergence [between us] springs from a difference in our assessment of Nasser's plans and intentions. May I set out our view of the position. In the nineteen-thirties Hitler established his position by a series of carefully planned movements. These began with occupation of the Rhineland and were followed by successive acts of aggression against Austria, Czechoslovakia. . . . Similarly the seizure of the Suez Canal is, we are convinced, the opening gambit in a planned campaign designed by Nasser to expel all Western influence and interests from Arab countries. . . . You may feel that even if we are right it would be better to wait until Nasser has unmistakably unveiled his intentions. But this was the argument which prevailed in 1936 and which we both rejected in 1948 [at the time of the Berlin blockade].

Again, a few weeks later, Eden sent a telegram to President Eisenhower which contained the following passage:

There is no doubt in our minds that Nasser, whether he likes it or not, is now effectively in Russian hands, just as Mussolini was in Hitler's. It would be as ineffective to show weakness to Nasser now in order to placate him as it was to show weakness to Mussolini. The only result was and would be to bring the two together.[17]

[17] *Full Circle*, pp. 517–21, 556.

Two years earlier, at the Geneva Conference on Indochina, the attitudes of Dulles and Eden regarding the use of force were almost exactly reversed as compared to the Suez crisis. The same analogies were used, but at this time it was Dulles who substituted the "Rhineland argument" in lieu of a military analysis as to how the use of force would turn out. Eden recalls from a discussion with Dulles: "I was not convinced by the assertion which Mr. Dulles then made, that the situation in Indochina was analogous to the Japanese invasion of Manchuria in 1931 and to Hitler's reoccupation of the Rhineland. I explained that the British Chiefs of Staff did not believe that allied intervention could be limited to the air and the sea."[18]

INTERNATIONAL AFFAIRS AS PERSONAL RELATIONS

The delegates who confront each other across the conference table may be subject to personal sympathies or dislikes. They respond not only to the relationship that exists between their countries but also to the *personal* relationship between each other. Their ideas and feelings about each other affect their conduct of negotiation in many small ways—and sometimes in major ways.

According to an optimistic view of the effect of personal relations in international affairs, friendly feelings between chief negotiators will enhance friendly relations between the states they represent. For instance, when Marshal Zhukov became Soviet Defense Minister in 1955, it was said that this might have a beneficial effect on American-Soviet relations, because Zhukov and Eisenhower had been on friendly terms at the end of World War II. Similarly the close collaboration between the American and the German governments in the 1950s has often been attributed to the special trust and liking that Chancellor Adenauer was said to have had for Secretary Dulles. There are many other examples, such as President Roosevelt's close relationship during World War II with Prime Minister Churchill, or—to cite a less successful case— Roosevelt's hope to establish some personal contact with Stalin.

It is worth exploring why and under what conditions good personal relations between negotiators might facilitate agreements

[18] *Ibid.,* p. 108.

between states. One explanation is that friendly interpersonal relations may strengthen the tendency to observe rules of accommodation and may make a larger set of these rules feasible. If you, as a diplomat, are personally acquainted with the opponent's representative, you have not only the bargaining reputation of your government to protect but also your personal reputation. You will expect that the other delegate will form certain ideas about your personality and accordingly estimate how you will act. He may have the corresponding expectation about you, thus establishing a pattern of reciprocal *personal* evaluations and expectations. The rules of personal behavior appropriate for close associates or friends therefore may be transferred to some extent to the affairs of state. This will give added strength and greater scope to the rules of accommodation observed between governments. In particular, debts of gratitude acquire the character of a personal obligation if the negotiators know each other well. Between Western negotiators, who may permit themselves to see a difference between the official position of their government and the national interest, this may encourage a spirit of camaraderie and almost turn negotiation into a joint mediation effort.

Yet, there are limits as to how useful a personal friendship can be in enhancing an accommodating style of negotiation. At one extreme, the delegate will sacrifice the interest of his government to satisfy his friend; at the other, he will be forced to abuse the friendship to advance the cause of his country.

Intimate acquaintance with a diplomat helps to assess his thoughts and motives. To put it crudely: friendship is a source of intelligence. In public as in private affairs, there is that intuitive understanding of a man which may reveal how strongly he means what he says and what his basic intentions are. Whereas a close personal relation between diplomats need not lead to greater frankness, it makes dissimulation more difficult. Between diplomats of friendly countries, it may strengthen reciprocal trust; and between hostile nations, it may at least make communication more meaningful for both sides. As Anthony Eden wrote, when recalling the ten-day visit of Marshal Bulganin and Khrushchev to England in 1956: "I have found it an advantage to know the man to whom I was addressing a communication through Ambassadors. . . . As a result of ten days spent together in almost constant contact, I felt that I knew these Russians as no volumes of despatches could have revealed them to me."[19]

But in making this connection between one's assessment of a negotiator as a person and as a government official, one is implicitly assuming that there is a close harmony between the two—that the person is all of a piece, so to speak. This assumption can bring disappointment. Western diplomats often seem to be surprised about the contrast between the human attractiveness of Communist delegates and their aggressive and frequently rude official behavior. If Westerners are optimistically inclined, they will put greater weight on the personal affability of the Communist diplomat than on his official acts, and they interpret his bellicose tactics as a show that he puts on for the benefit of some diehard forces in his government. It is the bad men behind the negotiator who have to be blamed.

When Khrushchev broke up the 1960 summit conference with his cantankerous performance, it was the "Stalinists" who made him do this, wasn't it? When the test-ban negotiations that had been going on almost four years were jolted in the summer of 1961 by the sudden Soviet resumption of testing, perhaps the Chinese had forced this move in Soviet policy? And when Stalin was still alive and Communist China did not yet exist, any discrepancy between the reasonable "Uncle Joe" and less reasonable Soviet policies could be explained by blaming some unidentified "bad men" behind Stalin. As Harry Hopkins told Robert E. Sherwood, about his own reaction to the Yalta Conference, where he was President Roosevelt's closest adviser:

We really believed in our hearts that this was the dawn of the new day. . . . The Russians had proved that they could be reasonable and farseeing and there wasn't any doubt in the minds of the President or any of us that we could live with them and get along with them peacefully. . . . But I have to make one amendment to that—I think we all had in our minds the reservation that we could not foretell what the results would be if anything should happen to Stalin. We felt sure that we could count on him to be reasonable and sensible and under-

19 *Ibid.*, pp. 404–5.

standing—but we never could be sure who or what might be in back of him there in the Kremlin.[20]

Sometimes, the Western tendency to personalize international relations leads to a paradoxical attitude: On the one hand, the negotiator may deny that he has any hard feelings against his adversary as a person, despite the latter's pugnacious behavior at the conference table; on the other hand, he often attributes the foreign policy of the opponent's government to highly personal emotions. When the opponent's government is under the sway of a dictator, this explanation may, in part, be correct. But even then, it is often dangerous to design one's diplomacy as a palliative for the psychic eccentricities of a hostile leader.

When the British statesman Halifax went to see Hitler and Goebbels in Berchtesgaden in November, 1937, he was concerned about such "questions arising out of the Versailles settlement" as Danzig, Austria, and Czechoslovakia. "On all these matters," Halifax wrote in his diary, "we were not necessarily concerned to stand for the *status quo* as of to-day, but we were very much concerned to secure the avoidance of such treatment of them as would be likely to cause trouble." And why should there be trouble? Goebbels had the answer: in contrast to Great Britain with her centuries of history, Nazi Germany was only five years old and very sensitive. Halifax was satisfied with this explanation: "This confirmed," he wrote, "what I had always been inclined to think about part of the Nazi attitude arising from an inferiority complex."[21]

If it is not an inferiority complex, perhaps there are certain moods which require satisfaction at the expense of the nation's foreign policies. A few months before Halifax's visit to Berchtesgaden, Prime Minister Neville Chamberlain wrote him a letter about Britain's relations with Fascist Italy. Eden, who received a copy, felt that Chamberlain "expressed a surprising opinion of the men we had to deal with. It was very necessary to remember, he [Chamberlain] wrote, that the dictators were men of moods. If we caught them in the right mood they would give us anything we

[20] *Roosevelt and Hopkins*, p. 870.
[21] Earl of Halifax, *Fulness of Days* (London: Collins, 1957), pp. 186–87, 191.

asked for. But if the mood changed they might shut up 'like an oyster.' The moral of this was, in the Prime Minister's opinion, that we must make Mussolini feel that things were moving all the time.''[22]

But on other occasions, Eden himself felt he had to conduct British foreign policy so as to satisfy what he thought were the moods and idiosyncrasies of the men in power. When he visited Moscow in December, 1941, Stalin pressed him to agree to the re-establishment of the boundaries that Russia had gained in the pact with Hitler, that is, to consent to the incorporation of the Baltic states and part of Finland and Poland into the Soviet Union. Eden felt he had to give in to this demand and urged the British ambassador in Washington to obtain the concurrence of the American government. "It is our belief," he cabled, that Stalin's demand "is put to us as a test of the sincerity of our avowed desire to work with him during and after the war. It is the fruit of a long period of suspicion and misunderstanding. . . . He [Stalin] pointed to 'plebiscites' in Baltic states. Our exchanges of views on this aspect of the subject would have been even less profitable than they were if I had suggested that those 'plebiscites' were faked. . . . I'm advised by Sir Stafford Cripps (and our experience of 1939 as you will remember will tend to confirm this) that any class of haggling may only increase his [Stalin's] suspicions."[23] As one dictator may have to be humored because he suffers from feelings of inferiority, so another one because he happens to have a suspicious personality.

One is tempted from the foregoing examples of diplomatic reasoning in the 1930s and early 40s (similar quotations could be found in diplomatic telegrams and official minutes of the present time) to conclude that the most successful negotiator would be someone who managed to give the impression of wanting to see things moving all the time, of suffering from an acute inferiority complex, being prone suddenly to shut up like an oyster, and having vast suspicions.

[22] Anthony Eden, *Facing the Dictators* (Boston: Houghton Mifflin, 1962), p. 514.
[23] U.S. Department of State, *Foreign Relations of the United States, 1942,* III, 514–15. Eden's failure to point out that the Baltic plebiscites were faked illustrates the tendency of Western diplomats not to confront the opponent with unpleasant facts.

CHAPTER 10

SHIFTING EVALUATIONS

There is nothing either good or bad,
but thinking makes it so.
Hamlet, II, 2

TO EXERCISE THEIR THREEFOLD CHOICE, NEGOTIATORS HAVE TO
aggregate many diverse estimates into three over-all values for each
of the three options: they must decide whether agreement on balance, with all the available terms taken together, is preferable to all
the likely consequences of no-agreement, as well as to all the prospects and risks of further bargaining. Normally, they will not tally
up these three aggregates consciously as if they were dealing with
three sums on an elaborate balance sheet. But intuitively they
must continue to size them up as they keep deciding which option
to choose. This means they must combine things that are nearly
incommensurable. Somehow they have to add up good terms and
bad ones, gains in territory and losses in lives, immediate opportunities and distant risks.

Historical hindsight sometimes reveals that both parties were
mistaken in the way they aggregated different aspects of an agreement. For instance, in the 1954 Geneva negotiations on Indochina,
the French negotiators were anxious that the agreed date for elections in North and South Vietnam be postponed as long as pos-

sible, whereas the Chinese and the North Vietnamese Communists wanted·an early election date to take advantage of disorganization and unrest. In the final bargaining sessions in this conference, the election date was traded off against the location of the demarcation line between North and South Vietnam: the sooner the date for elections, the further north would the Communists allow the line to be drawn. As it turned out, however, the elections were never held, whereas the demarcation line still divides the country. Evidently the French should not have considered an opportunity to push the Communists a hundred miles north as being outweighed by having to set the election date, say, half a year earlier (nor should the Communists—from their point of view—have surrendered territory in exchange for an earlier election date).

In addition to the difficulty of aggregating diverse aspects of an agreement, each party must weigh how its negotiating tactics affect its bargaining reputation. And at various junctures, the negotiator may also have to estimate whether it is worthwhile or not to observe some rule of accommodation. Naturally, there are no firm criteria for evaluating how one's bargaining reputation might be affected by the acceptance or rejection of certain terms. Likewise, the costs of violating rules of accommodation, or the gains from observing them, are hard to assess. In these evaluations the negotiators and those advising them are easily swayed by personal moods. At one time, a diplomat may feel angry at "world opinion" and be quite prepared to ignore rules of accommodation; at another time he may be impressed by public criticism alleging that his tactics are "unfair" and therefore become particularly accommodating toward his opponent.

UNCERTAIN CRITERIA

The distinction between *criteria* of evaluation and *objects* of evaluation is often blurred. Naturally, the objects of evaluation keep changing during negotiation: offered terms may be improved, threats may be withdrawn, new inducements may be added, commitments may be strengthened, and the balance of forces may shift. Also, the negotiator may learn of new facts concerning the opponent's strengths and weaknesses, he may see fresh alternatives, and he may discover new technical implications of the proposed terms.

Moreover, the negotiator's knowledge of his objects of evaluation is severely limited, particularly since his most important evaluations concern future events. If one judges diplomatic history from hindsight, one must be careful not to misinterpret as faulty negotiating tactics what were actually errors in prediction. Although the two types of errors are not clearly separable, one can usefully make a distinction.

When Roosevelt urged Churchill and Stalin, during World War II, to treat China as a great power and give her a permanent seat in the Security Council, his prediction about China's postwar contribution to world order was wrong; but there was nothing particularly amiss with his tactics in negotiating a Security Council seat for Chiang Kai-shek.[1] By contrast, when Roosevelt and Truman tried to secure Poland's independence at the Teheran, Yalta, and Potsdam conferences, their anticipation that Stalin might want to dominate and sovietize Poland was correct, but their negotiating tactics ineffective (mainly for failure to take advantage of the Soviet need to reach agreement with the Western powers).

Given the uncertainty of the negotiator's predictions and the changing content of his options, it is easy to recognize why he rarely holds to firm opinions in evaluating this threefold choice. What is less apparent is that he is adrift, too, in the *way* in which he evaluates his options. That is, at different moments he attaches different values to the same object.

The instability of evaluation criteria is harder to recognize, because we all depend on them in our everyday way of looking at negotiation, almost as we depend on the dimensions of time and space for looking at the world around us. The criteria provide the yardstick to measure how much the parties would gain or lose by

---

[1] Churchill's foresight on this point proved to be better. In August, 1944, he wrote in a minute to his Foreign Secretary: "That China is one of the world's four Great Powers is an absolute farce. I have told the President I would be reasonably polite about this American obsession, but I cannot agree that we should take a positive attitude on the matter. The latest information from inside China points to the rise already of a rival Government to supplant Chiang Kai-shek, and now there is always a Communist civil war impending there" (*Triumph and Tragedy,* p. 701).

accepting proposed terms; they indicate what kinds of trades are "equitable"; and they establish the bench mark by which we judge whether or not a demand is "reasonable," a concession "adequate," and a compromise "fair."

It is a common and cardinal fallacy to assume that these criteria exist independently of the negotiating process. Far from it, they are nothing but beliefs held by diplomats, their government colleagues, and various bystanders, and they are continually modified by the bargaining process. Hence these criteria cannot form a firm basis for evaluating negotiations. Quite to the contrary, it is negotiation that develops and changes them. Diplomats not only fight about terms that they evaluate in a given way; they also fight about the way of evaluation in order to fit it to their preferred terms. Even evaluations of mediators and outsiders are affected by the negotiation process. International diplomacy, in contrast to parlor games, has no score sheets or poker chips that record the gains and losses for each side. This is one of the most essential facts in understanding how nations negotiate.

Only some time after an agreement has been concluded can evaluations be made that are less dependent on the negotiating process. Historical hindsight may permit us to assess how an agreement worked out, as compared to the expectations the parties held when they reached it. It may be possible to say whether one party gained more than the other party meant to give, which aspects worked out better or worse than either party had thought, and which gambles paid off. But even with hindsight, the options that were not taken up can only be speculated on, and for many of the gains and losses the evaluation criteria will remain uncertain.

WHERE DOES A GAIN OR LOSS BEGIN?

Whenever a negotiator examines his options to see whether they would be advantageous or disadvantageous for his country, he must have some bench mark in the back of his mind that divides the plus side from the minus side. In other words, he cannot evaluate whether his country would be better off or worse by his accepting a certain term in an agreement, unless he has some notion as to what kind of terms would mean neither a gain nor a loss—something like a break-even point.

Negotiators often shift their break-even points in mid-course. This is one of the main reasons why their evaluations are so unstable. Yet, they are usually unaware that they change this basic criterion and think, instead, that their options have changed.

The Status Quo. A frequently used break-even point is the status quo. That is, any arrangement which does not change the existing situation will be evaluated as resulting in neither a gain nor a loss. However, since the world is always changing, maintaining the status quo on some isolated issue may seem like a gain or a loss from another vantage point. To the extent that a negotiator counts on things as they are at the moment, the ground is constantly shifting beneath him. Soon after a development for the worse (or better), governments and the public tend to view the new situation no longer as a departure from an earlier status quo but as a new status quo from which any improvement is evaluated as a gain and any deterioration as a loss. Here lies one reason why *faits accomplis* are feared; they can rapidly become the new break-even point.

This has happened, for example, with the Berlin wall. Immediately after the Communists had cut the city in two, the Western powers would still have considered it as a loss if, in a new agreement on Berlin, the wall had been allowed to remain. And if the Communists had agreed at that time to remove the wall, this would have been evaluated as nothing more than the restoration of the status quo—neither a plus nor a minus in a larger bargain. But two or three years later, many people in the West would consider the removal of the wall a big gain worth Western sacrifices in exchange; and it would be evaluated as neither a loss nor a gain if the wall was allowed to remain as part of a Berlin agreement.

Historical Trends. In some situations, negotiators do not use the status quo as the break-even point but regard a certain long-term development as natural or fixed in conformity with a fundamental historical trend. Although this trend may actually lead to a deterioration (or improvement) compared with the status quo, for purposes of negotiation such change is being evaluated as neither a loss nor a gain. What looks like a falling or rising curve to the historian is the break-even line for the diplomat.

Decolonization has become accepted as such a trend (but only in areas colonized by Western countries). If a native representative of an Asian or African colony travels to the metropolitan capital to negotiate on the future status of his country, he will evaluate any agreement which simply continues the status quo as a loss. In fact, both the metropolitan government and the colonial representatives will usually agree that the outcome must provide for some decolonization if it is to result in neither a gain nor a loss for either party, though they may disagree on the speed of decolonization which corresponds to such an outcome.

After the riots in the Panama Canal Zone in January, 1964, when the question of a renegotiation of the Panama Canal Treaty came up, most editorial commentators in the United States simply took it for granted that the historical trend was in the direction of increased Panamanian and decreased U.S. control. In other words, Panama had to *gain* more control in order not to *lose* in a new agreement with the United States. Or as a *New York Times* editorial put it (Jan. 19, 1964): "The big problem is who is going to control the Canal and how. Panama cannot run it alone. The United States cannot indefinitely run it, in the treaty's words, 'as if it were sovereign of the territory.' A genuinely joint United States-Panama control should be possible, and would probably be the best solution. . . . What is not possible is a continuation of the present situation without any change at all. . . ."

Initial Expectation. Quite a different break-even point, which offers an even less certain criterion of evaluation, is the negotiator's initial expectation as to how a particular term or the agreement as a whole will turn out. It is used in normalization and extension negotiations. This initial expectation, of course, is based on a number of other estimates and evaluations. It depends on precedents, on conceptions of the "normal" situation, on the estimated balance of forces (how bad the consequences would be from no-agreement), and perhaps on some ideas about a "fair" division of gains and losses.

A similar break-even point is the *opponent's* initial expectation. This point has to be estimated, of course, since the opponent may ask for more than he expects to get. The passive party in innovation negotiations frequently uses this bench mark by estimating what the initiating party expects to obtain and then measuring its gains and losses as departures from that point.

A similar approach may be used by the defensive party in re-distribution negotiations. Acting for the defensive side, the nego-tiator may base his evaluations on a break-even point that splits the difference between the status quo and the outcome that the opponent initially seemed to expect. Needless to say, the status quo cannot be defended with this criterion. Yet, negotiators who like to play the mediator tend to select this approach.

In the Berlin negotiations there were periods when American news media and commentators used this criterion as a break-even point. For example, in 1961, when many Westerners felt less hope-ful about Western presence and unimpaired freedom in West Ber-lin, an editorial in the *New York Times* (Sept. 8, 1961) suggested that agreement should be sought somewhere *between* the status quo (which the West was trying to defend!) and Khrushchev's initial demands: "The impasse will continue until and unless Khrushchev shows sincere interest in negotiation, in which both sides—not we alone—would make some concessions to the other." The same view was expressed in an editorial in *Newsweek* (Oct. 9, 1961): "Through the light and shadow of all these maneuvers had now emerged the visible trend of future negotiations. The Russians would try to obtain maximum Western recognition of East Ger-many with minimum recognition of the rights of West Berlin. The Western position would be exactly the opposite. Somewhere between the *two extremes* lay the *hopeful area* of agreement" (italics added). During the same period (Nov. 24, 1961) *The Times* (London) measured gains and losses as follows: "The essentials [of a new arrangement on Berlin] are freedom for the West Berliners, unrestricted access, economic (and hence politi-cal) links with West Germany, and the presence of Western troops. . . . To gain [*sic*] all this it would be no great sacrifice to give up espionage and provocative broadcasts, quietly to drop overt politi-cal activities such as the meeting of the West German Bundestag [in Berlin], and to accept some East German inspection of travel documents on the land and water routes."

HOW LARGE ARE THE GAINS AND LOSSES?

The negotiator, in addition to selecting a break-even point to separate the plus from the minus side, must evaluate how large his gains and losses are. In a sense, he will apply a scale or index to measure the magnitude of the advantages and disadvantages that his country would derive from the various options. He will not consciously pick a numerical scale, of course, but merely estimate these magnitudes intuitively—or feel them almost subconsciously. Various factors make these estimates subject to change as negotiations progress.

We have seen how a negotiator's infatuation with details may cause him to attach great importance to some minor issues, while neglecting issues that are of fundamental significance for his country. Also, if a great effort is required to obtain certain terms, these terms may seem more valuable than if they can be obtained easily. This is a common psychological reaction, as widespread in international relations as in everyday human affairs. Had the Russians agreed to a *partial* test-ban treaty in April, 1959—when the Western powers first proposed this solution to overcome the impasse on inspection arrangements—this would undoubtedly have seemed a less significant gain to the American government than the same treaty that was finally signed in August, 1963, after four and a half years of almost continuous negotiation.

A similar distortion occurs if a negotiator believes that an agreement is particularly valuable just because the available terms are the best he could conceivably have gotten. Such a negotiator makes the mistake of attributing to an outcome a higher value if he thinks he has pushed his opponent to the limit than if he does not think so. Even though he may be justified in deriving some personal satisfaction from having obtained the best possible terms, he should not conclude that these terms are preferable to no-agreement just because they are so close to the opponent's minimum. Getting a "good bargain" is not the same as getting a "good buy."

The converse reaction may occur if a party begins to feel that it cannot obtain what it has long tried to reach through negotiation. The disappointed party may console itself by placing a low value on the terms that now seem out of reach, although it had coveted them before. This has happened to some extent with the Western evaluation of German reunification. The reaction is illustrated by a report of a group of U.S. Senators to the Committee on

Foreign Relations. The group, concluding that the prospects for peaceful reunification of Germany through elections were remote, offered this consolation: "Obviously, the Russians do not desire it, and they are not necessarily alone in Europe in holding this position. Germany and Europe have managed to live with the division for many years."[2] (What about these grapes we tried so hard to get, but failed? Well, they are sour anyhow!)

Another source of distortion for the negotiator's evaluations is the emphasis on an even division. When a diplomat evaluates how large the gain (or loss) from a particular term of agreement would be, he will usually give special weight to that magnitude which seems to be equal to the opponent's gain (or loss). Each party will feel that its own advantage is small as long as the opponent receives more but that it is particularly large as soon as the opponent receives less. The same applies to disadvantages that both sides may incur as a result of an agreement. Indeed, the point of equality in itself is often felt to be particularly desirable. It is the point where an agreement becomes "equitable" or "fair." For diplomats who emphasize this criteria, it may almost appear more important that an agreement be "equitable" than that it enhance the national interest.

But whether two magnitudes are equal depends, of course, on the point from which they are measured. Terms can be made to offer equal advantages to both sides simply by shifting the break-even point.

In the Korean armistice negotiations, three different truce lines were advanced as being equitable, each one leading to an equal division of gains and losses in accordance with different criteria. At the very beginning of the armistice negotiations, the United Nations side proposed a truce line somewhat north (on the Communist side) of the line of ground contact, arguing that this would produce equality in terms of the military advantages and disadvantages. According to Admiral Joy, the senior delegate on the Western side, the UN team "contended that a northward adjustment of the ground-contact line was necessary to compensate for

---

[2] *Berlin in a Changing Europe*, Report of Senators Mansfield, Boggs, Pell, and Smith to the Committee on Foreign Relations (Washington: Government Printing Office, 1963), p. 8.

the withdrawal of United Nations Command air and naval operations, which ranged hundreds of miles north of the embattled ground forces." But somehow, the UN team felt ill-at-ease about this criterion and quickly shifted to another way of measuring equality. Admiral Joy wrote that this first proposal "was a bargaining position, and even while proposing it we made plain our interest in a solution on the line of ground contact."[3] This "solution" offered equality in the sense that neither side would gain territory, but it led to inequality in the sense that the United Nations forces would not be compensated for their withdrawal of air and naval operations.

The Communists thought of another criterion to make a truce line "equitable" that was more advantageous to them than this second UN proposal. They demanded that a line be drawn along the 38th Parallel, which would have given them territorial gains as compared with the line of ground contact. Although they argued for the 38th Parallel primarily on military grounds, the implication was clear that it would give equality in the sense that neither side would gain or lose in comparison with the status before the war. Incidentally, the Communists were not as shy about this proposal as the UN negotiators were about their first proposal. In contrast to what Admiral Joy reports about the way in which the UN team presented its case for a northward adjustment, the Communists did not "make plain their interest in another solution"; they vehemently and for a long time insisted on this southward adjustment of the line of ground contact.

Although a change in criteria can equalize the net gains of both sides for almost any set of terms, it may nonetheless be of great importance whether or not the negotiator thinks that the opponent's net gains are equal to his own. First, the point of imagined equality provides a focus for his expectations as to the outcome; it is like a resting point that can put an end to the infinite possibilities of dividing such things as territory, a sum of money, or voting power. Second, to depart from equality might have serious consequences for one's bargaining power. This is particularly true in antagonistic situations, where one does not wish to convey to the

---

[3] *How Communists Negotiate*, p. 60.

enemy—by accepting lesser gains than he—the idea that one evaluates one's own strength as being inferior to his.

In negotiation with an enemy, there is a further reason why the measurement of one's gains and losses is so uncertain. Whatever your foe gains in power, prestige, or wealth means a loss for you, even if you benefit yourself by cooperating with him at the time. And whatever your foe loses is *ipso facto* a gain for yourself because it weakens him. Hence, in evaluating whether an agreement—on balance—is to your advantage, you have to subtract something for your enemy's gains and add something to allow for the fact that his loss is your gain. What makes this evaluation so unstable is that the yardstick for measuring the opponent's losses often changes. First, you might measure whether he would suffer a loss compared with the situation before negotiation started, whereas later you might compare the possible outcome with the situation into which he maneuvered himself through his own bargaining moves. But have you gained if your enemy incurs a loss just because he breaks a commitment whose very purpose was to wrest a concession from you?

Where this slippery road of shifting evaluations might lead is illustrated by a report in the *New York Times* about a British proposal for an agreement with Khrushchev on Berlin. According to this story (which must be apocryphal!), the British Foreign Office reasoned in September, 1962, that the West should offer the Russians "presence" in West Berlin in exchange for a withdrawal of Soviet demands that the Western troops leave. Under one version, this Russian "presence" would have been established by permitting the Russian guards for the Soviet War Memorial (which lies in the British sector) to live in West Berlin and by giving the Russians control of a corridor from East Berlin to the War Memorial. Why this Western concession? Because, "for prestige reasons, the British believed Khrushchev could not give up his highly publicized demands for . . . removing the United States, British, and French garrisons unless he could show he had gained something in return."[4] That is, since your enemy would lose so much if he broke the commitment that he made in order to take something from you, you can reach a satisfactory agreement

[4] *New York Times,* Sept. 8, 1962.

by giving him only part of his "highly publicized demands," your loss being compensated by the fact that he will have to forgo the other part of his demands.

WHEN IS A COMMITMENT BROKEN?

When you have committed yourself not to yield on a certain point, your opponent may try to defeat the purpose of your commitment in two ways.[5] First, he may simply try to manipulate your threefold choice (e.g., by committing himself, erecting a deadline, or making threats) so that breaking your commitment will seem to you the lesser evil than the risks from holding on to your position. Second, your opponent may try to erode your commitment by permitting you to adhere to it in form while violating it in substance. The two methods are frequently combined: the first gives you the incentive to break the commitment; the second makes it easier to do so.

All commitments raise the question of criteria: What is the criterion that indicates whether or not a commitment has been broken? Since this criterion is frequently uncertain, the opponent can force his interpretation upon you, provided you are unable or unwilling to make a second commitment that will tie you to a firm interpretation of the first one.

Many commitments can be eroded because there is no firm criterion as to the time when the promised action should be taken. The fulfillment can thus be postponed indefinitely without incurring the costs of a clear-cut violation of one's commitment. The United Nations commitment to reunify Korea under free elections, which stemmed from the General Assembly resolution of October 7, 1950, was maintained in form in the Panmunjom Armistice agreement by adding an article which recommended to the governments concerned that they should hold a conference within three months "to settle through negotiation the questions of the withdrawal of all foreign forces from Korea, the peaceful settlement of the Korean question, etc."

Occasionally, however, it is possible to "freeze" firm criteria

---

[5] As defined before, a "commitment" is a move to convince one's opponent that one will maintain one's current position or implement one's prediction, by making it more difficult for oneself not to do so.

into one's commitment so as to prevent this erosion. On April 20, 1961, after the disastrous invasion attempt against Castro by Cuban refugees, President Kennedy declared: ". . . If the nations of this hemisphere should fail to meet their commitments against outside Communist penetration—then I want it clearly understood that this Government will not hesitate in meeting its primary obligations which are to the security of our Nation!" This commitment to act against Communist penetration was without firm criteria and hence did not strengthen the American bargaining position. However, on September 13, 1962, President Kennedy made a commitment that was much more specific, when he said: ". . . If Cuba should ever . . . become an offensive military base of significant capacity for the Soviet Union, then this country will do whatever must be done to protect its own security and that of its allies." As Khrushchev discovered a few weeks later in the negotiations following the Cuban crisis, this commitment provided the basis for a firm American position.

By way of example, a firm criterion could be "frozen" into the Western commitment to maintain troops in Berlin. The Western powers could promise to keep a specified number of troops in West Berlin rather than, as they do now, guarantee the presence of unspecified forces. Or to give another hypothetical illustration: In the test-ban negotiations, instead of insisting on "adequate inspection," President Kennedy could have declared that he would not accept an underground ban with less than, say, seven inspections. Yet these examples make it evident that commitments with "frozen" criteria suffer from another weakness. They make the negotiator vulnerable to the charge of clinging to symbolic positions. Whereas the criteria themselves cannot be eroded, the commitments as a whole might be scrapped more easily than if they had been based on broader principles that are more widely supported.

UNCERTAIN GOALS

The negotiator's evaluations depend of course to a large extent on his goals. As soon as he sets himself more modest goals, something that seemed to be a trifling advantage will look like a substantial profit; and should he choose new goals diametrically opposed to his old ones, anything that used to be evaluated as a gain will become a loss. This dependence of values on goals is common in everyday life and would not be worth mentioning if it were not for the fact that in negotiation the opponent often changes one's evaluations by changing one's goals.[6]

Naturally, governments frequently conceal their negotiating goals from their opponent. They may make only vague suggestions, even though they have a rather definite outcome in mind; or they may initially propose far more demanding terms (or deceptively modest ones), instead of revealing what they are trying to get. Nonetheless, the goals can be modified by a determined opponent.

WHAT IS WORTH NEGOTIATING FOR?

A government may enter into negotiation without having a specific outcome in mind. It may leave the initiative to its allies, or even to its opponent, and be concerned solely with the prevention of clauses that would be harmful to its interests. The defensive side in redistribution negotiations frequently takes such an attitude. It may only want to prevent a deterioration of the status quo without seeking any specific agreement. Likewise, the passive party in innovation negotiations may have come merely to see what the initiating party has to propose, planning to react to the alternatives as they unfold.

It is probably more common, however, for governments to pursue a more or less specific goal when they are negotiating. If it is an agreement they are trying to get, they will attempt to shape it in a certain way. Sometimes they may try to obtain one quite specific set of terms even though they are prepared to settle for less.

Given the diversity of objectives in foreign policy, it is natural that a specific negotiating goal, if it exists, must represent a compromise between several more or less conflicting aims of foreign policy. For example, in the negotiations that settled the Suez crisis in 1956, the American goal was to satisfy at least three partly

---

[6] Psychological experiments on bargaining behavior have investigated this dependence. See the literature on "level of aspiration" on p. 263 of the Bibliographic Note at the end of this book.

conflicting objectives of foreign policy: to restore harmonious relations with Great Britain and France, to safeguard the friendship
of the Arab nations, and to preserve Israel's independence.

Sometimes, negotiating goals emerge within a government more
by accident than by design. On other occasions, particularly if the
government takes the initiative for an innovation agreement, a
careful compromise among all relevant foreign policy objectives
may be worked out. Thus, the United Nations Organization—an
innovation largely the result of American initiative—was expected
by American policymakers to solve a large number of urgent postwar problems. The State Department planners who formulated
this initial American proposal for a world peace organization
selected their negotiating goal from among a wide range of possibilities. They considered whether the world organization should
be set up through a series of treaties or a single treaty, whether it
should be a revised and strengthened League of Nations or a new
organization, whether it should be based on regional groupings or
have a universal structure, and whether it should be confined to
issues of military security or include economic and other programs.
All these alternatives were evaluated in the preparatory committees
of the American government, long before the San Francisco
Conference.[7] By contrast, when the French government entered
the Geneva Conference on Indochina in 1954, it initially did not
have any image of what it wanted. At first, French leaders had
only vague ideas, such as to induce China to discontinue her aid
to the Viet Minh by offering her economic assistance and French
support for Peking's admission to the United Nations.

Governments usually do not negotiate for agreements that they
consider highly unlikely. They might engage in pseudo-negotia-
tions about totally improbable settlements for the sake of side-
effects only (e.g., the East-West negotiations about a treaty for
general and complete disarmament). But if a government is
seriously trying to reach a certain agreement, the terms that it has
in mind must not seem wholly unattainable. Partly, this is to
conserve resources: governments are limited in the amount of
attention, commitments, threats, and other pressures that they can

[7] U.S. Department of State, *Postwar Foreign Policy Preparation 1939–1945*
(Department of State Publication 3580 [Washington, 1949]), pp. 112–13.

bring to bear on various negotiations at any one time. Partly, the goals are kept realistic in order to avoid failure: diplomats prefer to negotiate only for what they expect to get, because they want the satisfaction of getting what they negotiate for.

Communist governments, it seems, are more willing than Western governments to pursue unattainable goals. The comparison, however, is complicated by two factors. First, to the extent that Communists take seriously a view of history according to which their total victory is foreordained, the attainability of any intermediate goal toward that ultimate outcome must appear to be only a matter of time. Second, it is hard for Western observers to discover the real goals of Communist negotiators, as distinct from their asking position. For instance, did the Russians really want to replace the UN Secretary-General with a "troika" in 1960–61, or did they merely want to obtain more influence in the UN Secretariat? And in the summer of 1963, did they really want to combine the partial nuclear test ban with an East-West nonaggression pact, or was the demand for a nonaggression pact just a tactical move?

To select "realistic" goals, you as the negotiator must evaluate your opportunities for influencing your opponent and assess the chances for a change in his strength and preferences. If you are unable to see any hope for moving toward your goal today, maybe tomorrow your opponent will change his mind, and your goal becomes "negotiable." Without really trying, you cannot know whether you estimated his and your strength correctly.

WHO DECIDES WHAT IS NEGOTIABLE?

Your opponent, of course, has an interest in changing your goals. If he dislikes your aims, he will try to discourage you from negotiating by making your original goal seem unattainable. On issues he does not want to have raised, he may give the impression of being so firmly committed to preserve the existing situation that you feel neither threats nor inducements could lead to a change. Being realistic, you will not attempt to bargain for what seems impossible to obtain.

This has happened to the West on the issue of self-determination in Eastern Europe. Many Westerners feel that Russia is so committed to maintain Communist regimes wherever they have once been established, that a change—if it comes at all—can only evolve over decades or perhaps longer. Since the 1950s, the Western powers have assumed that this issue is not negotiable. In spite of new opportunities (such as the 1953 uprisings in the Soviet zone of Germany or the 1956 revolution in Hungary), and in spite of new negotiating contexts (such as the Soviet demand for a change in West Berlin), the West never made a serious attempt, through pressures and incentives, to strike a bargain that would improve the situation. To cite just one characteristic formulation of the Western view:

> It is, of course, virtually impossible for the Russians to accept the "self-determination" of the German people, which is understandably the only form of reunification the West Germans will entertain. To allow the Germans to vote down communism by a huge majority would be such a disaster for Russia's leaders in eastern Europe and in the struggle with the Chinese that it is out of the question.[8]

To convince the West that a political change in Eastern Europe would be such a disaster for Russia that it is "out of the question" constitutes perhaps one of the most successful commitments in history. Curiously, it is not even clear whether this commitment was entirely the making of the Communist rulers or whether it was in part invented in the West. According to Khrushchev, for example, the leaders in Moscow were not always unanimous that a non-Communist East Germany was "out of the question." Khrushchev once said in reference to the 1953 uprisings in East Germany that Beria, together with Malenkov, "made the provocative proposal to liquidate East Germany as a Socialist state, to recommend to the East German Communist Party to abandon the struggle for the building of Socialism."[9] Similarly, regarding the Hungarian Revolution the Chinese Communist Party wrote in 1963 that "for a time" the Soviet leadership "intended to adopt a policy of capitulation and abandon Socialist Hungary to counter-revolution."[10] If this Chinese story is true, we must now sadly realize that the West took a more Stalinist view of the world than Khrushchev did. In

---

[8] *Economist,* Aug. 24, 1963, pp. 643–44.
[9] Speech of March 10, 1963.
[10] *Peking Review,* Sept. 13, 1963, p. 10.

a sense, the West collaborated with the Chinese, by solidifying the Soviet commitment according to which Russia *must* maintain Communist control in Eastern Europe—even at the cost of the most violent intervention. If the Chinese *and* the West say a change is out of the question, how could Moscow dare to consent to one?

The tendency to negotiate only for what seems attainable can lead to a self-reinforcing cycle. A nation that would like to alter a situation through negotiation but expects slight improvement at best may formulate rather modest goals: it will try to negotiate for small adjustments instead of for major gains. The opponent will usually discover this restraint and accordingly expect that his contribution need not be large. Then, if the first party becomes impressed by the opponent's confidence—which it unwittingly created—it will lower its expectations even further, leading to still lower goals. And so forth. Should this cycle continue, its end point would be that the first party finds the outlook for negotiation so unattractive that it will decide to leave the issue as is.

However, modest goals can also have compensating advantages. To the extent that genuine modesty can be conveyed to the opponent, it will reassure him that he need not fear a major challenge to his interests. This may make him more relaxed and friendlier and lead to a more accommodating negotiating style which will benefit the first party. Conversely, if the first party had communicated far-reaching aspirations to its opponent, this might have put him on his guard and increased his resistance.

Whether modest goals or ambitious ones will in the end bring better results depends on the opponent's political style and ideology. Certain opponents might always push to the limit without ever becoming more accommodating. The dilemma is familiar: Even though you curtail your negotiating goals, you may fail to divert your opponent from his antagonistic aims (much as you may fail to make him observe rules of accommodation by observing them yourself). This is the perennial dilemma of Western policy toward the Soviet Union.[11]

[11] Some writers have suggested that the West make a more deliberate effort to reduce Russia's hostility and to get away from mutually antagonistic aims. They recommend that the West should not only avoid goals that are threatening

AN EXAMPLE: EASTERN EUROPE

It is easy to show that negotiators are adrift when they evaluate gains and losses. Their criteria of evaluation are unstable and subject to the opponent's influence. So are the goals that they pursue through negotiation and on which their evaluations depend.

It is more difficult, however, to demonstrate how the evaluations have shifted in some actual negotiation and to separate changes in criteria from changes in the objective situations to which the criteria are applied. Negotiators rarely write down how they measure gains and losses, why they consider certain terms acceptable or "fair" while rejecting others, and what their goals really are as distinct from their demands and proposals. And even if these evaluations survive the fleeting moment by being recorded in some government document, they are not collected systematically but are scattered by chance among the vast materials in government archives. They might appear as a passage in an inter-office memorandum, a sentence in a telegram instructing a delegate, or a brief notation in a diary.

The East-West negotiations concerning the fate of Central and Eastern Europe, during World War II and since, provide a dramatic illustration of how evaluations change. Since the Soviet archives remain closed, we can trace these changes only for the Western powers, and even there the evidence is incomplete. These shifts were fundamental in shaping the postwar world, comparable in importance to the great situational or "objective" changes that took place during the same period, such as the buildup of American military power from 1943 to early 1945, the sweeping advances of the Red Army, the economic recovery in Western Europe, etc.

The story begins in November, 1941. (However, the traumatic experience of the British in August, 1939, when their negotiations with Russia were suddenly cut off by the Stalin-Hitler pact, has a bearing.) In October, 1941, we must remember, the German

---

to the Russians but also undertake unilateral moves to demonstrate its benevolence. See Charles E. Osgood, *An Alternative to War or Surrender* (Urbana, Ill.: University of Illinois Press, 1962).

armies had come within twenty miles of Moscow, and the Soviet government had been evacuated to Kuibyshev. Yet Stalin, in these days of his greatest crisis, began the diplomatic offensive which gradually led to Western acceptance of his control over Eastern and Central Europe up to the Elbe. On November 8, 1941, scarcely a month after a British-American delegation had concluded an agreement in Moscow for supplying Russia with badly needed arms, Stalin sent a telegram to Churchill which was so rude that Churchill did not answer it till he had received an apology three weeks later. Stalin began his list of accusations and reproaches by complaining that Great Britain lacked an understanding with the Soviet Union on war aims and on the organization of peace and that there could be no "mutual confidence" until this was settled.[12]

Stalin's diplomatic offensive was not without effect in the British Foreign Office. It started the slow process by which the Western goals were adapted to what Western diplomats perceived to be the Soviet goals, and Western evaluations were changed accordingly. A Foreign Office Document of that time records how British officials began to develop new criteria for evaluating future negotiations with Russia: "We did not know the Russian aims; they would probably ask for access to the Persian Gulf, the revision of the Montreux Convention, and the establishment of Russian bases in Norway, Finland, and the Baltic States. If efficient arrangements were made for general disarmament and security, they might ask for less. At present they might be content with some general resolution; if they wanted more than this, they would have to define their ideas to us and to the United States. We ought to let them see that we were treating them on an equality, and that the peace settlement would be dictated largely by the three Powers."[13]

The impact of Stalin's rude telegram was enhanced by the tendency, common among diplomats, to conduct affairs of state as if they were interpersonal relations. Both Foreign Secretary Eden and the British Ambassador in Moscow, Sir Stafford Cripps,

[12] Winston S. Churchill, *The Grand Alliance* (Boston: Houghton Mifflin, 1950), pp. 528–31.

[13] Sir Llewellyn Woodward, *British Foreign Policy in the Second World War* (London: H.M.S.O., 1962), p. 160. The document has been paraphrased by Woodward.

favored making concessions to allay what, they felt, were Stalin's suspicions. As Eden explained in a memorandum to the American Ambassador a month later, when he, Eden, was leaving for negotiations in Moscow: "The terms of the message were such as to leave no doubt that Stalin was in a mood of suspicion and even resentment to a degree that might adversely affect the cooperation of the two Governments in the prosecution of the war, and His Majesty's Government decided that every effort must be made to dissipate these feelings."[14] And after his visit to Moscow, Eden sent to Washington the telegram cited before (p. 163), in which he again stressed Stalin's "suspicion" as a reason for consenting to a westward move of Russia's boundary of some hundred miles or more.

In the meantime, British evaluations continued to be recalibrated in response to Stalin's goals. Indeed, not only Stalin's stated demands, but his *potential* demands, were used to evaluate the terms at which it would be in the interest of both Russia and the West to reach agreement. In February, 1942, a telegram from the British Foreign Office to Washington pleaded in behalf of Stalin's territorial demands: "It seems to us that the right method both of meeting this [Soviet] suspicion and of guarding so far as may be possible against the risk of Russia following entirely independent policy is to emphasize to the Soviet Government that . . . we and the United States Government would wish . . . to reach tripartite solutions. It must be remembered that Stalin might have asked for much more, e.g., control of the Dardanelles, spheres of influence in the Balkans, one-sided imposition on Poland of Russo-Polish frontiers, access to the Persian Gulf, access to the Atlantic involving cession of Norwegian territory."[15]

Winston Churchill, at first, did not share the views of Eden and the Foreign Office. While visiting Roosevelt, Churchill cabled to Eden, who had just come back from his negotiations in Moscow:

We have never recognised the 1941 frontiers of Russia except *de facto*. They were acquired by acts of aggression in shameful collusion

[14] U.S. Department of State, *Foreign Relations of the United States, 1941,* Vol. I (Washington, 1958), p. 192.
[15] U.S. Department of State, *Foreign Relations of the United States, 1942,* Vol. III (Washington, 1961), p. 518.

with Hitler. The transfer of the peoples of the Baltic States to Soviet Russia against their will would be contrary to all the principles for which we are fighting this war. . . . About the effect on Russia of our refusal . . . to depart from the principles of the Atlantic Charter, it must be observed that they entered the war only when attacked by Germany, having previously shown themselves utterly indifferent to our fate. . . . No one can foresee how the balance of power will lie or where the winning armies will stand at the end of the war. It seems probable however that the United States and the British Empire, far from being exhausted, will be the most powerfully armed and economic *bloc* the world has ever seen, and that the Soviet Union will need our aid for reconstruction far more than we shall then need theirs.

Nor was Churchill taken in by the idea that Stalin's "suspicions" should be humored: "If they harbour suspicions of us, it is only because of the guilt and self-reproach in their hearts."[16]

Three months later, however, Churchill changed his mind. On March 7, 1942, he wrote to Roosevelt: "The increase in gravity of the war has led me to feel that the principles of the Atlantic Charter ought not to be construed so as to deny Russia the frontiers she occupied when Germany attacked her. . . . I hope therefore that you will be able to give us a free hand to sign the treaty which Stalin desires as soon as possible."[17] Why did Churchill change his evaluation as to what would be a satisfactory agreement with Russia? Russia's position had not become much stronger, and that of Great Britain and the United States was by no means weaker. We may speculate that Churchill was swayed in a manner in which negotiators are often influenced: by thinking in terms of historical analogy. He must have remembered how, in August, 1939, the Anglo-French negotiations in Moscow ended when Stalin made his pact with Hitler. He may have recalled his own words earlier that year, when he had warned Chamberlain quickly to conclude an agreement with Russia. The failure of the Ango-French negotiations in Moscow in 1939 must have also influenced the Foreign Office, since some of the same officials were involved then as were involved in 1942. As the American Chargé in London observed in March, 1942: "They are still bitterly con-

---

[16] *The Grand Alliance*, pp. 695–96, 473.
[17] Winston S. Churchill, *The Hinge of Fate*, p. 327.

scious that to their minds their own haggling tactics during the 1939 negotiations—and over these very Baltic States—were the real cause of Stalin's agreement with the Germans."[18]

Whatever caused Churchill to change his mind, he would have given in to the Russian demands when Molotov arrived in London in 1942 had it not been for American opposition. As it turned out, this opposition was sufficient to put the Russians off, and on May 26 a treaty of alliance was signed without any territorial provisions. To Churchill, who had just lowered his evaluation criteria in the last few months, this outcome now seemed like a gain: "This was a great relief to me, and a far better solution that I had dared to hope."[19]

Thus ended the first act. On the surface, the American position, that the Atlantic Charter should also apply to Eastern Europe, had won out. Underneath, however, the evaluation criteria had now been permanently altered. Russia was now expected to want these territories in Eastern Europe. Her goal gradually became the expected outcome, and the expected outcome became the new break-even point from which gains and losses would be measured in the future. By initiating his most successful series of negotiations at the time of his greatest weakness, Stalin had demonstrated the fallacy of the Western cliché that one must negotiate from strength.

The beginning of the second act might be traced to the first American-British review of war aims between Eden and Roosevelt in March, 1943. Eden told Roosevelt he thought that the Soviet Union would insist on absorbing the Baltic states. Roosevelt remarked that they might have to agree to this absorption but, if so, this ought to be used as a bargaining counter with Russia. On Poland, Eden thought that the Soviet Union would claim for itself some of the territory that had been part of Poland in 1939— possibly up to the Curzon line.[20]

Half a year later, Roosevelt remarked to Secretary of State Cordell Hull (who was about to leave for the Moscow Conference

[18] *Foreign Relations of the United States, 1942,* III, 533.
[19] *The Hinge of Fate,* p. 336.
[20] Herbert Feis, *Churchill-Roosevelt-Stalin* (Princeton, N.J.: Princeton University Press, 1957), p. 122.

of October, 1943) that his, Roosevelt's, inclination would be to tell Stalin, "that neither Britain nor we would fight Russia over the Baltic states. . . ." Although Roosevelt still wanted the Russians to promise a plebiscite over the absorption of the Baltic states, his earlier reluctance and the idea of a *quid pro quo* was gone. But on the Soviet-Polish boundary, Roosevelt still thought, as he told Hull, that it should be "somewhat east of the so-called Curzon line, with Lemberg going to Poland."[21]

This view prevailed in the American government up to the Yalta Conference in February, 1945. A U.S. policy paper in preparation for Yalta stated: "We should support a frontier settlement which in the east would take the Curzon Line as a basis but would, if possible, include the Province of Lwów [Lemberg] in Poland. . . . We should resist the exaggerated claims now being advanced by [the Polish Communists] for compensation from Germany which would include the cities of Stettin and Breslau in Poland and make necessary the transfer of from eight to ten million Germans." As to Hungary, another U.S. policy paper for Yalta evaluated possible gains and losses much as today they might be evaluated, say, for Finland. It recognized that the Soviet interest in Hungary was "more direct" than the American interest but added: "We do not, however, consider that the Soviet Union has any special privileged or dominant position in Hungary." Churchill, on the other hand, in his famous percentage deal with Stalin, had already agreed to a fifty-fifty sharing of dominance in Hungary. But even this was a far greater Western influence than the United States acceded to after the war and has taken for granted ever since.[22]

It would make this digression too long to trace the shifting Western evaluations regarding Eastern Europe through the Yalta and Potsdam Conferences and thence through the early postwar years. The story has been told often and well. But the vast changes in Eastern Europe have frequently been explained as though the only cause was that the Soviet forces got there first. Of course, without this military outcome most of the changes would probably

---

[21] *The Memoirs of Cordell Hull* (New York: Macmillan, 1948) II, 1266.
[22] *The Conferences at Malta and Yalta 1945*, pp. 230, 245. Churchill, *Triumph and Tragedy*, p. 227.

not have occurred. Yet the military outcome was in part determined by those negotiations in which the Western evaluations kept eroding.

Cause and effect are often intertwined. In a number of areas now part of Communist Europe, Western forces could have entered first, had these areas by that time not become regarded as belonging to the Soviet sphere of influence. In other areas, such as Bornholm and Northern Iran, the Soviets actually were in full military control, but were induced through negotiation to withdraw, partly because Western evaluations remained firm. By contrast, in Czechoslovakia, which was free of Soviet troops and far more accessible to American and British military strength than isolated Iran, the West tolerated Soviet interference and eventually the coup of 1948, precisely because Washington had already come to regard the Sovietization of Czechoslovakia as the expected and tolerable outcome.

Perhaps one more episode ought to be added to this tale, that of the 1948 Berlin blockade. Here, the Western evaluations changed in the opposite direction: at first it seemed like a gain if Stalin could be induced to settle for only a *limited* control over West Berlin, later any Soviet interference in West Berlin looked like a serious loss.

On July 30, 1948, a month and a half after Stalin had imposed the Berlin blockade, the Western powers started negotiating in Moscow in order to have the blockade removed. Stalin said he was willing to lift the blockade, provided the Western powers would simultaneously replace the West German mark in West Berlin with the Soviet mark.[23] The Western ambassadors accepted Stalin's proposal, but they reached an impasse with Molotov when trying to work out four-power control over the regulation of the Soviet marks that were to be used throughout Berlin. Stalin again intervened and assured the Western ambassadors that the bank in the Soviet zone which would issue and control the money for all

[23] Shortly after the first blockade measures, the Western powers had instituted a currency reform within their zones of Germany and a few days later introduced the new West German mark in West Berlin (after a new Soviet German mark had been introduced in East Berlin and in the Soviet zone of Germany).

of Berlin would itself be controlled by a four-power financial commission under the four commanders in Berlin.

What seems striking today is that in the summer of 1948 the Western evaluation criteria were such that it seemed worthwhile to accept Soviet currency in West Berlin (tempered with some Western controls) in exchange for Stalin's promise to discontinue the blockade. More than that, the American negotiator, Walter Bedell Smith, felt that Stalin's proposal "sounded very good indeed."[24]

As it turned out, this "very good" arrangement never materialized. The task of working out the practical implementation of the currency arrangement was left to the four military governors in Berlin. There, Soviet stubbornness saved the Western powers from what would have been a very undesirable trade (evaluated by today's criteria). The Soviet commander in Berlin not only objected to a four-power finance committee for controlling the bank in the Soviet zone that would have regulated the currency in West Berlin, but he wanted to restrict civil air traffic to Berlin and establish complete control over trade with Berlin.[25]

As W. P. Davison explained, the Western powers were so defeatist in the summer of 1948 because they greatly underrated the potentialities of the airlift and the strength of popular morale in Berlin.[26] But these erroneous estimates alone do not explain why, in August, 1948, Stalin's currency arrangement was acceptable to the Western capitals and looked "very good" to Ambassador Smith, whereas already in the spring of 1949 it would have looked like a serious loss. Parallel with the successful development of the airlift, but not just because of it, Western evaluations changed. For one thing, the very effort to preserve West Berlin made it seem more valuable. And the prolonged negotiations made the status quo assume permanent interest; it became the break-even point for measuring gains and losses. West Berlin was no longer

[24] Walter Bedell Smith, *My Three Years in Moscow* (Philadelphia: Lippincott, 1950), p. 249.

[25] Lucius D. Clay, *Decision in Germany* (Garden City, N.Y.: Doubleday, 1950), p. 371.

[26] W. Phillips Davison, *The Berlin Blockade* (Princeton, N.J.: Princeton University Press, 1958), p. 193.

a transient outpost behind the Russian lines accidentally left over from World War II.

Since then, Western evaluations regarding Berlin have continued to fluctuate. In 1959, for example, the Western powers proposed a new agreement on Berlin which would have guaranteed free access to West Berlin for five years (to expire in July, 1964!) and would have envisaged curbs on intelligence and "subversive" activities, with these controls to be monitored by the United Nations.[27] But the Russians saw to it that the Berlin negotiations would continue, and as a result the Western evaluations, instead of eroding further, became more assertive again. After 1961, the Western powers would certainly have considered their 1959 proposal a bad bargain.

There is nothing either a gain or a loss, but negotiating makes it so!

[27] When this interim agreement would have lapsed, the Russians could have refused to renew it except under conditions unacceptable to the West. Even though the old rights would then have been reinstated according to the Western view, the Western position would have seemed much weaker. As Henry Kissinger pointed out, it was doubtful that "the West would after a five-year interval defend rights for which it was not prepared to contend when they were first challenged and which were specifically altered by the interim agreement" (*The Necessity for Choice*, p. 143). And during the five years, the Communists could have used the curb on "subversive" activities to demand censorship and the restriction of political activity in West Berlin.

CHAPTER 11

HOW THE PARTIES COME TO TERMS

UNTIL AGREEMENT EMERGES, EACH PARTY KEEPS PROPOSING terms to the opponent while trying to find out what terms he would settle for. It is an essential feature of negotiation that the process of finding out the opponent's terms (and of revealing one's own) is also part of the process of inducing him to soften his terms (and of making one's own terms more acceptable to him).

The Anticipated Minimum. People not familiar with the way in which nations negotiate assume that each party has its minimum position. They imagine the existence of a borderline dividing the terms at which a party would accept agreement from those at which it would inevitably reject. This borderline is thought to remain fixed except on those rare occasions when a government deliberately revises it up or down.

Reality is more complicated and more subtle. Objective minimum positions, in the sense just explained, normally do not exist for three reasons. First, governments do not face two choices only, agreement and no-agreement, that a minimum position could separate like a watershed. From the beginning of every negotiation to its very end, they keep choosing between three options, so that the watershed between the first two depends on the outlook for the third one: the prospects for further bargaining. Second, in deciding their threefold choice, governments must be concerned with more than the probable gains from further bargaining and the comparison of agreement with no-agreement. They must also consider how their negotiating will affect their bargaining reputation and to what extent they should observe or ignore rules of accommodation. Third, as discussed before, all evaluations and expectations—and even the goals—keep shifting.

Instead of fixed minimum positions, each party can have only an *anticipated minimum*. The negotiator anticipates that he will not choose agreement at terms below his "minimum," but he cannot know whether he might not eventually accept agreement at lesser terms or choose no-agreement even though the available terms were better than this "minimum." For example, in the negotiations about an inspection system for a ban on underground nuclear tests, the American negotiators might have anticipated that they would accept a treaty with, say, five inspections but not with four. If the time had come, however, either to sign a treaty prohibiting underground tests or to stop negotiating, even three inspections might have been found adequate or six insufficient.

There is a further complication: the anticipated minimum is usually blurred. Normally, the parties have only a vague anticipation of the terms that they expect to consider sufficiently desirable for preferring agreement over no-agreement. Frequently, this anticipation is very faint. Indeed, even when a negotiator has given up further bargaining and is actually choosing agreement (or no-agreement), he may not be fully aware how much worse (or better) the terms would have to be to reverse his choice. All the more reason to reject the popular notion of fixed minima, which stand immovable from the beginning to the end of a conference like goal posts in a ball game. To revert to the hypothetical example, should a treaty providing for six inspections be signed on underground tests, the American negotiators would probably not know whether they would have rejected the treaty if it had provided for only four, three, or one inspection.

It is not an uncommon negotiating tactic, however, to create a commitment to a position by treating it *as if* it were a fixed minimum. Government officials often talk about certain terms as being their firm minimum, pretending to know that agreement at inferior terms would *always* be undesirable. Actually, if these officials analyzed their beliefs, they would have to admit that they are not at all so clear as to where they should place the watershed between agreement and no-agreement. It is expedient for them, however, not to be fully aware of this indeterminacy and to talk themselves into believing that they know exactly where their "minimum position" lies. To cut short any erosive re-examination of this "minimum" among themselves, they might argue that "one has to stop somewhere."

THE FUNCTION OF PROPOSALS

Proposals play a key role in the process through which the parties come to terms. Indeed, the confrontation, revisions, and final acceptance of proposals at the conference table is sometimes all that is meant by "negotiation." Even in the broader definition used in this book, explicit proposals are an essential feature of "negotiation," for they distinguish it from tacit bargaining. Certainly, if there is to be an explicit agreement, there must first be at least one explicit proposal.

Proposals, however, are not the whole story of negotiation; rather, they are markers on the surface which indicate more substantial developments underneath. It should also be recalled that governments prepare proposals in part or entirely for the purpose of producing certain side-effects: to spread propaganda, to maintain contact, to stave off violent actions, or for similar reasons that do not concern agreement. Here these side-effects will be ignored in order to concentrate on the ways in which governments use proposals to reach favorable terms of agreement.

Ostensibly, proposals *always* represent an offer; they give a description of the terms that are allegedly being made available to the opponent. But in fact, proposals are frequently meant as an offer only toward the final phases of a conference. And even then they are binding only to the extent that the parties observe the rule of accommodation according to which an accepted offer should not be withdrawn. In contrast to business negotiations, governments can always withdraw their offers after they have been accepted, albeit with some cost to their bargaining reputation.

If you are engaged in international negotiation, many of your proposals do not serve as offers. Instead they are meant to influence your opponent so that he will make better terms available to you than he was originally disposed to or, conversely, so that he will come to accept greater demands of yours. In other words, your proposals serve either as path-breakers for an eventual offer of yours or as stimuli to make your opponent produce an offer favorable to you.

Your proposals must change your opponent's expectations. They must make him believe that you will insist on certain demands. More than that, they must accustom him to the idea that he wants to reach agreement by meeting what seem to be your irreducible terms. Thus your proposals should accomplish two things with your opponent: they should change his expectations about *your* anticipated minimum, and they should change his anticipations concerning *his* minimum terms. As suggested earlier, the first change will help to bring about the second change. If your opponent changes his expectation as to what *you* intend to settle for, he may change his mind as to what *he* is trying to get.

In the nuclear test-ban conference, for example, the Western insistence early in 1963 on more than just three on-site inspections may have changed Khrushchev's expectations as to the minimum inspection arrangements that the Western powers would accept for banning underground tests. And this may have helped to change his mind about his accepting a partial treaty permitting underground tests, once he had become anxious to have a treaty.

To keep the opponent interested in negotiating, diplomats often formulate their proposals in a flexible fashion. The marked preference for flexibility among many Western diplomats results, in part, from the fear that the opponent might suddenly choose no-agreement if faced with a firm position. In part, Western diplomats keep their proposals flexible because they feel that this is the proper way to negotiate.

But this tactic is self-defeating if the diplomats on the opponent's side want to prove their mettle by showing that they pushed you as far as possible. They cannot satisfy themselves (or their government) that they have reached the limit as long as you offer them a menu of choices, particularly if the menu keeps changing. This is the reason why Westerners have been warned against trying out many variant proposals in negotiating with the Russians. Occasionally, though, a variant proposal may have helped to get a satisfactory agreement with the Soviet Union, for instance the Western proposal for a partial test ban.

However, if your opponent is under domestic pressure to reach agreement and to demonstrate his own flexibility, your flexibility can be used to hasten agreement. You may ensnare him into accepting one of your proposals by putting many alternatives before him.

Tacit bargaining moves may add firmness to negotiations that are otherwise conducted in a flexible manner. The reason is that the opponent usually cannot tell how flexible or firm a tacit move is meant to be as long as it does not become the subject of explicit negotiation. Statesmen who feel constrained by tradition or by domestic opinion to maintain an appearance of flexibility, therefore, can profit from tacit moves that they link to, but do not mention in, their proposals. Also, whereas rigid explicit proposals might antagonize the opponent and cause him to break off negotiations, tacit moves might be tolerated by him because he does not know whether the lack of flexibility is intentional or not.

Such effects of tacit moves may have helped to resolve the Cuba crisis in 1962. Many observers feel that what really compelled Khrushchev to withdraw his missiles was the intelligence he received of American military preparations suggesting that an air strike against his Cuban bases was imminent. Since this threat was tacit (as far as can be judged from the published exchange between Khrushchev and Kennedy), it gave Khrushchev no hint as to how firm or flexible it was.[1] Therefore, it endowed the key American demand for the withdrawal of missiles (which was, of course, explicit) with particular firmness. All the other explicit positions —both the American and the Soviet ones—turned out to be so flexible that they practically melted away. Take the American demand for United Nations inspection. After being exposed to U Thant's mediation, Castro's haggling, and Khrushchev's counter-

---

[1] In a speech in 1963, Attorney General Robert Kennedy remarked that "notification" was sent to Khrushchev of "overwhelming retaliatory action" if the missiles were not pulled out. However, the *New York Times* quotes "high officials" as saying that the "notification" was by way of deeds, not words. "What got the message through to Khrushchev was action." The calling up of Air Force reservists and the movement of military equipment to Florida was deliberately done rather openly (*New York Times*, April 26, 1963).

offer for Red Cross inspection, it finally led to the curious agreement for distant and discreet observation of Soviet ships by the U.S. Navy. Likewise, Khrushchev's demand for the withdrawal of American missiles from Turkey was quietly abandoned. And his demand for an American pledge not to invade or interfere with Cuba became lost in the shuffle, when the UN inspection (on which American negotiators made such a pledge conditional) never materialized. (Khrushchev, however, likes to pretend that the pledge had actually been given.)

Firmness in negotiating proposals can be a deliberate tactic, just like flexibility. It may be used to make the opponent think that one's proposal is close to one's anticipated minimum or, at any rate, that one firmly expects to have one's proposal accepted and will not make further concessions. A way of expressing firmness —though not always a successful one—is repetition. Communist diplomats never tire of reiterating the same position over and over again. Westerners, on the other hand, often try to convey firmness by using new arguments and minor variations; perhaps the feeling that the public is listening in makes sheer repetition of their proposals embarrassing to them. Westerners feel free to be repetitious only when asserting a governing principle, such as the need for verification of disarmament measures or the legality of Western rights of access to Berlin.

But firmness is not always a tactic deliberately chosen to impress the opponent. Negotiators may be firm and keep on repeating their demands simply because their government is unable to furnish them with new instructions. When the representatives of the Algerian FLN negotiated with France about Algeria's independence, they first held on rigidly to sweeping positions (e.g., "complete independence") and could not come to grips with the many details that had to be settled to implement the granting of independence in an orderly fashion. This was not so much the result of their tenacity as of the inability of the Algerian rebels to make the decisions necessary for negotiation. The French practically had to teach their Algerian adversaries that concessions could be traded and that positions might be modified here or there without becoming less desirable.

THE FUNCTION OF ARGUMENTS

Anyone who has worked his way through verbatim records of an international conference must have wondered what, really, was the purpose of all the words that were exchanged over the green baize. At times diplomats seem to talk for the love of their own rhetoric, with no other purpose in mind than to make well-sounding speeches or to win a debating point. At other times they talk for the sake of some side-effect, say, to maintain contact with the opponent or to spread propaganda. Only part of their arguments serve the central purpose of improving the opponent's offers or of making him accept their own. Sometimes diplomats—like other human beings—talk without really knowing what they wish to accomplish with their words.

But, it is possible to concentrate on the arguments designed to improve the terms of agreement and to disregard all the talking done for other purposes or for no purpose at all. The negotiator can use such arguments in several ways, each of which represents a slightly different tactic. Quite likely he will mix these tactics intuitively, moving from one to the other like an experienced driver shifting gears, without consciously calculating what he is doing.

ARGUMENTS TO MAKE ONE'S PROPOSALS ATTRACTIVE

Of course, governments are not swayed by sales talk in the way a naïve consumer might be swayed by advertising. Nonetheless, a negotiator can say things about his offers that will make them seem more attractive to the opponent. One reason is that arguments may be like supplementary offers. That is, the words a negotiator uses in praising his proposal may be viewed as more or less binding amplifications which spell out further details of his offer. Such amplifications are binding for the same reason that an agreement itself is binding, though to a lesser extent. Should a party succeed in having its proposal accepted but later violate the interpretations and amplifications it has given, it will not be believed in the future when it tries to "sell" another proposal.[2]

[2] Decisions of the International Court support the notion that explanations given during negotiations are binding. The Court has held, however, that the

Another way in which a diplomat might make his proposals more attractive merely by talking about them is to convince his opponent that he is motivated by friendly intentions. This is particularly important for proposals aimed at a redistribution agreement, since the defensive side will be opposed to a redistribution that would strengthen an enemy but might tolerate one to win a friend.

Yet, in a way it is curious that talk at the conference table should make any difference. A customer shopping for a rug in a bazaar will not find the price more acceptable just because the merchant claims to be his friend. Perhaps the arguments of diplomats form part of the mosaic of intelligence on the basis of which governments try to size up their opponents. When a diplomat maintains that his proposals stem from the best of intentions, this will not be accepted as a definitive explanation, but it is an item that will be put on the plus side in evaluating his proposal. Remonstrations of good intentions are especially influential during those turning points in international relations when the question whether a country is one's friend or foe hangs in the balance.

Shortly after he became President, Harry Truman sent Harry Hopkins to see Stalin in Moscow. Truman considered this mission of "primary importance . . . to know whether the death of Roosevelt had brought any important changes in the attitudes of Stalin. . . ."[3] One of the most important problems for Hopkins to discuss was the disagreement about Poland. After Hopkins had explained the American desire for a free Poland, Stalin pointed out that in the course of twenty-five years the Germans had twice invaded Russia via Poland. It was therefore in Russia's vital interest that Poland should be both strong and friendly. And he added that "there was no intention on the part of the Soviet Union to interfere in Poland's internal affairs, that Poland would live under the parliamentary system which is like Czechoslovakia, Belgium, and Holland and that any talk of an intention to Sovietize

---

negotiatory history may be used for treaty interpretation only if the treaty itself is not clear and if all parties before the Court participated in the negotiations. (J. L. Brierly, The Law of Nations [Oxford: Clarendon Press, 1949], p. 235; Georg Schwarzenberger, International Law [London: Stevens, 1949], I, 218.)

[3] Truman, Memoirs, I, 110.

Poland was stupid."[4] Hopkins' report did of course not fully persuade Truman as to the benevolence of the Soviet position, but neither was Truman convinced—as he became two years later—that Stalin did indeed want to Sovietize Poland.

About the same time, the Soviet government was engaged in some other redistribution negotiations. At the end of World War II Stalin tried to take some territory from Turkey. This aroused British and American opposition, and the way in which Soviet diplomats argued for their demand did not help. For instance, in a discussion with the Soviet ambassador in Ankara, the Turkish foreign minister inquired "whether the Soviet Union which possesses a respectable portion of the earth's surface really needed any additional territory." The Soviet ambassador replied that "the Soviet Union did not need additional territory but the Armenian Soviet Socialist Republic was very small and needed additional territory." The Turkish foreign minister simply retorted that he "could not accept such a statement."[5]

A more subtle way of making one's proposals more attractive is to influence the opponent's evaluation criteria, rather than to protest one's good intentions or to offer favorable amplifications.

Some time before the Soviets demanded a slice of Turkish territory, they had requested that the Montreux Convention be revised so as to remove all restrictions on the passage of Russian warships through the Turkish Straits. At Yalta, Stalin argued that "it was impossible to accept a situation in which Turkey had a hand on Russia's throat [but that the Convention should be revised] in such a manner as not to harm the legitimate interests of Turkey." Churchill did not deny the validity of these arguments and took a rather favorable view of the Russian request for a revision of the Convention. The Russian arguments also seem to have encouraged a re-evaluation in the U.S. government. A U.S. policy paper for the Yalta Conference argued that the Montreux Convention has "worked well" and that "any major changes probably would violate Turkish sovereignty." But a few months after Yalta, in preparation for the Potsdam Conference, another U.S. policy paper

[4] *Foreign Relations of the United States: The Conference of Berlin (Potsdam) 1945*, I, 39 (quotation as paraphrased in the official minutes).
[5] *Ibid.*, p. 1025.

stated: "The Government of the United States believes that following the present war the Montreux Convention to some extent will be outmoded."[6]

On the issue of the revision of the Panama Canal Treaty, it is in Panama's interest to use arguments that will change the American evaluation criteria to make the treaty appear as an instance of colonialism—an inequity that ought to be remedied. Such an evaluation would make a redistribution in favor of Panama more attractive to the United States, because it would seem to be in line with a historical trend. Changes in favor of Panama would be viewed as an even outcome by the United States, not as a Panamanian gain and an American loss.

To sum up, arguments may induce the opponent to recalibrate his evaluations if he is already inclined to do so. He may be persuaded to shift his break-even point because he has no firm views as to where his gains and losses begin. But he will not be talked into reversing his preferences on major issues. Words are not enough to convert a government or the negotiators representing it.

Although experienced diplomats should know better, a great deal of time is wasted in international conferences as one delegate exhorts another delegate that his government should prefer what it dislikes and should shun what it pursues. International diplomacy is not like a high school debate where people change sides because they listen to some convincing sentences. Thus, one wonders what Secretary Byrnes sought to accomplish when he argued with Molotov that an independent Poland was better for Russia than one under Soviet control. Almost with disappointment Byrnes recalls: "I could not impress [Molotov] with my views that Soviet security would be better assured by having in Poland a people who are friendly, rather than a government that was friendly only because it was dictated by the Soviet Union. Unsuccessfully, I argued that governments would come and go, but that if the Soviet Government's conduct in Poland won the friendship of the people, the friendship of the government would be assured."[7]

---

[6] *Ibid., The Conferences at Malta and Yalta 1945*, p. 903 and p. 328; and *The Conference of Berlin (Potsdam) 1945*, I, 1014.

[7] Byrnes, *Speaking Frankly*, p. 32.

ARGUMENTS EXPRESSING FIRMNESS

An important function of arguments is to impress the opponent that one's proposal is firm and that no concessions can be forthcoming. A commitment may actually be reinforced by the act of explaining it in a public conference, because the negotiator will be afraid of domestic criticism if he makes a concession after having argued that his proposal was vital.

A common way of demonstrating one's commitment is to argue that domestic forces would oppose a change in one's position. Harry Hopkins, during his mission to Moscow in May, 1945, tried to demonstrate the firmness of the American position on Poland primarily by pointing out that public opinion in the United States was disturbed and that Truman might lose the public support that Roosevelt enjoyed for a friendly policy toward the Soviet Union. However, Hopkins probably weakened his argument by dissociating himself from this body of opinion and by implying that the President, for himself, really had no strong views on Poland. He told Stalin that "rightly or wrongly" there was a strong feeling among the American people that the Soviet Union wished to dominate Poland but added that this was not his point of view. Hopkins argued that friendly American-Soviet relations were threatened by the public reaction in the United States to the events in Poland but reminded Stalin that "many minority groups in America" were not sympathetic to Russia anyhow, "that Poland was only a symbol," and that Stalin "should not assume that the *Chicago Tribune* or the Hearst Press had any real influence on American public opinion."[8]

The domestic-opinion argument is effective only if it conveys the idea that the domestic views are held by people who can influence policy. At the 1955 summit meeting Bulganin used a domestic-opinion argument on Eden that seemed to meet this requirement. He told Eden in private—as if he were imparting a great secret—that "it would really not be possible for his Government to return to Moscow from this Conference if they agreed to the immediate unification of Germany. They were a united Government and

[8] *The Conference of Berlin (Potsdam) 1945*, pp. 56–58 (quotes as paraphrased in Bohlen's memorandum).

reasonably solidly based in the country, but this was something that Russia would not accept; and if they were to agree to it neither the army nor the people would understand, and this was no time to weaken the Government."[9]

The domestic-opinion argument was again used on Eden by Secretary Dulles during the Suez crisis in 1956. According to Eden, Dulles "stated that he could not release us from our obligation to withdraw [the British forces from the Canal zone], since to do so would be 'in some sense a breach of faith on the part of the Administration with Congress and United States public opinion.' He maintained that our action had caused revulsion throughout the United States." But this time Eden was not impressed with the argument: "This was strong language," he writes, "and at variance with the reports of our own representatives, who considered that the sharp feelings displayed at that time in Washington had not really represented American opinion."[10]

Another way of expressing firmness is to maintain that one's position accords with legal or scientific principles. At least, this is the principal function of legal and scientific arguments; for you do not usually make your proposal more attractive to your opponent by telling him that what you are proposing is in accordance with scientific facts or international law. However, if you make your opponent believe that *you* think your proposal is grounded on such principles, you may have conveyed to him that your proposal is firm. If your opponent believes that you view your position as being part of a larger, coherent system, he must expect that you will refuse a concession for fear of undermining other positions that are connected with this system of yours. The American negotiators in the nuclear test-ban conference may have used scientific arguments with some success for this reason. They were able to demonstrate a strong commitment to many minor details of the inspection system because they maintained the stance that the system, in its entirety, had to be in accordance with scientific requirements. During the early part of the test-ban negotiations the Russians gave in on several such details, not so much because they cared whether or not the system was scientifically sound, but

[9] Anthony Eden, *Full Circle,* p. 334.
[10] *Ibid.,* p. 664.

because they were impressed with the American commitment to a scientifically grounded system.

Procedural arguments or arguments against a new precedent are often used for the same purpose. If you can show that a concession would violate established procedure or set a new precedent, your position may look firmer than if your opponent thought that you would only be conceding some of the substance of your position.

Another tactic for dissuading your opponent from further bargaining is to argue that you know he is willing to settle for your terms, if pressed to do so. In other words, you pretend to know that his anticipated minimum terms are compatible with your offer, thus suggesting that you will be quite stubborn in clinging to your terms.

Firmness can also be expressed by telling your opponent that you are not at all eager to reach agreement, so that he will think he has to meet your terms to make agreement worthwhile for you. Up to the atomic bombing of Hiroshima, the United States was anxious to obtain Soviet participation in defeating Japan. This wish resulted from faulty intelligence about Japan's military strength, ignoring of Japanese peace feelers, and the unimaginative insistence on "unconditional surrender." But these errors are not the ones that concern us here.

American diplomacy committed another error in negotiating with Stalin for Soviet entry into the war against Japan—regardless of whether or not Soviet participation was necessary for a quick victory. This was the American belief that Stalin was not eager to come into the war and hence would do so only if rewarded by territorial gains. Foreign Secretary Eden, for one, did not share this view, as he explained to Secretary of State Stettinius when they met at Malta to prepare for the Yalta Conference (where Stalin was promised his reward for entering the war against Japan). According to the minutes of the Malta meeting, Eden told Stettinius: ". . . if the Russians decided to enter the war against Japan they would take the decision because they considered it in their interests that the Japanese war should not be successfully finished by the U.S. and Great Britain alone. There was therefore no need for us to offer a high price for their participation, and if we were prepared to agree to their territorial demands in the Far East we should see to it that we obtained a good return in respect of the points on which we required concessions from them."[11]

At Yalta, Stalin skillfully avoided giving any support to Eden's thesis that it was in Russia's own interest to enter the war against Japan. He argued that if his demands in the Far East were not met, "it would be difficult for him and Molotov to explain to the Soviet people why Russia was entering the war against Japan . . . ; however, if these political conditions were met, the people would understand the national interest involved and it would be very much easier to explain the decision to a Supreme Soviet."[12] And when Hopkins came to see him in Moscow a few months later, Stalin, to make sure that his conditions would be met, again used the argument that he was not eager to enter the war against Japan.

ARGUMENTS ABOUT RULES OF ACCOMMODATION

Negotiators argue a great deal about rules of accommodation. Appeals are made to the opponent that he ought to be more flexible, that he should not impugn one's motives, that it is his turn to reciprocate a concession, and so forth. Negotiators of the European Communities are wont to plead for their proposals by appealing to the *esprit communautaire,* implying that a higher standard of accommodation should apply within the Communities.

In multilateral negotiations, arguments about rules of accommodation have greater effect than in bilateral ones. The other parties may act as mediators who will turn against a party that can be shown to have violated these rules. Hence, negotiators not only will argue that the opponent ought to observe certain rules (or has failed to do so) but will try to demonstrate that they themselves are beyond reproach. They will use what is sometimes called "diplomatic language"—meticulously polite, never blunt, and always flexible. A negotiator who wants to veto a proposal in a multilateral conference without incurring blame may say, for example, that the issue has not yet been adequately discussed and therefore must be postponed.

[11] *The Conferences at Malta and Yalta 1945,* p. 501.

[12] *Ibid.,* p. 769 (quote as paraphrased in the minutes). Earlier, at Teheran, Stalin had promised to participate in the Pacific war without mentioning territorial compensation. (For further details of this story, see Herbert Feis, *The China Tangle* [Princeton, N.J.: Princeton University Press, 1953], pp. 226–39.)

Moreover, to gain the approval of third parties who might have a mediating influence in multilateral negotiation, diplomats will usually see to it that their arguments sound reasonable. They will not commit gross violations of logic, brazenly distort well-known facts, or offend common standards of justice and fairness. Western participants in the Eighteen-Nation Disarmament Conference felt that the presence of neutral nations forced the Communist negotiators to use more reasonable arguments than in earlier conferences without neutral participation. By contrast, if there are no mediators around, it sometimes pays to use a totally unreasonable argument to demonstrate that one's position is independent of the reasons that are being discussed and therefore cannot be shaken by the opponent's arguments. This is what Tsarapkin may have had in mind when he maintained at the nuclear test-ban conference (prior to the participation of neutral nations): "I must repeat that whether the staff of control posts, or of other parts of the control system, consists of foreigners or of citizens of the country on whose territory the control post is located, the work of control will not suffer in any way. This is an absolutely indisputable proposition, which you cannot possibly refute."[13] The question whether citizens could be trusted to report a violation by their own country is blithely ignored.

REACHING POINTS OF AGREEMENT

As the parties bring their positions into agreement, they adapt their proposals to a single agreed set of terms, out in the open at the conference table. But this is only the surface manifestation of the process of reaching agreement. The rest takes place in the negotiators' minds and in the inner councils of governments. The terms of agreement are reached through a contest of wills, wits, and interests—much of which remains concealed from the opponent—in which the parties keep revising their expectations about each other, shift their evaluations for measuring gains and losses, and continually weigh (as long as they seek agreement) the

[13] Conference on the Discontinuance of Nuclear Weapon Tests, 23d Plenary Meeting, Dec. 11, 1958, p. 16.

choice between accepting the available terms and further bargaining.

The open confrontation of proposals may be clarified by, first, examining how parties come to terms on a single, indivisible issue and by, later, considering how they connect several issues to arrive at more complex agreements. A variety of different maneuvers are used to come to terms on a single issue. These maneuvers usually take place in various combinations, but for the sake of clarity they will be discussed one by one.

THE COMPROMISE

Edward Stettinius wrote in defense of the Yalta Conference, which he attended as Roosevelt's Secretary of State, that the Russians made more concessions than the United States and Great Britain made to them. "On certain issues, of course," he goes on to say, "each of the three Great Powers modified its original position in order to reach agreement. Although it is sometimes alleged that there is something evil in compromise, actually, of course, compromise is necessary for progress as any sensible man knows. Compromise, when reached honorably and in a spirit of honesty by all concerned, is the only fair and rational way of reaching a reasonable agreement between two differing points of view."[14]

It is a recurrent theme in Western writings on diplomacy that compromise is not only desirable but even necessary for reaching agreement. The fact is that agreement can be reached in other ways, some of which might well be considered more desirable. The Yalta Agreement should be neither defended nor attacked because parts of it were reached through compromise. Moreover, it is an egregious error to call compromise a "fair" or "rational" method without comparing the "fairness" of the initial positions from which the parties started. Perhaps Stettinius' phrase "in a spirit of honesty" implies such a comparison. But honesty is not the discriminating criterion here, since all negotiation naturally includes some deception.

A "compromise" usually means an agreement reached through

---

[14] Edward R. Stettinius, Jr., *Roosevelt and the Russians* (Garden City, N.Y.: Doubleday, 1949), p. 6.

concessions by both sides. And a party is said to make a "concession" when it changes its proposal so as to bring it closer to that of the opponent. However, the fact that a party has made a concession only means that it has lowered the terms it first stated —not the ones it expected to get. When a party reaches a compromise, its expectations may actually move in a direction opposite to the movement of its proposals. While the proposals become more modest, the expectations may become more demanding. For example, a negotiator may have been ready to make a large concession when he discovers that the opponent is asking much less than expected. The negotiator will then *raise* his expectations, while *lowering* his demands by only the small concession necessary to reach agreement. Evidently, there is nothing either fair or foul in moving one's proposal closer to that of the opponent, nor does an agreement become reasonable merely because it has been reached through such mutual revisions of proposals.

The mutual concessions required for a compromise, moreover, may have quite a different meaning for each of the parties. Your opponent may never have expected to obtain more than the point of compromise, but he asked for more initially in order to have a "bargaining position." You, on the other hand, may have expected to settle at your initial position, or very close to it, and therefore had to change your expectations when you saw how far apart you were from your opponent and how determined he was. Now, from your point of view, surely, this compromise maneuver did not make the outcome particularly "fair."

It is one of the most common negotiating tactics to ask for more than one expects to receive, in order to move the point of compromise in one's favor. Of course, if both sides use this tactic, its effect may well cancel out. Your opponent will not accept your proposal as long as he thinks that it is only a "bargaining position"; in fact, he may not even make concessions from his "bargaining position" until you have lowered yours. It is still worse for you if your opponent thinks that you have been asking for far more than you would settle for, whereas actually you have left yourself very little room between your initial proposal and your anticipated minimum. Khrushchev alleged that this was happening to him with his proposals on Berlin:

They [Adenauer and Brentano] say that negotiations with the Soviet Union should follow the principle of concession for concession. But that is a mercantile approach. When working out our proposals we did not approach the matter as hucksters would, who name the price with a "margin," at thrice the cost, and then, after bargaining, sell their goods at a much cheaper price than the one they named at the beginning. . . . We have no reason to make any concessions, since we have not made our proposals for the purpose of bargaining.[15]

A special form of the compromise maneuver is *haggling* (also known as "bazaar" bargaining and, in French, as *marchandage*). In haggling, both parties more or less admit that they are starting with "bargaining positions." They alternate in making many separate, and usually small, concessions until the point of compromise is reached. Haggling is rather customary for reaching agreement on numbers, such as amounts of money or tariff rates. The region of compromise can often be projected long before the compromise has been settled, because both sides may reveal the rate at which they are making concessions. If this is the case, a tentative agreement has in fact been reached in the initial phases of haggling, and the exchange of the additional concessions merely confirms and perhaps refines the point of compromise. For this reason, if you are involved in a situation where the opponent expects you to haggle and you have made the first proposal, you may refuse to make any concessions until your opponent has raised his initial proposal to a level from which your joint haggling promises to converge on a point that will meet your expectations. If your opponent should fail to improve his first counter-offer, you will tell him that you "refuse to consider it," because you know that a compromise between his and your position would not satisfy you.

Sometimes negotiators try to reach a favorable compromise by asking for something that is of little value to them but highly undesirable to the opponent. The objective is not to obtain part of what they are asking for but to receive a concession from the opponent in return for abandoning their demand entirely. One might call such positions "extortionary" demands.

[15] Speech in Tirana, May 30, 1959 (N. S. Khrushchev, *World without Arms, World without Wars,* Book 1, p. 374).

In the Korean truce talks the United Nations negotiators were faced with such a demand. After prolonged wrangling, it was agreed that a Neutral Nations Supervisory Commission be established to check on the implementation of the truce terms and that each side was to nominate three neutral nations acceptable to the opponent. The United Nations nominated Sweden, Switzerland, and Norway; the Communists nominated Poland, Czechoslovakia—and the Soviet Union! The Communists did not need Soviet members in the Supervisory Commission in addition to Czechs and Poles, and they must have been well aware that the West could not accept the Soviet Union as a neutral nation. Nonetheless, they argued stubbornly in favor of their proposal: "If the Soviet Union could not be nominated as a neutral nation, there would be no neutral nation at all existing in the world. What is more strange is that your side should object to the Soviet Union when it has agreed to Poland and Czechoslovakia."

For some strange reason the U.S. government (which instructed the UN Command) forbade the UN negotiators to mention the real reason why the Soviet Union was unacceptable as a neutral nation—namely, that it was the main logistics base for the Communist forces. This inhibition did not go unnoticed by the Communists: "Why do you give no logical reason for opposing the great, peace-loving U.S.S.R. as a member of the Neutral Nations? You give no reason because you have none. You are unable to deny that the U.S.S.R. is a true neutral in the Korean conflict."

While the UN labored under its self-imposed handicap, this debate went on for weeks and weeks. The UN side tried to eliminate the Soviet Union as a neutral nation by suggesting that both the Soviet Union and Norway be dropped. But this was rejected, and the UN Command did not insist. In the end, the UN Command felt it had to pay the ransom to get rid of this "extortionary" demand and swapped a position to which it had attached great importance: the prohibition of the repair and construction of airfields after the truce.[16]

A more effective riposte to an "extortionary" demand is to raise an "extortionary" demand of one's own. With a little more

[16] Vatcher, *Panmunjom*, pp. 108–13, and Joy, *How Communists Negotiate*, pp. 89–99.

daring and imagination, the U.S. government could have instructed the UN negotiators differently. It could have replied to the Communists, for example, that the inclusion of the Soviet Union among the neutral nations required that it be balanced with another Far Eastern power—namely, Nationalist China (while explaining to its allies that it expected to trade the nomination of Nationalist China against that of the Soviet Union). Since Communist China would not have accepted Nationalist China as a neutral nation, this coupling—if maintained with firmness—might have saved the UN side from buying off the Communist demand by conceding something that it really wanted.

Like all evaluations in negotiation, evaluations of a compromise are dependent on, and changed by, the negotiation process. What started out as your "bargaining position" may later become an essential part of your anticipated minimum and vice versa. Your opponent may consider your "bargaining position" as a modest demand on one issue, but on another issue he may mistake for an "extortionary" demand a position that you consider essential. Since the difference between a "bargaining position" and an essential position or between a modest and an immodest one depends on expectations and evaluation criteria, and since these expectations and criteria change as a result of negotiation, all the bench marks for assessing a compromise are really adrift.

CATCHING UP WITH RISING DEMANDS

A compromise is not the only way in which parties can converge on the terms of agreement. One party, far from making concessions, may add new demands to its proposal. If the other party wishes to reach agreement nonetheless, it will have to continue conceding and in the end settle for less favorable terms than those initially proposed by the first party.

This tactic was already known in ancient mythology. The prophetess Sibyl of Cumae offered Tarquin the Proud, last of the legendary kings of Rome, nine books containing prophecies. Tarquin thought the price so high that he refused to buy. Sibyl then burned three of the books and offered the remaining six at the same price. When Tarquin refused again, she burned three more, and Tarquin, fearing that she might destroy them all, bought the last three books at the price originally asked for the nine.

The tactic of the Sibylline Books serves to discourage the opponent from further bargaining. He may quickly accept the offered terms for fear of continually missing better opportunities. It is particularly effective when the prospects for no-agreement look increasingly worse to the opponent.

This happened to the Finns when they were defending themselves against the Russian invasion in the winter of 1939–40. The Finnish government continued to negotiate with Moscow in order to halt the Soviet attack. The Soviets, too, preferred a negotiated settlement, since they had discovered that conquering all of Finland would be very difficult (owing to the surprisingly effective Finnish resistance) and risky (because of the possibility of Anglo-French intervention). When Molotov made his first peace offer, he warned the Swedish Foreign Minister who acted as intermediary: "If these terms are not now accepted, the demands will be increased." Two weeks later, he repeated this warning and made no concessions at all. And when the Finnish negotiators arrived in Moscow a few days later, new demands, indeed, were added. The Finns felt forced to accept.[17]

In other situations, the Sibylline Books tactic may have the advantage of drawing the opponent into the negotiations through the modest initial proposals, whereas starting with the more demanding final position might have repelled him. Once the opponent is negotiating, the gradually increasing demands may help shift his evaluations and eventually make the final position acceptable to him. This happened during 1961–62 in the prolonged nuclear test-ban conference. On the detection system, the Russian position for a while moved further away from the Western position, while the Western powers, up to a point, were catching up with the rising demands. (The issue of the detection system became immaterial, however, when the partial treaty was signed in 1963.)

The Sibylline Books tactic violates rules of accommodation and hence may antagonize public opinion or stir up the opponent's

[17] Max Jakobson, *The Diplomacy of the Winter War* (Cambridge, Mass.: Harvard University Press, 1961), pp. 234–35, 249–50.

hostility. If this is a drawback, however, it can be minimized by couching the initial proposal in ambiguous language and by arguing that the ensuing demands are justified by changed conditions. In this way it will also be easier for the opponent to swallow the increased demands because his bargaining reputation will be less impaired.

ACCEPTING THE FIRST PROPOSAL

When negotiating an agreement, you may settle many of its terms simply by accepting the first proposal that your opponent puts forward, either immediately or after having made some proposals of your own. You may do so because (1) you have no desire to improve the terms, (2) you fear the opponent might add to his demands, or (3) you are convinced that your opponent will not improve his first offer. Your opponent may even present his first proposal as an ultimatum; that is, he may commit his bargaining reputation to his prediction that he would rather break off negotiations than change his proposal.[18]

Not just minor points but important issues are frequently settled through acceptance of the first proposal. In fact, more examples could probably be found than of settlements through compromise. To cite just one instance, the purchase price for Alaska was fixed in this manner. Secretary of State Seward offered $5,000,000, but the Russian Ambassador asked initially for $7,000,000 and refused to lower his price (although he was authorized to go down to $5,000,000). Seward therefore accepted the initial Russian demand for $7,000,000. (Afterwards Seward also purchased the cancellation of all claims that the Russian-American Company had in Alaska by adding another $200,000.)

[18] In labor-management negotiation, an elaborated version of the tactic of making one's first proposal the final one has become known as Boulwareism (after Lemuel Boulware of the General Electric Corporation). The company carefully prepares a proposal which in many ways corresponds to the wishes and attitudes of the employees, takes precedents and analogous situations into account, and is widely advertised among the employees. Naturally, labor leaders dislike this procedure because they cannot obtain better terms than those originally offered by management. See Carl M. Stevens, *Strategy and Collective Bargaining Negotiation* (New York: McGraw-Hill, 1963), pp. 34–37, and Allan Weisenfeld and Monroe Berkowitz, "A New Look in Collective Bargaining," *Labor Law Journal* (Aug., 1955), pp. 561–71.

FOCAL POINTS AND MEDIATION

Among the many alternatives for settling an issue, there are often a few which seem particularly prominent to the parties. These focal points are like a notch where a compromise might converge, a resting place where rising demands might come to a halt, or a barrier over which an initial proposal cannot be budged. In *tacit* bargaining, focal points help the parties to coordinate their expectations and positions. In negotiation, since coordination can be achieved through the exchange of proposals, focal points serve to reduce the alternatives that the parties must consider.[19]

Round figures in monetary settlements, apart from satisfying the common preference for simplicity and neatness, are easier to justify. Secretary of State Seward and the Russian Ambassador might have agreed on a purchase price for Alaska of $6,000,000 or $8,000,000 without needing any reason for the particular last six digits. But had they settled on, say, $7,169,315, they would have wanted to justify the $169,315. Indeed, the final price for Alaska of $7,200,000 was the sum of two separately justifiable round figures.

Another reason why negotiators tend to agree on focal points is that they can better anchor their commitments at places that are set apart from neighboring points by some particular feature. Boundary disputes are frequently settled on focal points based on precedent or geographic features. For example, in settling the Oregon boundary dispute of 1846 between the United States and Great Britain, the line was drawn along the 49th Parallel up to the Juan de Fuca Strait and thence through the middle of the Strait to the Pacific. The 49th Parallel was prominent because it extended the U.S.-Canadian boundary that existed east of the disputed area, and the Strait was an obvious geographic feature.

Where precedents or geography do not provide focal points, negotiators often construe some points so as to make them prominent. For example, delegates haggling about import quotas often first decide to reduce the infinite number of quantities on which they could possibly agree to a few figures, such as a quota

[19] Focal points, and particularly their role in coordination, have first been dealt with by Thomas C. Schelling (*The Strategy of Conflict*, pp. 67–73).

equal to last year's imports, one equal to the average of the last five years, and perhaps one equal to the import quota of a third country. As if by tacit agreement, bargaining will then be confined to these artificially created focal points.

In multilateral negotiation, a preliminary agreement between some of the participants can act as a focal point. Those who have reached a preliminary accord will look at their point of agreement as the prominent feasible solution and be reluctant to change their positions. Unless the disagreeing parties give in, they may find themselves excluded from the agreement or at least being blamed for obstructing unanimity. To prevent this, it may sometimes seem preferable to withdraw from negotiations or to break them up before the other parties have formed such a focal point. When President de Gaulle suddenly vetoed Britain's application for entry into the Common Market in January, 1963, many people wondered why he had not chosen the more "subtle" method of insisting on terms that would be rejected by Great Britain. The answer may be that he expected the other five Common Market members and Great Britain soon to agree on a set of terms, so that France would have had to veto a "ready agreement" instead of breaking off "fruitless negotiations."

A related effect occurs in *mediation:* the mediator's suggestions are influential mainly because they create focal points.[20] This becomes particularly evident when the parties are trying to arrive at a complex agreement which has to settle many interrelated details. The Common Market agreements on agricultural integration of January, 1962, and December, 1963, were both based on a comprehensive proposal by the Common Market Commission. On both occasions, the Commission made its proposal before formal negotiations among the six member states had started (as it was requested to do), and as the negotiators approached their deadline while their draft agreement was still full of gaps, the original Commission proposal—with some revisions—was the only complete arrangement on which they all could quickly converge. The mediating power of the Commission is enhanced by the fact that it possesses better technical knowledge about such intricate agreements than any of the six governments.

[20] *The Strategy of Conflict,* p. 144.

DEDUCTION FROM A FRAMEWORK AGREEMENT

Friendly nations often use a two-stage process to arrive at points of agreement. By means of a compromise (or some other maneuver involving a confrontation of proposals) they first reach agreement on a framework of broad objectives and principles. Then they deduce detailed points of agreement from this framework by applying mutually acceptable methods of reasoning (simple logic, methods of an appropriate scientific discipline, or legal reasoning).

Since the outcome from the application of these methods is roughly predetermined, the parties, by settling on the framework, in fact agree on a certain range within which the final terms will fall. Thereafter they leave the determination of the specific terms to the deductive process. Of course, even the most scrupulous application of mutually acceptable methods of deduction frequently leaves some uncertainties that will have to be settled in other ways (through a compromise, for example).

In a climate of acute antagonism, the "deductive method" is likely to break down because the opponents will be tempted to depart from the agreed framework or from the methods of deduction in order to shift the outcome to their advantage. The "deductive method" is most effective when the parties observe many rules of accommodation.

In negotiations between Western nations deduction from an agreed framework is often delegated to experts who are more conversant with the applicable methods than political negotiators. This does not mean that the experts are impartial; they may have strong preferences regarding the outcome and may feel obligated to seek favorable terms for their government. However, each party expects its experts not to violate the standards of their profession —at least not flagrantly.

Between East and West, a famous attempt to delegate the "deductive method" to experts was the 1958 Experts' Conference for a nuclear test-detection system. This conference was expected (at least by the Western participants) to settle various details of a detection system by applying the methods of physical sciences to the framework agreement, according to which the system should discover nuclear weapon tests in any environment that seemed physically accessible for testing. The restriction in methods to physical sciences excluded, for example, consideration of psychological questions, such as the capabilities and national bias of the technical and administrative staff. Almost at once, however, the participants were dealing with topics which do not ordinarily crop up in a physics colloquium. In part, personnel questions were settled by exchanging proposals. For instance, the American participants proposed that inspection posts should have thirty technicians, and the Soviets accepted this number. In part, personnel questions were called "political," meaning that they were out of bounds for the Experts' Conference. Thus the American participants insisted that the experts ought to say nothing about the question of whether the control posts should be manned by technicians who were *not* nationals of the country in which the posts were to be located.

A notable instance where the 1958 Experts' Conference departed from the "deductive method" was in singling out a detection system which was expected to have only a poor capacity for underground tests below five kilotons. The selection of this particular system could, of course, not be based on the laws of physics, nor did the agreed principles (terms of reference) justify it. The solution appropriate to the "deductive method" would have been to show how the system had to vary depending on the size of tests to be detected. This is what the American participants initially favored. But in order to keep the number of control posts acceptable to the Russians, the Americans and the British suggested settling for a system with a reduced performance. In doing this, they acted as negotiators, not as scientific experts.[21]

---

[21] This change in roles need not be criticized if it was authorized and fully understood in Washington. See Robert Gilpin, *American Scientists and Nuclear Weapons Policy* (Princeton, N.J.: Princeton University Press, 1962), pp. 202–14; and Earl H. Voss, *Nuclear Ambush* (Chicago: Regnery, 1963), pp. 183, 214–19. A comprehensive analysis of the 1958 Experts' Conference and the subsequent role of experts will be found in Harold Jacobson and Eric Stein, *Diplomats, Scientists and Politicians: The United States and the Nuclear Test Ban Negotiations* (Ann Arbor: University of Michigan Press, 1964). On the difficulties of separating "political" from "technical" issues see Ciro E. Zoppo, *Technical and Political Aspects of Arms Control Negotiation: The 1958 Experts' Conference* (RAND Corporation Research Memorandum 3286 [Santa Monica, Calif., 1962]).

Non-controversial Solutions

Diplomats like to stress that in practicing the art of negotiation one must be able to overcome sticky issues of conflict through the discovery of "new solutions" or the invention of "new formulae." What is usually meant by a "new solution" is an outcome that is less controversial than any of the alternatives which have been the subject of dispute. By contrast, a compromise is "controversial" because it picks an outcome from a range of alternatives where each improvement for one party means some deterioration for the other party. A "non-controversial" solution avoids this choice entirely: it puts an end to the dispute by picking an outcome so that the losses and gains of the parties remain unaffected or indeterminate.

In 1943, Great Britain, the United States, and the Soviet Union formed the European Advisory Commission, which served as an important negotiating body for detailed agreements on the termination of hostilities in Europe. Lord Strang, the British representative at this Commission, reports that it was often possible to reach agreement with the Russians by changes in wording which they found objectionable but which was of little consequence to the other parties. Lord Strang wrote that when the parties had reached an impasse:

I would sometimes suggest that we should leave our formulae entirely aside for the moment and try to explain to each other exactly what were, in practice, the results that we wished to achieve by this particular clause in the agreement. If each of us could have his own way, what was it that we wanted to see happening when the time came to apply the clause? By this procedure, it would sometimes appear that, for all that we were at variance in our drafting, our practical aims were in fact not irreconcilable. On this basis, a new and usually simpler form of words could be found which was acceptable to all.[22]

Another form of a non-controversial solution is to leave the settlement to a chance process. This maneuver is well known in everyday life. If two people cannot agree on how to allocate between themselves some indivisible piece of property, they may

[22] Lord [William] Strang, *Home and Abroad* (London: André Deutsch, 1956), pp. 205–6.

nonetheless agree on flipping a coin or drawing lots to settle the issue. The counterpart in international negotiation is to turn an issue over to arbitration or to let it be decided by a plebiscite, provided the outcome of either of these processes is unpredictable for both parties (if it is predictable, the solution will be controversial).

Arbitration is widely used for settling boundary disputes. In the Venezuelan boundary dispute of 1897 between the United States and Great Britain, the parties were unable to foresee the outcome of the arbitration procedure to which they agreed. Great Britain, in fact, accepted arbitration only reluctantly but then was awarded most of the disputed territory. In the prolonged Franco-German dispute about the Saar, the French and German governments agreed in 1954 to let the Saar population vote on a statute providing for the Europeanization of the Saar. The rejection of this statute came somewhat as a surprise for both governments and paved the way for the return of the Saar to Germany.[23] In the Kashmir dispute between India and Pakistan, the Indian government has withdrawn its consent to a plebiscite precisely because it considers its outcome predictable.

MANIPULATION OF ISSUES

Governments usually have considerable freedom in the way in which they formulate the issues. Their delegates may spend more time and effort in trying to agree on what the issues are than in settling them. For good reason! The formulation of an issue may stake out the starting points and limits for concessions, fix the bench marks for evaluating gains and losses, and circumscribe the areas where pressures, threats, and inducements can be used.

At the beginning of the Korean truce talks the Communists proposed the following four-point agenda: "(1) The establishment of the 38th Parallel as the military demarcation line. . . . (2) Withdrawal of all armed forces of foreign countries from Korea. (3) Concrete arrangements for the realization of a cease-fire. . . . (4) Arrangements relating to prisoners of war follow-

---

[23] Jacques Freymond, *The Saar Conflict, 1945–1955*, pp. 172 ff.

ing the armistice."[24] Evidently, the first two agenda items were not issues for negotiation but the Communist-preferred terms for a settlement. The UN side was not deceived by this tactic and rejected this "agenda."

When Panama broke diplomatic relations with the United States after the disturbances in the Canal Zone in January, 1964, it tried to maneuver the United States into accepting revision of the 1903 Treaty as a subject of negotiation. Presumably this would have focused negotiations on the question of how extensively the 1903 Treaty should be revised. Failing agreement on this question, the United States might then have been accused of breaking its promise to revise the treaty, and third countries as well as many people in Panama and the United States would thereafter have considered the treaty less valid.

Instead of formulating an issue so that one's terms are already built into it, one may protect one's position by making it into a condition for negotiation. Jean Monnet, as noted before, successfully made the acceptance of the principle of a supra-national authority a condition for participation in the negotiations on the Schuman Plan. In the Free Trade Area Negotiations in 1957–58, the countries in favor of a free trade area (Great Britain and the other present EFTA members) tried to confine the negotiations to the detailed implementation of their objective to avoid a dispute about its desirability and feasibility. However, the tactic failed in this case.

In the 1958 Experts' Conference the Russians initially maintained that the conference should start by coming out in favor of test cessation. As the leader of the Soviet delegation put it: "If we do not assume that tests must and will be halted, then our work is quite fruitless."[25] The American scientists countered that the Experts' Conference should only examine techniques for detecting nuclear tests without reaching a conclusion on the desirability of test cessation. The American position won out, and the issue whether or not tests were to be stopped was left to the political test-ban conference.

The order in which issues are dealt with has several implica-

[24] Vatcher, *Panmunjom*, p. 33.
[25] Conference of Experts, July 2, 1958, P.V. 2, p. 46.

tions. To increase the chances for agreement, negotiators tend to take up the less controversial issues first, in the hope that the parties will become increasingly desirous of an agreement and therefore willing to make greater sacrifices in solving the hard issues. With only a few refractory issues left, the negotiators may take pride in seeing their efforts succeed and be afraid of public censure should they fail. When the six members of the Common Market had to settle a long list of tariff positions in 1959–60, the Common Market Commission carefully arranged to start with discussion of those products on which agreement could be reached most easily. In the end, when the parties were left with only a few remaining products, they felt under pressure to compromise their differences.[26]

Proposals for an agenda can of course be confronted with counter-proposals. This may permit a compromise maneuver on some issues before they have even been debated. For example, "extortionary" demands and counter-demands may be canceled out at this stage rather than after the substantive matter has been brought up by both sides.

A related tactic is to make the inclusion of an undesirable agenda item so difficult that other parties will not find it worthwhile to press the issue. Stalin succeeded in preventing the British from bringing up the Yugoslav question at the Potsdam Conference by exploiting Truman's impatience. When Eden first wanted to put this question on the agenda, Stalin argued that Yugoslavia was an allied country and that it was not possible to settle this matter without the Yugoslavs being present. Since Truman wondered whether the matter was serious enough to warrant sending for Yugoslav representatives, Churchill pointed out that the Yalta agreements on this subject had not been carried out: there had been no elections, juridical procedure had not been restored, etc. Stalin then reiterated he would agree to discuss the subject but that it was "not possible to try the Yugoslav state without hearing its representatives." Here Truman intervened and said that "he

---

[26] Leon N. Lindberg, *The Political Dynamics of European Economic Integration* (Stanford, Calif.: Stanford University Press, 1963), p. 215. The tariff positions were those of the so-called List G. This list was in itself a refractory residue from the Treaty of Rome negotiations.

was here as a representative of the United States to discuss world affairs. He did not wish to sit here as a court to settle matters which will eventually be settled by the United Nations Organization. If we do that, we shall become involved in trying to settle every political difficulty and will have to listen to a succession of representatives, De Gaulle, Franco, and others. He did not wish to waste time listening to complaints but wished to deal with the problems which the three Heads of Government had come here to settle."[27] This marked pretty much the end of the Yugoslav question at Potsdam.

As noted before, however, an agreed agenda is important only to the extent that the parties feel constrained to observe the rule that one ought to adhere to it. In multilateral negotiation this rule is more difficult to violate than is the case in two-party meetings. Furthermore, partial agreement is harder to reverse in multilateral negotiation, since all the parties would have to consent to the change. Hence, the ordering of issues tends to be more important than in a bilateral conference.

In the Paris Peace Conference of 1919, the British war aims were dealt with at the beginning, and Clemenceau was criticized for being tardy in securing the French demands. But as John Maynard Keynes pointed out (in his biographical sketches of Clemenceau, Lloyd George, and Woodrow Wilson), the more modest British aims served to accustom the President to the controversial French demands. Furthermore, this order of procedure also laid Lloyd George "open to the charge, whenever he seemed too critical of French demands, that, having first secured every conceivable thing that he wanted himself, he was now ready with characteristic treachery to abandon his undertakings to his French comrades. In the atmosphere of Paris this seemed a much more potent taunt than it really was."[28]

An accentuation of this tactic is the *last-minute demand*, which a party presents in a multilateral conference only after all the other outstanding issues have been settled and the agreement is ready for signing. If the other parties are anxious to preserve and

---

[27] *The Conference of Berlin (Potsdam) 1945*, II, 127–29.
[28] John Maynard Keynes, *Essays in Biography* (London: Rupert Hart-Davis, 1951), p. 37.

conclude the agreement reached, they may feel forced to give in. At the end of the 1954 Geneva Conference on Indochina, the Cambodians waited until last, after the French, the Chinese, and all the other parties had practically settled the agreements on Laos and Vietnam. Anthony Eden recalled that he, Molotov, and Mendès-France, already exhausted from negotiating all the other settlements, had to hold a long meeting with the Cambodians and the Viet Minh. "It was a gruelling session. At two o'clock on the morning of the 21st [of July], after hard bargaining and some surprising last-minute concessions by Molotov, we succeeded in resolving the remaining differences between them."[29]

The government whose demands are dealt with at the end of a conference does not, of course, always gain. If it cannot convincingly threaten to choose no-agreement, its demands may be left unsatisfied, particularly if it should come under pressure at home not to become responsible for a breakdown in the negotiations. This seems to have happened to the Dutch when the detailed agricultural accords were settled in Brussels in December, 1963. After the other Common Market countries had accepted in part the proposal of the Commission and in part agreed to modify this proposal here and there, the Dutch still held on to a position that differed from the "focal point" created by the Commission proposal. Unfortunately, the disagreement was about the unlofty subject of the price difference between butter and margarine. When it came to the showdown, the Dutch government did not want to become responsible (as the French negotiators skillfully made it appear) for holding up the progress of Europe because of the price of margarine.[30]

More important perhaps than the ordering of issues is the linking of separable issues into *package deals* and *tie-ins*. In a package deal a party proposes simultaneously to settle several issues that are considered part of the agreement under negotiation. In a tie-in a party introduces an issue considered extraneous by the opponent and offers to accept a certain settlement provided this extraneous issue will also be settled to its satisfaction. For example, in 1961 the new American administration offered the Russians a package

[29] *Full Circle*, p. 159.
[30] *Le Monde*, Dec. 24, 1963, p. 1.

deal to settle some of the important outstanding issues of the test ban; whereas in the summer of 1963 Khrushchev first wanted a tie-in between a partial test ban and a nonaggression pact.

The time to propose a package deal is when your opponent fears that he may not get his way on an issue of particular interest to him unless he concedes you something in return. If you are willing to give in on the first issue anyhow, you might as well tie it together with another issue where you could make some gains. There was an interesting incident at the Potsdam Conference which suggests that President Truman may have missed an opportunity for a package deal in which he could have made his consent to the new Western frontiers of Poland conditional on Soviet concessions on German reparations. Truman and Churchill, after all, did accept the Polish frontiers that Stalin had asked for. Before this issue was settled, however, President Truman made a remark which Stalin seems to have misunderstood as a hinted proposal for a package deal. Stating that the German occupation zones should not be changed in favor of Poland, Truman argued that "any other course will make reparations very difficult, particularly if part of the German territory is gone before agreement is reached on what reparations should be." According to the minutes of this meeting, Stalin replied "that the Soviet Union was not afraid of the reparations question and would if necessary renounce them." Instead of exploring whether Stalin was indeed willing to make a package deal Truman simply added "that the United States would get no reparations anyhow. This made no difference. We were trying to keep from paying more, as we did before [after World War I?]."[31]

The opposite of a tie-in is to carve an issue out of a larger context, leaving the related issues unsettled. This involves certain risks, however. The related issues may be settled by default because postponing them may make a temporary arrangement permanent or the limited settlement may create a strong precedent for the issues which have been left out. In addition, by settling one issue in isolation, the negotiator may surrender his leverage for obtaining a satisfactory settlement of the other issues—the opportunity for a package deal will be permanently lost.

[31] *The Conference of Berlin (Potsdam) 1945,* II, 209.

Excluding underground tests from the nuclear test-ban treaty surely facilitated agreement. But until the summer of 1963 Khrushchev vigorously opposed this separation of issues. He must have realized that once a partial treaty had been signed, the Western powers would feel under much less pressure to accept his minimal detection arrangements for banning underground tests.

Apart from avoiding disputes that are hard to resolve, the separation of issues may make it easier for both parties to offer concessions. If the issue appears to be isolated, the terms on which it is settled will not create "focal points" that might affect the outcome of other disputes.[32]

[32] For a stimulating discussion that stresses the advantages of separating issues, see Roger Fisher, "Fractionating Conflict," in *International Conflict and Behavioral Science,* ed. R. Fisher (New York: Basic Books, 1964).

CHAPTER 12

NEGOTIATING SKILL: EAST AND WEST

IT IS MEANINGFUL TO CONTRAST THE SOVIET STYLE OF NEGOTI-
ation with that of Western governments, for there are enough
unique characteristics to set the two apart. But between the styles
of Western governments the differences are normally overshadowed
by those between individual negotiators. In the current era something like a national style emerges in the West only in a case
such as De Gaulle's France, where the particular style of the man
at the top is executed in detail by a centralized government with
disciplined and experienced officials.

Western diplomats differ of course in their training and cultural
traditions. These differences may find some reflection in their
methods of negotiation, but usually they are not pervasive enough
to produce a distinctly recognizable negotiation style. More important are the differences in government structure determining
the domestic constraints under which each negotiator must operate.
These, however, vary from issue to issue. An example of a somewhat more constant national characteristic is the high sensitivity of
American diplomats to public opinion, which might derive both
from cultural factors and the particular features of American
political life. French diplomats are prone to elaborate historical-
philosophical themes as a background to their negotiating strategies, perhaps because their education puts such stress on the
composition of synthesizing essays. German and American negotiators at times place a greater emphasis on legal aspects than the

diplomats of most other Western countries, probably because of the important role that lawyers play in the conduct of foreign policy in Bonn and Washington.[1]

HOW SHREWD ARE SOVIET NEGOTIATORS?

Soviet foreign policy has been highly successful in the last twenty years, if measured by the expansion of the Communist-controlled area and by Russia's newly won influence in many parts of the world. Yet the combined military and economic strength of the West has remained superior to that of the Communist camp during this same period of expansion. Small wonder that many people think Soviet negotiators are far shrewder and more skillful than their Western opponents and that conferences with the Russians are traps to be avoided rather than opportunities to be sought.[2]

Undoubtedly, Soviet negotiators have certain advantages over their Western adversaries because they are backed by an authoritarian government. Western capitals, and Washington in particular, cannot develop a negotiating position on a major issue without letting the public in one some of the internal controversies. This gives Soviet delegates valuable intelligence about the strength

---

[1] Kenneth W. Thompson stresses this point for the American diplomatic style (*American Diplomacy and Emergent Patterns* [New York: New York University Press, 1962], pp. 37–38). Charles W. Thayer also believes that one can scarcely distinguish different styles of diplomacy among the great powers, except for the Soviet style (*Diplomat* [New York: Harper, 1959], pp. 83–84). Harold Nicolson, however, maintains that there are certain constant characteristics that distinguish the practice of negotiation by such powers as Great Britain, Germany, France, and Italy. As a good Englishman, Nicolson of course finds that the British type of diplomacy "is on the whole the type which is most conducive to the maintenance of peaceful relations"; but as not such a good historian he forgets 1914 and the 1930s when he writes that the British diplomatist "almost always succeeds" (*Diplomacy*, pp. 144, 131). Raymond Aron contrasts the methods by which the British and the French negotiate with the United States: the British try to influence American policies through discussion and public opinion, the French through obstructions (i.e., the threat of no-agreement) (*Paix et Guerre entre les Nations* [Paris: Calmann-Lévy, 1962], pp. 461–63).

[2] Apart from additions and changes, this section has appeared as an article in the *New York Times*, Dec. 9, 1963 (Magazine section). © 1962 by The New York Times Company. Reprinted by permission.

with which Western positions are held. Moscow, of course, permits no leaks about any differences that might exist between, say, Gromyko and Malinovsky over how to approach the West on disarmament or on Berlin. Its fall-back positions remain secret, not only from newspapermen but frequently also from its own delegations. Western diplomats often complain about this wall of secrecy that makes it so difficult to find out how firmly a Soviet position is held and what sort of modifications in the Western position might lead to agreement.

Moreover, Soviet diplomats need not feel constrained by domestic public opinion as much as Westerners do. The public in Communist countries is normally poorly informed about negotiations. Knowing their lack of influence on foreign affairs, Soviet citizens hardly attempt to make their views heard—or even to formulate a view of their own. This permits Soviet diplomats to choose their negotiating tactics with greater freedom. Only in the long run, perhaps, do Communist leaders require some domestic backing for their foreign policy.

Soviet negotiators enjoy a further advantage in that they can support their long-term strategy and day-to-day tactics with fully coordinated propaganda machinery, whereas Western countries speak always with many voices. Frequently at conferences the Russians delight in citing statements by Western opposition leaders, scientists, or journalists to refute a position of a Western government.

In short, Soviet negotiators seem to command all that is required for carrying out the most cunning strategies: complete secrecy in planning, freedom from domestic interference in execution, and the coordinated support of a powerful authoritarian regime. Given all these advantages, have Soviet negotiators really shown proportionate cunning and skill? An examination of their record, comparing some of their opportunities with the results they actually obtained, is in order.

The Marshall Plan, to take one case, will long be remembered as one of the most successful and farsighted programs of American foreign policy. What is almost forgotten is that the Russians were initially invited to participate. After Marshall's historic speech in June, 1947, British Foreign Secretary Bevin quickly seized the initiative, met with his French colleague Bidault, and asked Moscow to join in a conference at which Europe would work out its answer to the American offer. Stalin sent Molotov to Paris with a delegation of eighty-nine aides.

What did the skillful Soviet negotiator make of this decisive opportunity? He did not try to postpone West European recovery and European-American cooperation by more than five days!

True, Bevin made it clear that he would not be delayed by Soviet stalling. But why did Molotov make it so easy for Bevin? Why did he reject outright the American offer for a coordinated recovery program, instead of accepting it in principle and then discussing the details later? Why did he fail to exploit the suggestion made by some groups in the West that the United Nations should play the leading role in European recovery? Or he could have shown some interest when Bidault (conscious of pressure on his government by the powerful French Communist Party) made a last-minute effort to save the conference. With reluctant agreement from Bevin, Bidault's proposal attempted to meet some of the Soviet objections by emphasizing that the organization for European recovery would not interfere with a country's internal affairs. Yet Molotov would not give an inch, and the conference broke up. Thus Russia lost its chance to delay or influence an integrated West European recovery.

To realize the enormity of this Russian blunder, we must recall that the implementation of the Marshall Plan was not assured at that time. On the one hand, U.S. Congressional support was far from certain. On the other hand, there was considerable European backing for Russia's participation. Prior to the conference which brought Molotov to Paris, an editorial in the London *Times* said: "The strongest argument which could be placed in Mr. Marshall's hands for delivery to Congress would be the firm hope of a sound integration of the whole European economy effected by all the countries which are to benefit from American aid, and led by Britain, France, and the Soviet Union." Similarly, the *Economist* proposed that the United Nations Economic Commission for Europe be used—"in spite of its shortcomings"—as the machinery to administer Marshall aid: "Might it not therefore be the course of wisdom to reach a compromise between the Russian and the Western views?"[3]

Khrushchev showed himself an equally unskillful negotiator with his tactics on the Berlin issue, though his mistakes were of a different kind from Stalin's and Molotov's. As noted before, Khrushchev spoiled his bargaining reputation by repeating again and again his threat to sign a peace treaty with the Communist regime in East Germany, each time specifying the period within which he would do so but doing nothing each time his bluff was called. An explicit threat with a time limit can be a potent weapon; however, prudent negotiators use it only when they are fully prepared to carry it out or are certain that they will not be challenged. A time limit makes it all too apparent if they are caught bluffing, and this damages the credibility of their threats in the future. History recounts few examples of a senior statesman who squandered and blunted his power to use such threats so completely as Khrushchev did.

This was not Khrushchev's only blunder. When he broke up the summit meeting in May, 1960, he spoiled a unique opportunity to extract concessions from the United States. Only a few days before he flew to Paris to meet with Eisenhower, Macmillan, and De Gaulle, he was able to denounce the United States roundly for the U-2 flights, causing major repercussions in the whole world and skillfully trapping the U.S. government in a lie. On the first day in Paris, Khrushchev played his cards well; with righteous indignation he asked for an apology from the President, which he must have known he could not get. But he did get the promise

[3] The *Times* (London), June 24, 1947; the *Economist*, June 28, 1947. A French diplomat noted in his diary just a few days before Molotov's final *nyet:* "With a little Machiavellism, the Soviets ought to . . . insert themselves in the preparatory plan because their accession would immediately provoke its failure" (Jacques Dumaine, *Quai d'Orsay: 1945–51* [Paris: Julliard, 1955], p. 204). And two years later McGeorge Bundy reflected: "How much of the original impetus of the plan would have survived if Molotov had really sat down at Paris, deployed the enormous retinue he took with him (and one still wonders what they were doing there if this notion was not considered) and cooperated in form but not in fact?" In the mood of 1949 Bundy goes on to ask: "And if we are grateful, are we perhaps also safe for the present, from the effects of a policy of deceptive friendliness by Russia?" ("The Test of Yalta," *Foreign Affairs* [July, 1949], pp. 627, 629.)

that the U-2 flights would be discontinued, while Macmillan and De Gaulle pleaded with him to start the summit meeting.

What a reversal of roles, after Khrushchev had been calling for a summit conference so long! What a chance for Khrushchev to drop the demand for apology grudgingly, as if making a generous concession, and then to confront the Western statesmen and ask for reciprocal concessions!

Khrushchev chose another tactic. He put on his rambunctious show in Paris, throwing away his dignity and his trump card. In the end it was, in a sense, he who apologized—two days later in East Berlin. To the glum East German Communists who had expected the long-announced peace treaty, he said the existing situation would have to be preserved until another summit meeting could take place.

Later, Khrushchev hinted that he had anticipated the failure of the Paris summit meeting but that his colleagues wanted him to go all the same. Perhaps Khrushchev realized that his earlier expectations were too optimistic and that the Western powers would not abandon Berlin completely. But this was a poor reason for bringing back from Paris even less than he could have gotten. Had he chosen a shrewder tactic, generously "forgiving" the U-2 incident, the Western powers could not have broken up the meeting without making at least some concessions—perhaps quite substantial ones.

According to a recent Soviet handbook on diplomacy:

[Communist diplomacy] is invariably successful in exposing the aggressive intentions of the imperialist governments. . . . It does this from the tribunes of diplomatic conferences, in official diplomatic statements and documents, as well as in the press. [This] is one of the important methods of socialist diplomacy by means of which it mobilizes democratic social opinion and the masses of people all over the world against the aggressive policies of the imperialist governments.[4]

Yet, when faced with some unusual opportunity for mobilizing "the masses of people all over the world," Soviet diplomacy is not "invariably successful."

[4] *Diplomaticheskii Slovar* (Moscow: State Publishing House for Political Literature, 1960), I, 466.

Along came the issue of atmospheric nuclear tests in the spring of 1962, for example. For the previous six months the United States had confined itself to underground testing, although the Soviet Union had resumed nuclear tests in the atmosphere the summer before. But in March, 1962, the American government decided the self-imposed handicap was too great, and President Kennedy announced twelve days before the disarmament confer-ence convened that the United States would soon have to resume nuclear testing in the atmosphere. He promised, however, that if the Soviet Union would accept a treaty with appropriate controls, "sign it before the latter part of April, and apply it immediately . . . , there would be no need for our tests to begin." Some people feared that the Russians might take advantage of that offer and make some last-minute concessions which would trap the American government into further negotiations whose only result would be postponement of its tests.

As it turned out, the Soviets were far too clumsy. Whatever their real aims, they failed to delay the U.S. tests, they did not inflict a propaganda defeat on the West, and they did not get a control-free ban against underground nuclear testing. Although at the time they probably preferred to remain free to resume their own tests later in 1962 rather than to commit themselves at once to test cessation under a treaty, they must surely have been interested in making propaganda gains and in increasing dissension between the United States and neutralist nations. For this, they had some real opportunities.

They could have encouraged the interest the British negotiators showed in a further reduction of the inspection system. "We are ready to negotiate upon any proposals for an adequate minimum of international verification," said the British Foreign Secretary Lord Home. "We are flexible and ready for reasonable com-promise." Nyet—no international verification at all, was the Soviet reply.

Opportunity for the Soviets to make some political and propa-ganda gains became even greater when the eight neutral nations proposed their compromise plan for a test ban. That plan essentially accepted the Soviet position that there should be no foreign in-spectors in Russia but added an "international commission" to evaluate the data from national systems. The commission could, in a vaguely defined way, call on a suspected country to furnish more information and *perhaps* arrange an on-site inspection. Obviously, the United States had some serious reservations about the proposal but refrained from rejecting it.

At that juncture, Premier Khrushchev could have announced dramatically that he was not only ready to accept the neutrals' proposal but also that he would consent to combine it with the "best elements" of the Western draft, provided President Kennedy kept his word and did not start atmospheric tests, now that a treaty could be signed "before the latter part of April." Had the President rejected this outright, beginning the tests a few days later, he would have met with a worldwide storm of protest and probably with serious disagreement from Macmillan. On the other hand, had the President postponed the tests, Khrushchev would not have been committed to any treaty he did not want. As the Western negotiators were urgently trying to nail down a specific treaty text (while the expensive task force in the Pacific was kept waiting), the Soviet negotiators could have become evasive or simply have stuck to the neutrals' proposal until American patience ran out. In the end, the United States might have been forced to resume atmospheric tests with a propaganda loss far greater than it actually suffered in April, 1962.

The Soviet negotiators were not imaginative enough to try for these almost riskless gains. To be sure, they urged negotiations on the basis of the neutrals' proposal, but they refused to accept obligatory international inspection (although, without detailed specifications, "international inspection" is just a vague phrase). And while they made some threats to discourage the American tests, they failed to couple them with a dramatic offer.

Another tactical mistake of Soviet negotiators is that they often fail to exploit an "extortionary" demand before it has become obsolete. After World War II they maintained their opposition to the cession of the Saar to France, apparently in the hope that France would have to ransom the Saar from the Soviet veto at a high political price. As late as 1947 it looked as if this tactic would work. Secretary Byrnes expected that: "Russia will maintain its opposition to the cession of the Saar until the final hours and then seek to secure, in exchange for agreement, French support on some other question."[5] The Soviet negotiators missed this final hour. Instead they unwittingly made possible the transfer of the Saar to Germany and thus contributed to Franco-German reconciliation.

Related to the mistake of letting an "extortionary" demand become obsolete is the failure to revise an unacceptable demand in time to make gains through a compromise. For example, in 1945 Stalin faced Turkey with a double demand. As we have seen, he not only requested a revision of the Montreux Convention but also asked for a slice of Turkish territory and a Russian base in the Straits. Originally, the United States was willing to support a revision of the Montreux Convention in Russia's favor, Great Britain was ready to go along, and Turkey would probably not have been able to resist by herself.

But Stalin's additional demands for a slice of Turkish territory and a base stirred up British and American opposition. As a result, Stalin failed at the Potsdam Conference to consolidate any gain regarding the Straits. All he obtained was American and British consent to "recognize" the need for revision of the Montreux Convention. It was agreed that the next step should be the subject of direct conversations between the three powers and Turkey. But then in 1946 Stalin made the fatal mistake of renewing *all* his demands against Turkey. This aroused American opposition, and a year later Turkey received full American support under the Truman Doctrine. When in 1953 the Russians at last withdrew their demands for Turkish territory and a base in the Straits, what good was this belated concession? Turkey was now firmly in NATO, and the Western support for changing the Montreux Convention had long since evaporated.

The mistake of clinging to unacceptable demands for too long is related to the self-defeating way in which the Russians sometimes negotiate a tie-in. The tactic of a tie-in will not work if the opponent is asked to surrender more than he expects to receive.

[5] *Speaking Frankly*, p. 170.

When the French negotiators at Brussels linked their consent to the Second Stage of the Common Market with an agreement on agriculture, they managed this tie-in successfully, because the sacrifices they asked of the Germans for the common agricultural policy were not such as to outweigh German interest in continued progress of the Common Market. But when Russian negotiators tried to obtain more influence in the United Nations Secretariat, they totally mismanaged the tie-in tactic. As discussed earlier, they tried to tie their consent to a successor for Dag Hammarskjöld to their demand for a "troika." A troika, however, would have canceled all interest the United States and other United Nations members had in replacing Hammarskjöld, whereas a more modest Soviet demand (such as for a "troika" of Deputy Secretaries) might have been accepted, particularly if it had found favor with the uncommitted nations. (In fact, the Western nations did accept some changes in the UN Secretariat in favor of the Afro-Asians.)

We can find some common elements in the shortcomings of Soviet negotiators. They often ask for a whole loaf where they could get half a loaf—and wind up with nothing. They fritter away the credibility of their threats and the value of their promises, the two key tools for every diplomat. They cannot find the right dosage of demands and inducements. Curiously, they walk out of negotiations when they should stay in, while at other times they keep on talking in violation of their own deadlines. They insult those whose good will they ought to cultivate, and become self-righteous and rigid where they ought to be ingratiating and inventive. They fight furious battles against an empty phrase or a vague principle, although they are past masters at twisting the meaning of words and at utilizing agreements-in-principle for their own ends.

In short, the shrewd and skillful negotiating style of the Soviet government turns out to be a myth. However, Western diplomats should not be too sanguine about Soviet blunders, for many of these blunders are simply a failure to take advantage of Western vulnerabilities. On such occasions the East-West performance resembles that of two novice chess players. If one player leaves his queen unprotected and the other fails to take it, neither can be called a master.

Moreover, the very idiosyncrasies of Soviet negotiators that account for their blunders can also work to their advantage. If they are careless in having their bluffs called, they are also carefree in trying to gain through bluffing. If they miss many a chance to obligate the West by being a little more generous, they correspondingly feel no obligations to be generous where it would hurt them. And if they do not have the French dexterity in managing a tie-in so as to come out ahead, their rigidity also prevents them from becoming entangled in an exchange where they are left holding the short end. It is true, sometimes they are so stubborn that they cling to an unacceptable demand until they have missed the opportunity for a profitable compromise. But at other times, they are stubborn enough to repeat what seems to be an unacceptable demand until the opponent has changed his evaluations and accepts all or most of what they asked for. Sometimes, certainly, they are too obtuse to force Western governments into a substantial concession by beguiling Western opinion with a small concession of their own. At other times, nonetheless, this obtuseness saves them from disaster, when they can salvage a crucial position only by defying public opinion throughout the world.

Contrary to a popular image in the West, Soviet negotiators are bold rather than shrewd, brazen rather than cunning. It is not the skills attributed to a Talleyrand that the West must fear from Communist diplomats, nor are the Russians brilliant disciples of Machiavelli. What the West must beware of is the brazenness that allowed Stalin to negotiate for his East European empire while the Germans were at the gates of Moscow, the boldness that permitted Khrushchev to make this empire "unnegotiable" while trying to negotiate for Communist control over West Berlin and for the retention of his troops (if not missiles) in Cuba.

WESTERN TALENTS

Dante's description of Heaven may strike us as somewhat lackluster and contrived in comparison with the rich detail and vividness of his Hell. Whoever has tried to describe Heaven will understand why even a Dante might fail. Certainly, for as mundane a topic as negotiating skill, Hell is much easier to paint than Heaven.

Perhaps the faults of negotiators can be more readily identified than their virtues, because in diplomacy failure usually makes news while success is undramatic. Perhaps the weaknesses of our negotiators stand out more sharply because they are spiced with our frustrations, whereas their strengths seem so bland since they are taken for granted. Perhaps the Faustian devil in all our souls, who makes us sooner tire of one page of praise than of a hundred pages of criticism, beguiles us into thinking that in any comparison of virtues and vices, the vices alone tell an interesting story.

It seems natural to evaluate the diplomatic talents and faults of Western governments primarily by comparing them with those of the Soviet government, because among modern negotiating styles the principal distinction is that between East and West. Actually, the Western fortes show up mainly in negotiations with other Western governments but are of little value with Communist opponents; and conversely, the Western faults are harmful in dealing with Communist diplomats but less serious in negotiations within the West. That is to say, the talents of Western diplomacy are largely confined to negotiations with more or less friendly nations, whereas its weaknesses show up in coping with an adversary.

An important talent of Western diplomats that Communists largely lack is the ability to negotiate within the framework of an international organization and to take advantage of international institutions for settling disputes. Through various alliances, Western nations are able to coordinate their activities and to maintain an effective unity in policy execution, even though they might never be fully agreed on all the details of a policy or on a unified doctrine. In fact, it is precisely because they do not insist on a unity of dogma that they can negotiate their differences so as to avoid both schism and *diktat*. The Warsaw Pact cannot embrace Yugoslavia, and for all practical purposes it now excludes Albania. But NATO was able to survive the Suez crisis, it has lost neither Greece nor Turkey so far in spite of their quarrel over Cyprus, it contains such diverse nations as Norway and Portugal, and unless Paris and Washington descend to the negotiating methods used between Mao Tse-tung and Khrushchev, NATO will also be able to weather the American-French dispute.

Western diplomats are skillful also in dealing with conflicts in isolation. Within an alliance tied by an intimate fabric of military, commercial, financial, and cultural relations, they understand how to negotiate about a conflict in one of these spheres without impairing their relationship in the other spheres. This means they must be willing not to bring in other matters even when this might strengthen their case.

Related to the adeptness with which Western diplomats negotiate within international organizations is their capacity for utilizing rules of accommodation. Many rules are observed among Western allies as a matter of routine, thus preserving a tradition of reciprocation that is both efficient and profitable in the long run. Perhaps their familiarity with constitutional procedures in domestic affairs helps Western officials to work with and benefit from an accommodating style in international affairs. Of course, this presumes a mutual and lasting willingness to use restraint in making gains at the expense of the other parties. When this restraint breaks down, all the short-run accommodations nevertheless proffered become gratuitous losses.

Negotiation in this *esprit communautaire* is greatly facilitated through legal arrangements which set limits to the parties' expectations and thus to the range of conflict over which they bargain. It is also helped by common institutions that can take on a mediating function or provide experts to settle terms of agreement through the "deductive method." And as Jean Monnet pointed out, the life of institutions is longer than the life of people, so that institutions can, if they are well constructed, accumulate and transmit the wisdom of succeeding generations.[6] In the case of negotiations between France and Germany, for example, the special relationship based on the rapport between De Gaulle and Adenauer is already a thing of the past. But the collaboration based on the common institutions in Brussels has survived, and in the long run it may well turn out to be the principal driving force for Franco-German unity.

[6] Jean Monnet, *Les Etats-Unis d'Europe Ont Commencé* (Paris: Laffont, 1955), p. 22.

As with Soviet diplomacy, however, the idiosyncracies that account for Western negotiating skill are, on other occasions, responsible for Western weaknesses. Most of the Western talents
cannot weather highly antagonistic situations.

WESTERN WEAKNESSES

The following inventory of Western weaknesses is illustrated
mostly with examples from American and British diplomacy.
Perhaps other Western negotiators—be they French or Finnish,
Turkish or Italian—might protest that this portrait does not fit
them. But since the diplomacy of the United States (and to a
somewhat lesser extent that of Great Britain) plays such a leading
role, American or British weaknesses are certainly highly relevant
for the West.

LETTING THE OPPONENT DETERMINE THE ISSUES

In a news conference on July 12, 1962, Secretary of State Rusk
complained, when talking about the Berlin issue, that "the other
side seems not to want to talk about a great many things which are
of interest to us, the permanent peace settlement for Germany
as a whole, for example, or arrangements with respect to Berlin as
a whole, because they have simply said that certain matters are
just not discussable." One of the newspaper correspondents present
thought he had detected something new. He started fishing for
more: "You have now reintroduced the elements of an all-German
settlement and of a Berlin accord that involves all of Berlin. Is
this perhaps an interesting outcome of your recent European trip?"
But the Secretary retreated quickly: "No, I didn't intend to make
that much news with that remark. I was reflecting on the general
attitude of the West over a considerable period of time. . . . The
West has been trying to . . . find a permanent satisfactory German settlement which would bring peace to Central Europe. But
that has not been pursued because, as you will recall, I did say
that was the kind of thing that the other side has not been willing
to discuss. They say, 'This is not discussable. Now let's talk about
your position here in West Berlin.' "[7]

[7] *Department of State Bulletin,* July 30, 1962, pp. 172–73.

And what does the West do? It talks about its position in West Berlin and agrees that East Berlin and Eastern Europe are not discussable.

It is, of course, often impossible to prevent the opponent from making an issue out of something that one would prefer to have left alone. And if the opponent can make no-agreement unpleasant enough, it may even be desirable to negotiate about such issues. But this does not mean that one must abstain from raising other issues where the tables would be turned.

The neutralization of Laos was an unavoidable issue. Because the Communists committed more force than the United States was willing to commit, they could have achieved an outcome favorable to them without an agreement. Likewise, the neutralization of South Vietnam has become an issue for the United States, in part because of the difficulty of achieving a military victory and in part because of De Gaulle's attempt to gain influence at the expense of his American ally. Yet the West scarcely tries to make an issue out of the neutralization of North Vietnam. During the Laos Conference of 1961–62, the neutralization of North Vietnam was never seriously raised as an issue, and in connection with the possibility of a negotiated settlement for South Vietnam it was raised only belatedly and rather gingerly. For example in his press conference of February 1, 1964, President Johnson said that if there was a proposal from any side to neutralize both North and South Vietnam, "the United States would consider it sympathetically." Why not *make* a proposal for a neutral North Vietnam and press for it?

Similarly, it may be impossible for the United States to prevent the notion of returning Okinawa to Japanese control from persisting as at least a latent issue. There seems to be no need, however, to accept as a law of nature the point of view that the return of the Soviet-held Kuril Islands to Japan is no longer an issue.

To compare the case of the Panama Canal Zone with that of the formerly Finnish port of Petsamo is instructive. In both cases there is the same overwhelming disparity of strength between the country in possession of each of the areas (the United States and the Soviet Union) and the country that claims or might claim the area (Panama and Finland, respectively). In both cases the country in possession acquired permanent sovereign rights through a clear-cut treaty (although Stalin showed more foresight than Teddy Roosevelt in not leaving Finland "titular sovereignty" over Petsamo). And the difference in the history of the two treaties is not such that the renegotiation of one should be an obvious issue whereas the renegotiation of the other is never mentioned. The Soviet-Finnish treaty ended a war, it is true, in which Finland had joined in an attack on the Soviet Union. But the Soviet Union had attacked Finland and taken territory from her only fifteen months earlier, whereas Panama owes its existence as a nation independent of Colombia to Theodore Roosevelt's intervention.

It can be said, of course, that little Finland is anxious not to make an issue out of the return of Petsamo (although without this port Finland has no access to the Arctic Sea), because she would rather live in peace with Russia and because she has not the faintest hope of ever getting Petsamo back anyway. But this is precisely the point. The Finns know that Soviet negotiators would not permit them to make an issue out of Petsamo;[8] the Panamanians know that it is quite profitable to make an issue out of their treaty with the United States.

The tendency to let the opponent determine the issue shows itself not only in the selection of subjects for negotiation but also in the terminology adopted and the concepts used. This may be a more serious consequence, for it can affect the thinking of negotiators without their being aware of it.

An interesting illustration is the development of the concept "colonialism." Western negotiators talk and think of "decolonization" only in reference to areas in Africa, Asia, or Latin America that have been colonized by a Western country. When referring to Eastern Europe, on the other hand, they talk in terms of "stabilization," or at best "liberalization," and it is a rather rare occasion when they bring up the very recent colonization of Tibet or the nineteenth-century colonization by Russia of vast areas in Central Asia. Western diplomats maintain that it would be futile to make an issue out of Tibet or Uzbekistan or to compare the

---

[8] Actually the Russians did relent on other issues. For example, in 1962 the Finns succeeded in getting permission to lease the Saimaa Canal, which they had lost in the peace treaty with Russia.

desirability of self-determination for Angola with that for East Germany. The Western effort to win the support and friendship of Afro-Asian nations, it is argued, would not be helped by raising such issues, because the Afro-Asians do not wish to become involved in the East-West "cold war" but are only interested in those manifestations of colonialism that are part of their own experience.

Western negotiators who think this way seem to forget that whether or not a subject seems relevant to one's own experience depends on how it is presented. When the U.S. government consented in December, 1962, to the removal of the Hungarian question from the UN agenda and to having the position of a UN Representative on Hungary abolished, it merely intended to abandon what seemed like a useless irritant against the Soviet Union. But unintentionally, it confirmed the view of the Afro-Asian nations that colonialism in Hungary had nothing to do with the colonialism they were fighting.

Mental associations are formed by repetition. If the West consents to the removal of the Hungarian question from the UN agenda (which has a long and growing list of other colonial issues) and almost never raises such issues as the fate of the Asian Muslims in Soviet Uzbekistan, it teaches the Afro-Asians to associate "colonialism" only with those issues in which it is the accused party.

SHY ABOUT COUNTER-DEMANDS

Western negotiators assume that it would be clearly improper not to be flexible. It is widely felt in the West that concessions ought to be reciprocated and that compromise is the ideal way of reaching agreement. At the same time, Western governments (except France under De Gaulle) are reluctant to refuse negotiation if confronted with a redistribution demand. However, if one engages in redistribution negotiations while observing the rule of flexibility, there is only one way of avoiding a net loss: to make counter-demands. But this, Western negotiators are reluctant to do.

Counter-demands are requests for a redistribution in one's favor, either on an issue related to the one raised by the opponent or possibly on a quite unrelated issue. They are essential, not only to permit oneself to be flexible without incurring a net loss, but also to protect oneself against mediators who simply split the difference between the opposing proposals—as most mediators are wont to do. How, for example, would U Thant have mediated the Berlin negotiations? "There are various other issues like Berlin," he said on December 2, 1962, "on which it may become imperative to reach solutions on the basis of compromise and the principle of give-and-take on both sides."

On those rare occasions when Western negotiators do confront the opponent with a counter-demand, they tend to convey a lack of conviction—almost as if they acted with a bad conscience. They do not push the counter-demand with the same vigor that the opponent puts behind his initial demand, nor do they repeat it anywhere nearly as often.

For example, after the Soviet demands against West Berlin in November, 1958, the Western allies, in their notes of December 31, 1958, hinted at a counter-demand for the areas now in East Germany which were evacuated by the Western troops:

The Soviet Union has directly and through its [East German] puppet regime . . . consolidated its hold over the large areas which the Western Alliance relinquished to it. It now demands that the Western Alliance should relinquish the positions in Berlin which in effect were the *quid pro quo*. The three Western Powers are there as occupying powers, and they are not prepared to relinquish the rights . . . , just as they assume the Soviet Union is not willing now to restore to the occupancy of the Western Powers the position which they had won in Mecklenburg, Saxony, Thuringia and Anhalt and which, under the agreements, of 1944 and 1945, they turned over for occupation by the Soviet Union.[9]

But little has been heard of this potential counter-demand since.

Similarly, after the Berlin wall went up, the Western allies occasionally suggested that freedom of circulation should be restored in all Berlin in accordance with the Four-Power Agreements. But this has remained a wish rather than a demand, and even the wish was quickly suppressed when it met with the expected Soviet rebuff.

[9] U.S. note to the Soviet Union of Dec. 31, 1958 (*Department of State Bulletin*, Jan. 19, 1959, p. 79).

The reluctance to make counter-demands is not confined to East-West negotiations. The United States made no counter-demands, for example, in the negotiations with Panama after the riots in the Canal Zone in January, 1964. It is true that the incident touching off these riots can be blamed on the American side (the refusal of American students to observe the U.S.-Panamanian agreement on flags). But afterwards, mobs from Panama attacked the Canal Zone, and sniper fire from *outside* the Zone caused casualties among U.S. forces. As President Johnson pointed out, the role of the U.S. forces "was one of resisting aggression, and not committing it."[10]

Resisting aggression? The negotiations were opened with Panamanian charges of U.S. aggression, and the United States made no demands of its own. One wonders whether American interests might not have been better protected, and the negotiations actually facilitated, had the U.S. government immediately come forth with a series of counter-demands. For example, Washington might have requested that Panama take steps to prevent a recurrence of mob attacks on the Canal Zone; it might have raised the question of compensation for the property destroyed; and it might have hinted that the violence by Panamanian mobs made it inadvisable to offer further concessions, inasmuch as the flag incident would not have occurred had the United States refused to accept Panamanian flags in the Zone a number of years ago. In short, Washington could have assumed the posture of the aggrieved party instead of meekly accepting the role of the accused. By abstaining from any counter-demands, the U.S. government might actually have done a disservice to the Panamanian government, because for domestic reasons the Panamanian government needed to win concessions from the United States, and counter-demands would have allowed Washington to concede more.

Western negotiators give various justifications for not raising counter-demands or for abandoning them so meekly. Counter-demands, it is said, would widen the area of conflict. This is of course true when they are first raised. Indeed, it is the purpose of counter-demands to prevent the area of conflict from lying entirely on one's

---

[10] President Johnson's statement of Jan. 23, 1964.

own side of the fence. But later, counter-demands may facilitate agreement by putting some pressure on the opponent and permitting greater flexibility in one's own position.

Another justification for avoiding counter-demands, which is used primarily in the United States, is that Congress and the public would object if the counter-demand were later dropped in exchange for the withdrawal of the opponent's original demand. This justification is weak for three reasons. First, effective negotiation requires a willingness to become committed and to occasionally absorb the cost of breaking one's commitment. Second, the objections to dropping counter-demands can often be avoided by identifying one's counter-demands as such. Where this is feasible, the public will accept, if not urge, that they be dropped as soon as the opponent withdraws his original demand. Third, there is something disingenuous in arguing that Congress or the public would not accept the withdrawal of counter-demands. Unless the negotiator also refuses to be flexible, he is in fact implying that a concession on a counter-demand would be noticed, whereas a concession at the expense of the status quo could be concealed.

As a result of their shyness about counter-demands, Western negotiators frequently miss opportunities for making tie-ins. (Unlike the counter-demand in redistribution negotiations, which wards off the opponent's demand, the counter-demand in a tie-in is used to gain some objective by making the fulfillment of a demand by the opponent conditional on the fulfillment of one's own demand.)

In the postwar negotiations with the Soviet Union on European problems, the Western powers were anxious to work out a treaty for re-establishing Austria's independence. In 1946 the Western powers and the Soviet Union negotiated the peace treaties with Bulgaria, Romania, Hungary, and Italy, about which the Russians were just as anxious. The Soviet Union wished to conclude peace treaties with the three Balkan states in order to solidify and formalize Communist control, and it wanted a peace treaty with Italy in order to obtain Italian reparations.

While these peace treaties were being negotiated, Secretary Byrnes tried in vain to bring up the Austrian treaty. At the first session of the Council of Foreign Ministers meeting in April,

1946, Byrnes asked that the Austrian question be included on the agenda, but Molotov immediately objected, saying he was not ready to give it consideration at this time. Byrnes tried again in April and at the next session of the Council of Foreign Ministers in June. At this latter session, Molotov contended that it was inadvisable to consider the Austrian treaty because the parties would have their hands full with the treaties under consideration. As Secretary Byrnes recalled in his memoirs, Molotov exclaimed: "May God help us to complete the work on the treaties which are now before us." And then Byrnes continued in his memoirs: "Since it was clear that Mr. Molotov was lending little assistance, I could only reply that I hoped, indeed, that God would do so."[11]

But this was not the only reply Byrnes could have given. He could have firmly refused to discuss any other treaties unless the Austrian treaty were included. Since the Soviet Union still had considerable interest in these other treaties, the tie-in might have worked.

A more recent example of neglecting a tie-in is provided by the British negotiations with Egypt in 1954, concerning the Egyptian demand for the withdrawal of British troops from the Suez Canal area ahead of the time specified in the Anglo-Egyptian treaty. Surely, the British negotiators must have thought about the possibility that Egypt might want to nationalize the Canal. Yet, they did not attempt to tie guaranties against nationalization to the withdrawal of their troops. They were of course under American pressure to give in to the Egyptian demand, and even if they had obtained an Egyptian promise against nationalization, it might later have been broken. Nonetheless, by tying in their counter-demand at that time, they might have accomplished one of two things. With an Egyptian promise against nationalization, British intervention against a breach of this promise would have been easier to justify at home and harder to oppose by the United States (and Egypt, knowing this, might well have kept the promise). If, on the other hand, Egypt had refused to give such a promise, the British-Egyptian conflict would have come to a head at a time far more favorable to Britain: there would have been no need to attempt a landing of troops in the Suez Canal Zone, for the troops were still there.

[11] *Speaking Frankly*, p. 164.

AFRAID OF MAKING UNACCEPTABLE PROPOSALS

Related to the shyness about counter-demands is the aversion of Western negotiators to push proposals that they consider unacceptable to the opponent. This aversion applies to major positions only, not to proposals on some details within a larger position. On details, Western diplomats of course frequently make demands which they expect to be unacceptable—only in order to have room for concessions when seeking a compromise.

As noted before, Communist negotiators are more willing to exert themselves for unattainable goals. Or perhaps they are more aware of the fact that what the opponent will ultimately accept is in part a function of what is being proposed to him. Sometimes they even admit that they do not expect their proposals to be accepted. Khrushchev once wrote to Macmillan: "In sending this message [suggesting a German peace treaty and withdrawal of foreign forces], I ask myself the question, what will be your reaction? Will you accept our proposals? I will tell you frankly, I have no belief in this because I do not believe in the wisdom of those circles which now determine the policy of the Western powers. It seems that the time is not yet ripe. . . ."[12]

Various reasons may account for the aversion of Western diplomats to unacceptable proposals. They may feel that it would look foolhardy to advance such proposals. They may fear they would needlessly antagonize the opponent. Or they may think that they could be accused of not negotiating "in good faith."

The notion that one should not push unacceptable proposals has for Westerners almost the quality of a moral rule, even where this "moral" way of negotiating comes in conflict with the morality of one's negotiating position. Paradoxically, this rule—far from facilitating negotiation—may sometimes destroy the possibility for negotiating at all. On certain issues, Western diplomats prefer to avoid negotiation altogether because they would either have to push unacceptable proposals or take the initiative in proposing an outcome that would be inferior to no-agreement.

What these Western negotiators overlook is that by refusing to press a certain proposal because it seems unacceptable, they may

[12] Letter to Macmillan of April 12, 1962.

actually make it so or at least maintain it so. They strengthen the opponent's commitment by conveying to him that he is not expected to yield. And they forgo pressures that might erode the opponent's evaluations.

Western diplomats could learn a lesson from their colleagues in the new African states. There are several similarities between the posture of the new African states with regard to their grievances about the Union of South Africa and the posture of the Western powers with regard to their grievances about Eastern Europe. The goals that the Africans favor—abolishing apartheid and wresting Southwest Africa's independence from the Union of South Africa —are now totally unacceptable to the government of South Africa. Likewise, the goals that the Western powers favor in Eastern Europe are now totally unacceptable to Moscow: self-determination in the Soviet Zone of Germany and independence in Eastern Europe such that, say, the Hungarians could choose neutrality as they tried to in 1956. The African states have nowhere near the military and economic powers needed to force the government of South Africa to give in. In the same way, the local populations in East and Central Europe do not have the power to force Moscow to give in (as demonstrated on June 17, 1953, and in October, 1956). If South Africa were to be defeated by a full-scale Soviet intervention, this might bring an East-West war into the heart of Africa. And if the West attempted a full-scale military intervention against Soviet control in Eastern Europe, this, correspondingly, would probably lead to an East-West war in the heart of Europe that might well become nuclear.

The difference between the African negotiators and the Western ones is that the Africans keep pushing day after day their proposals for abolishing apartheid or detaching Southwest Africa from the Union, whereas Western negotiators act in the belief that self-determination for the Soviet Zone of Germany or full independence for Budapest is out of their reach, if not out of the question. The Africans feel confident that the trend of history is in their favor, regardless of the present imbalance in power. The Western powers either do not look for a favorable trend (they settle for "stabilization"), or they hope for internal "liberalization" (a trend which would permit them to continue their passive role). Thus they forget that historical trends are shaped by the expectations of men and that these expectations can be shaped, in part, by pushing unacceptable proposals.

But what about the objection that unacceptable proposals will make a favorable outcome even less likely by provoking the opponent and exacerbating his feelings of hostility? There is, of course, no pat answer to this familiar risk. The choice between modesty and aggressiveness depends on the merits of the issue and on the prospects for changing the opponent's attitudes. It is not a foregone conclusion that relations with the opponent will become more difficult if he is being confronted with unacceptable proposals. Westerners often wish that the Soviet Union were more of a "status quo power"—that is, interested in preserving only its present influence and possessions, not in adding to them. Is it not possible to stimulate such an interest more by challenging the Soviet stake in the status quo than by guaranteeing it?

DENYING ONESELF AVAILABLE THREATS

From April, 1939, until the announcement of the Hitler-Stalin pact on August 21 of that year, the British and the French tried to negotiate an agreement with Russia against the likelihood of German aggression. This was not an easy assignment, since the Poles, Romanians, and Baltic states—the potential victims of Hitler's next move—were adamantly opposed to automatic Soviet assistance, fearing (not unreasonably as shown by later events) that once Soviet armies entered their countries to fight the Germans, they might never leave.

According to a Foreign Office memorandum of May 22, 1939, the British in their own right were not sanguine about negotiating with Moscow: "Even though we may not be able to count implicitly on the Soviet Government either honestly wishing to fulfill, or being capable of fulfilling, their treaty obligations, nevertheless, the alternative of a Soviet Union completely untrammelled and exposed continually to the temptation of intriguing with both sides . . . might present a no less, perhaps more, dangerous situation than that produced by collaborating with a dishonest or an incompetent partner."

Nor did the British have much confidence in the strength of their negotiating position. On July 20, 1939, William Strang, the British emissary in Moscow, reported to London:

> Our need for an agreement is more immediate than theirs. Unlike them we have assumed obligations which we may be obliged to fulfill any day; and some of the obligations we have undertaken are of benefit to the Soviet Union since they protect a good part of their Western frontier. Having committed ourselves to these obligations, we have no other policy open to us than that of building up the Peace Front. The Russians have, in the last resort, at least two alternative policies, namely, the policy of isolation, and the policy of accommodation with Germany.[13]

By assuming that they had "no other policy open" to them, the British denied themselves the capacity to threaten. Scarcely nine months before, the same British government and the French had signed an agreement with Hitler at Munich, in violation of their commitment to Czechoslovakia and excluding the Soviet Union, permitting the Germans to expand eastward while keeping peace in the west. If the Soviets were as suspicious as Strang reported they were in his dispatch from Moscow, it should have been easy for the British to make the Soviets suspect that unless they showed more interest in reaching agreement on the Peace Front, there might be another Munich which would bring the German army up to the Soviet border. The British seem to have forgotten that a threat has to be credible only to the opponent; it does not have to be agreeable to oneself or satisfy all one's commitments. Who can say whether hints of such a threat would not have led to an Anglo-French-Soviet agreement before Stalin signed the pact with Hitler? The puzzling thing is that the British never even considered whether or not they should make use of it.

Western negotiators have no particular difficulty in using threats that are merely an extension of warnings (i.e., when the threatened action is an addition only to the action that would be taken anyhow in one's self-interest if the opponent failed to comply). Such threats Western negotiators often use to good effects, and, in contrast to Khrushchev's negotiating style, they wisely prefer to leave them implicit, where feasible, instead of making explicit threats.

[13] E. L. Woodward and R. Butler (eds.), *Documents on British Foreign Policy 1919–1939* (Third Series), V, 646; VI, 422.

On those occasions, however, when the Western negotiator could make an effective threat only by envisaging a radical departure from his basic policy, he often denies himself the capacity to threaten, even though these occasions are frequently decisive junctures in important negotiations. Of course, if you are pursuing certain aims through negotiation, it is not an inviting prospect to contemplate a complete reversal of your policies in conflict with your present aims—merely for the purpose of hurting your opponent. But your opponent may not know how attached you are to your present policies and how unlikely such a reversal is. Just because you do not wish to switch to the opposite policy does not mean that you should guarantee to your opponent that you will not do so.

Such self-denial is desirable only in dealing with close allies or trustworthy friendly nations, when it is more important to maintain the opponent's long-term confidence than to exert pressures by threatening a reversal of one's joint policies or a reversal even of the alliance itself. Where this long-term confidence is lacking, nothing is lost by letting your opponent fear that you might do an about-face unless he becomes more accommodating. In 1942, to cite a previous example, Churchill was won over to Eden's idea that Stalin should be granted territorial gains in Eastern Europe in exchange for a pact with Great Britain. Churchill changed his mind not because he felt confident about Stalin's long-term policies but for precisely the opposite reason: he feared Stalin might make another deal with Hitler.

American negotiators have deprived themselves of threats on a number of occasions because they did not want to envisage reversing a basic policy. In the Far East as in Europe, the United States has adhered to the policy of leaving the Communists certain sanctuaries—areas where it will not interfere—to avoid a direct great-power conflict, to reduce the risks of expanding hostilities, and occasionally to preserve Western sanctuaries as a *quid pro quo*. Much as this may have been a wise policy, it was foolish to guarantee to the opponent in every instance that this policy would not be reversed.

The Korean armistice negotiations might have ended faster or on terms more favorable to the West had Peking been left in greater doubt whether or not the Chinese mainland (then exceedingly vulnerable) might be attacked from the air or the sea. At least the threat should have been kept alive that the United Nations forces would try to regain part of North Korea. On February 3, 1951, months before the armistice talks had even started, the State Department declared (according to the *New York Times*) "that the restoration of peace in Korea would not be helped by 'speculation' about whether U.N. forces would or would not cross the 38th Parallel if they reached it in a new offensive." The restoration of peace might indeed have been helped if just such speculation had been encouraged very loudly in Washington!

Again, in the negotiations for the neutralization of Laos in 1961, the Americans would have been in a stronger bargaining position if they had not deprived themselves so much of their capacity to threaten. When the American negotiators set out to attend the Laos Conference, Washington could simply have expressed mild interest in neutralization. Instead, the United States gave obvious signs that it would pursue nothing but neutralization and make no more attempts, for instance, to include Laos in a Western alliance. Nor were the Communists given much reason to fear an expansion of hostilities into their sanctuary in North Vietnam.

The Russians, by contrast, do not give the United States the comfort of curtailing their capacity to threaten. One reason why the United States is cautious in asserting itself in Panama or in helping anti-Communist forces in Cuba is the fear that the Russians might intervene, either by supporting local opposition or with action elsewhere. Khrushchev likes to encourage speculation about Soviet intervention rather than to snuff it out. Even after his retreat in the 1962 Cuba crisis, he promised to intervene in Cuba if the United States ever acted against Castro.

But when asserting themselves on Eastern Europe, the Russians have no American threats to worry about. In October, 1956, while the Kremlin leaders formulated plans to crush the Hungarian Revolution, they might at first have been somewhat worried that the West would help the Hungarians. Then, as the West continued to negotiate only for propaganda effects in the United Nations, this risk must have looked increasingly smaller. And, as if to assure everyone that the United States all along had been negotiating merely for side-effects, President Eisenhower guaranteed to the Russians that as long as they maintained superior local force, their sanctuary in Eastern Europe was under no threat from the West, either at that time or on any similar occasion in the future. "Nothing, of course, has so disturbed the American people as the events in Hungary," he remarked in his press conference on November 14, 1956. "Our hearts have gone out to them, and we have done everything it is possible to, in the way of alleviating suffering. But I must make one thing clear: the United States doesn't now—and never has—advocate open rebellion by an undefended populace against force over which they could not possibly prevail."

Robert Murphy's account of the atmosphere in the U.S. State Department during the Hungarian Revolution is much to the point. There were "fears of terrible reprisals" by the Soviet army against the Hungarians, but no thought seems to have been given as to how the United States might instill some fears into the Soviet leaders when they debated whether to order military intervention. There was much concern that "the Russians were trying to blame Americans for the human slaughter" [sic!]—this concern, in fact, prompted the Eisenhower statement just quoted—but little concern that the United States might be blamed for having lost all interest in the liberation of Eastern Europe. The idea of flying supplies to the Hungarians was conveniently dismissed by the argument that Austria opposed any overflights, but how many planes would Austria have shot down? And the suggestion of *threatening* American intervention was equated with the *certainty* of war. Although it is obvious that "the American people did not desire to go to war against the Soviet Union," would the Russian leaders have desired to go to war against the United States if offered a more attractive compromise settlement? During the Cuban missile crisis in 1962, President Kennedy could also have argued that the American people did not "desire" to go to war against Russia and confined himself to negotiating for ephemeral side-effects in the United Nations.[14]

[14] Robert Murphy, *Diplomat among Warriors* (Garden City, N.Y.: Doubleday, 1964), pp. 428–32. Murphy's pages merely reflect State Department thinking during those days. Had Murphy been in charge of the Hungarian crisis, he might have acted differently. His memoirs suggest that he did not usually share the

We can detect some underlying characteristics that the weaknesses of Western negotiators have in common. There is a somewhat passive attitude toward conflict, a tendency to avoid conflict rather than to win it and a readiness to quit while gains might still be made. Where the West has to negotiate from weakness, it often lacks the self-confidence and boldness to push for success; where it can negotiate from strength, it is frequently too squeamish to exploit its advantages. More fundamental, however, is the tendency to overlook the fact that negotiation changes evaluations. He who mistakes his eroding evaluations for the trend of history can be made to believe that slowing down his retreat is a gain, that preventing further enemy advances must be the limit of his ambitions, and that trying to recover what has been lost would be utter recklessness.

THE COMPLEAT NEGOTIATOR

The compleat negotiator, according to seventeenth- and eighteenth-century manuals on diplomacy, should have a quick mind but unlimited patience, know how to dissemble without being a liar, inspire trust without trusting others, be modest but assertive, charm others without succumbing to their charm, and possess plenty of money and a beautiful wife while remaining indifferent to all temptations of riches and women.

It is easy to add to this garland of virtues, but difficult in the real world to judge a good negotiator from a bad one. One cannot evaluate a negotiator merely by asking how close he came to realizing the aims of his government; for if he came close, he may owe his success to modest aims or favorable conditions rather than to his skill. Nor can one be sure that he has done well just because his gains and losses compare favorably with those of the opponent; for it is an essential task of negotiators to change the evaluation of gains and losses.

Frequently one judges a negotiator by comparing the results he obtained with results he might have obtained had he acted differently. In doing so, however, one should distinguish between

Western weakness of denying oneself available threats (e.g., his recommendation to challenge the 1948 Berlin blockade on the ground, pp. 316–17).

errors in negotiation, on the one hand, and errors in prediction and foreign-policy planning, on the other. Furthermore, one has to allow for domestic constraints which limit the alternatives that the negotiator could have chosen. Even though a skillful negotiator will guide and strengthen his domestic support, he cannot escape these constraints completely.

On occasion, the outcome of an international conference seems predetermined by the balance of military strength, by economic factors, or by other forces beyond the negotiator's control. For example, George Kennan argued that the establishment of Soviet military power in Eastern Europe and the entry of Soviet forces into Manchuria did not result from the wartime conferences of Moscow, Teheran, and Yalta, but from the military operations during the concluding phases of the war when the Western democracies were not in a position to enter these areas first.[15] One can surely agree with Kennan that only a limited range of alternatives was open at these conferences. But one should question how narrow this range actually was and whether the negotiators did not take for granted bounds that they drew themselves.

Imagine, for instance, a reverse of the situation in Iran and in Korea—that Iran was the country divided into a Communist North and a pro-Western South but that Korea was unified under a government friendly to the West. If this were the situation today, we would probably feel that the Western democracies could have done nothing to prevent the Russians from staying in Northern Iran (an area they occupied first, after all!) but that in Korea the West had a better chance to keep the country unified and friendly (obviously! Russia having entered the war against Japan so late and Korea being more accessible to American military strength than Iran).

Many of the clichés about the perfect negotiator might be revised rather than discarded. A good negotiator should be *realistic*, yes, but not in the sense of accepting an outcome as being determined by the balance of forces without trying to re-interpret

[15] George F. Kennan, *American Diplomacy, 1900–1950* (Chicago: University of Chicago Press, 1951), p. 85. Regarding Europe, Kennan conceded that "the postwar line of division between East and West might have lain somewhat farther east than it does today, and that would certainly be a relief to everyone concerned" (*ibid.*, p. 87).

this "balance" in his favor. Instead of taking a situation for granted, he should be realistic in recognizing that his opponent's evaluations as well as his own are constantly adrift, that issues are not created by Nature but by himself and by his opponent, and that there are ways of negotiating from weakness as well as from strength.

A good negotiator should also be *flexible*—not by being without a firm position but by utilizing both firm and flexible proposals. He should be flexible in his tactics by discriminating between occasions when it pays to adhere to rules of accommodation and when it does not. He must distinguish situations where it would be disastrous to make a threat from others where it is essential to threaten or even to bluff. He must know when to humor the personal quirks of his opponent and when to ignore them. He must be willing to disregard propaganda losses at one time and to negotiate merely for propaganda at another time. He must be prepared to follow domestic opinion at home as well as to encourage a new consensus both in his government and in his country.

And a good negotiator should be *patient*—though not primarily in order to sit in Geneva for months at a time hearing the opponent repeat speeches and repeating his own. He should be patient in working for seemingly lost causes, because by doing so he may slowly change the opponent's views and objectives. He should be patient to live with conflict and uncertainty and know that he may have succeeded even if (or precisely because) his negotiations failed. Above all, he must maintain the will to win.

BIBLIOGRAPHIC NOTE

TECHNIQUES OF DIPLOMATIC NEGOTIATION

The formalities of negotiation are listed in the traditional manuals on diplomat practices. For example: Sir Ernest Satow, *A Guide to Diplomatic Practice* (rev. ed.; London: Longmans, Green, 1958); and Graham H. Stuart, *American Diplomatic and Consular Practice* (New York: Appleton-Century-Crofts, 1952).

The *history* of diplomatic practices and of the conduct of foreign relations is dealt with in Garrett Mattingly, *Renaissance Diplomacy* (London: Jonathan Cape, 1955); and Harold Nicolson, *The Evolution of Diplomatic Method* (Glasgow: The University Press, 1954). Heinrich Wildner, *Die Technik der Diplomatie: L'art de négocier* (Vienna: Springer-Verlag, 1959) treas both history and current aspects of negotiation techniques and contains an extensive, annoted bibliography of earlier guides for the "perfect negotiator." In view of this bibliography, only three such guides are here mentioned that contain observations still of some interest today: François de Callières, *De la Manière de Négocier avec les Souverains* (1716 [English translation published by University of Notre Dame Press, 1963]); Fortune-Barthelemy de Félice, *Des Négociations ou de l'Art de Négocier,* reproduced in Karl von Martens, *Le Guide Diplomatique,* Vol. I (Paris: Gavelot, 1851); Antoine Pecquet, *De l'Art de Négocier avec les Souverains* (The Hague: J. van Duren, 1738).

On modern problems of negotiating methods: Dean Acheson, *Meetings at the Summit: A Study in Diplomatic Method* (Durham, N.H.: University of New Hampshire, 1958), an address at the University of New Hampshire, is excellent on summitry. Wipert von Blücher, *Wege und Irrwege der Diplomatie* (Wiesbaden: Limes Verlag, 1953); Jules Cambon, *Le Diplomate* (Paris: Hachette, 1926); Sir Maurice Hankey (Lord Hankey), *Diplomacy by Conference, Studies in Public Affairs, 1920–1946* (London: E. Benn, 1946); Sir William Hayter, *The Diplomacy of the Great*

Powers (New York: Macmillan, 1961), impressions of U.S., Soviet, French, and British negotiating styles; Norman L. Hill, *The Public International Conference* (Stanford, Calif.: Stanford University Press, 1929), interesting observations on pre- and post-World War II conferences and on the role of experts. *Journal of International Affairs,* special issue on "Diplomacy in Transition," XVII, No. 1 (1963); Stephen D. Kertesz and M. A. Fitzsimons (eds.), *Diplomacy in a Changing World* (Notre Dame, Ind.: University of Notre Dame Press, 1959); R. B. Mowat, *Diplomacy and Peace* (London: Williams & Norgate, 1935); Harold Nicolson, *Diplomacy* (New York: Harcourt, Brace, 1939); Dean Rusk, "The President," *Foreign Affairs,* XXXVIII, No. 3 (April, 1960), 353–69 on summitry; Charles W. Thayer, *Diplomat* (New York: Harper & Brothers, 1959).

For a novel on negotiating techniques: Francis Walder, *Saint-Germain ou la Négociation* (Paris: Gallimard, 1958 [English translation: *The Negotiators,* published by McDowell, Obolensky in 1959]).

For a sweeping analysis of the relation between diplomatic and military bargaining, with many keen observations on methods of diplomatic negotiation: Raymond Aron, *Paix et Guerre entre les Nations* (Paris: Calmann-Lévy, 1962).

FOREIGN POLICY, PUBLIC OPINION, AND THE CONDUCT OF FOREIGN AFFAIRS

Even though the literature on foreign policy is vast, not many of the books deal with methods and principles of negotiation. A recent bibliography can be found in Elmer Plischke, *Conduct of American Diplomacy* (Princeton, N.J.: Van Nostrand, 1961), and this book also describes the organization of U.S. diplomacy. Special aspects of U.S. diplomacy are dealt with in Michael H. Cardozo, *Diplomats in International Cooperation: Stepchildren of the Foreign Service* (Ithaca, N.Y.: Cornell University Press, 1962); and Robert Gilpin, *American Scientists and Nuclear Weapons Policy* (Princeton, N.J.: Princeton University Press, 1962).

For the influence of domestic opinion on negotiations: Andrew Berding, *Foreign Affairs and You! How American Policy Is Made and What It Means to You* (Garden City, N.Y.: Doubleday,

1962), which is illustrative but uncritical of the public-opinion influence; Bernard C. Cohen, *The Political Process and Foreign Policy: The Making of the Japanese Peace Settlement* (Princeton, N.J.: Princeton University Press, 1957); Bernard C. Cohen, *The Press and Foreign Policy* (Princeton, N.J.: Princeton University Press, 1963); Cecil V. Crabb, Jr., *American Foreign Policy in the Nuclear Age* (Evanston, Ill.: Row, Peterson, 1960), Chap. 7; H. Bradford Westerfield, *Foreign Policy and Party Politics* (New Haven: Yale University Press, 1958).

The following deal with the American negotiating style and recent problems in U.S. diplomacy: Dean Acheson, *Power and Diplomacy* (Cambridge, Mass.: Harvard University Press, 1958); Henry Kissinger, *The Necessity for Choice* (New York: Harper & Brothers, 1960), which contains many interesting observations on the weaknesses of the American style; Thomas Molnar, *The Two Faces of American Foreign Policy* (New York and Indianapolis: Bobbs-Merrill, 1962); Kenneth W. Thompson, *American Diplomacy and Emergent Patterns* (New York: New York University Press, 1962).

The atmosphere of the late 1950s is recaptured in Coral Bell, *Negotiation from Strength: A Study in the Politics of Power* (London: Chatto and Windus, 1962). In contrast with the inability to negotiate from strength, case histories of skillful negotiation from weakness are most instructive, such as Annette Baker Fox, *The Power of Small States: Diplomacy in World War II* (Chicago: University of Chicago Press, 1959).

Applicable to the conduct of diplomacy in general (not just U.S. diplomacy) are: Joseph Frankel, *The Making of Foreign Policy: An Analysis of Decision-Making* (London: Oxford University Press, 1963); Lester B. Pearson, *Diplomacy in the Nuclear Age* (Cambridge, Mass.: Harvard University Press, 1959); and Arnold Wolfers, *Discord and Collaboration: Essays on International Politics* (Baltimore, Md.: Johns Hopkins Press, 1962). A rich but diverse source of historical material is Alfred Vagts, *Defense and Diplomacy; The Soldier and the Conduct of Foreign Relations* (New York: King's Crown Press, 1956).

THE COMMUNIST STYLE OF NEGOTIATION

Primarily analytical: Dean Acheson, "On Dealing with Russia: An Inside View," *New York Times* (April 12, 1959), Magazine section, pp. 27, 88–89; McGeorge Bundy, "The Test of Yalta," *Foreign Affairs,* XXVII, No. 4 (July, 1949), 618–29; John C. Campbell, "Negotiation with the Soviets: Some Lessons of the War Period," *Foreign Affairs,* XXXIV, No. 1 (Jan., 1956), 305–19; Philip E. Mosely, *The Kremlin and World Politics* (New York: Vintage, 1960), Chap. 1, "Some Soviet Techniques of Negotiation," and Chaps. 5 through 10, for an excellent analysis; Gordon Craig, "Techniques of Negotiation," in Ivo J. Lederer (ed.), *Russian Foreign Policy, Essays in Historical Perspective* (New Haven, Conn.: Yale University Press, 1962), pp. 351–73; Gordon Craig, "Totalitarian Approaches to Diplomatic Negotiation," in A. O. Sarkissian (ed.), *Studies in Diplomatic History and Historiography in Honour of G. P. Gooch* (London: Longmans, Green, 1961), pp. 107–25, for an interesting comparison between Soviet and Fascist style; Stephen D. Kertesz, "American and Soviet Negotiating Behavior," in Stephen D. Kertesz and M. A. Fitzsimons (eds.), *Diplomacy in a Changing World* (Notre Dame, Ind.: University of Notre Dame Press, 1959), pp. 133–71, for good contrasts between East and West; Raymond Dennett and Joseph E. Johnson (eds.), *Negotiating with the Russians* (Boston: World Peace Foundation, 1951); John W. Spanier and Joseph L. Nogee, *The Politics of Disarmament: A Study in Soviet-American Gamesmanship* (New York: Praeger, 1962); William H. Vatcher, Jr., *Panmunjom: The Story of the Korean Military Armistice Negotiation* (New York: Praeger, 1958).

Primarily memoirs: James F. Byrnes, *Speaking Frankly* (New York: Harper & Brothers, 1947); General George Catroux, *J'ai vu tomber le Raideau de Fer: Moscou 1945–1948* (Paris: Hachette, 1952) French Ambassador; Mark W. Clark, *Calculated Risk* (New York: Harper & Brothers, 1950), relating to 1946–47; Mark W. Clark, *From the Danube to the Yalu* (New York: Harper & Brothers, 1954), Korea and criticism of policies in Washington; John R. Deane, *The Strange Alliance* (New York: Viking Press, 1947), lend-lease negotiations; Admiral C. Turner Joy, *How*

Communists Negotiate (New York: Macmillan, 1955), Korean armistice; U. S. Ambassador Walter Bedell Smith, *My Three Years in Moscow* (Philadelphia: J. B. Lippincott, 1950); Lord F. William Strang, *Home and Abroad* (London: André Deutsch, 1956), on Franco-British negotiations in Moscow in 1939 and European Advisory Commission, 1943–44.

EUROPEAN INTEGRATION

Since this book contains many illustrations from the history of European integration, some studies relevant for these negotiating methods deserve to be listed here: Achille Albonetti, *Préhistoire des États-Unis de l'Europe* (Paris: Editions Sirey, 1963); Miriam Camps, *The Free Trade Area Negotiations* (Occasional Paper No. 2 [London: Political and Economic Planning, 1959]); Amitai Etzioni, "The Dialectics of Supranational Unification," *The Amercan Political Science Review*, LVI, No. 4 (Dec., 1962), 927–35; Great Britain, *Negotiations for a European Free Trade Area; Documents Relating to the Negotiations from July, 1956, to December, 1958* (Cmnd. 641 [London: H.M.S.O., 1959]); Ernst B. Haas, *The Uniting of Europe* (Stanford, Calif.: Stanford University Press, 1958); Ernst B. Haas, "International Integration, The European and the Universal Process," *International Organization*, XV, No. 3 (Summer, 1961), 366–92; Karl Kaiser, *EWG und Freihandelszone; England und der Kontinent in der Europäischen Integration* (Leiden: A. W. Sythoff, 1963); Leon N. Lindberg, *The Political Dynamics of European Economic Integration* (Stanford, Calif.: Stanford University Press, 1962); Anthony Nutting, *Europe Will Not Wait: A Warning and a Way Out* (London: Hollis & Carter, 1960).

ACCOUNTS OF SPECIFIC NEGOTIATIONS, BIOGRAPHIES, AND OTHER SOURCES

It would be pointless to begin listing here memoirs of senior negotiators and statesmen, such as those by Churchill, Truman, Eden, Cordell Hull, etc. These autobiographies are, of course, important sources for the study of negotiations. So are good biographies. To list just a few that are particularly relevant for methods of negotiation: Gordon A. Craig and Felix Gilbert (eds.), *The*

Diplomats: 1919–1939 (Princeton, N.J.: Princeton University Press, 1953); Alexander DeConde, *The American Secretary of State, an Interpretation* (New York: Praeger, 1962) contains good essays on the relationship between Secretaries and their Presidents; Harold Nicolson, *Curzon: The Last Phase 1919–1925* (London: Constable, 1934), which gives a fascinating analysis of Curzon's techniques at the Lausanne Conference; Charles Webster, *The Art and Practice of Diplomacy* (New York: Barnes & Noble, 1962), content is less ambitious than title, on Palmerston and autobiographical.

The literature on many specific conferences is also large. Specialized bibliographies can be consulted for the Congress of Vienna, the Paris Peace Conference of 1919, etc. For more recent conferences: Herbert Feis, *Between War and Peace, the Potsdam Conference* (Princeton, N.J.: Princeton University Press, 1960); Edward J. Rozek, *Allied Wartime Diplomacy: A Pattern in Poland* (New York: John Wiley, 1958); Amelia C. Leiss and Raymond Dennett (eds.), *European Peace Treaties after World War II: Negotiations and Texts of Treaties with Italy, Bulgaria, Hungary, Rumania, and Finland* (Boston: World Peace Foundation, 1954); Jacques Freymond, *The Saar Conflict, 1944–1955* (New York: Praeger, 1960); Jean Edward Smith, *The Defense of Berlin* (Baltimore, Md.: Johns Hopkins Press, 1963), which offers a bibliography of other studies on Berlin.

Two studies on financial negotiations are: Edward W. Bennett, *Germany and the Diplomacy of the Financial Crisis, 1931* (Cambridge, Mass.: Harvard University Press, 1962); and Richard N. Gardner, *Sterling-Dollar Diplomacy* (Oxford: Clarendon Press, 1956).

On disarmament negotiations: Merze Tate, *The Disarmament Illusion, the Movement for a Limitation of Armaments to 1907* (New York: Macmillan, 1942); Andrew D. White, *The First Hague Conference* (Boston: World Peace Foundation, 1912); Calvin De Armond Davis, *The United States and the First Hague Peace Conference* (Ithaca, N.Y.: Cornell University Press, 1962); Raymond G. O'Connor, *Perilous Equilibrium: The United States and the London Naval Conference of 1930* (Lawrence, Kan.: University of Kansas Press, 1962); Bernard G. Bechhoefer, "Ne-

gotiating the Status of the International Atomic Energy Agency,"
International Organization, XIII (Winter, 1959), 38–59; Bernard G. Bechhoefer, *Postwar Negotiations for Arms Control*
(Washington: The Brookings Institution, 1961); Joseph L. Nogee,
Soviet Policy towards International Control of Atomic Energy
(Notre Dame, Ind.: University of Notre Dame Press, 1961); and
Spanier and Nogee listed above in Section 3; Earl H. Voss, *Nuclear Ambush* (Chicago, Ill.: Regnery, 1963) on test-ban conference; Harold Jacobson and Eric Stein, *Diplomats, Scientists and
Politicians: The United States and the Nuclear Test Ban Negotiations* (Ann Arbor, Mich.: University of Michigan Press, 1966).

BARGAINING THEORY AND ANALYSES OF DECISION-MAKING

Some of the more recent publications presenting or making use
of game theory and related approaches are: Kenneth E. Boulding,
Conflict and Defense: A General Theory (New York: Harper &
Row, 1962); James Buchan and G. Tullock, *The Calculus of Consent* (Ann Arbor, Mich.: University of Michigan Press, 1962);
John C. Harsanyi, "On the Rationality Postulates Underlying the
Theory of Cooperative Games," *The Journal of Conflict Resolution,* V, No. 2 (June, 1961), 179–96; R. Duncan Luce and
Howard Raiffa, *Games and Decision* (New York: John Wiley,
1957), which is an excellent and comprehensive treatment of
game theory but, as with all pure game theory, scarcely relevant
for political negotiation; J. Pen, "A General Theory of Bargaining," *American Economic Review,* XLII (March, 1952), 24–42,
which makes interesting points on the bargainer's satisfaction and
the "ludic" element in bargaining; Anatol Rapoport, *Fights,
Games, and Debates* (Ann Arbor, Mich.: University of Michigan
Press, 1960); William H. Riker, *The Theory of Political Coalitions*
(New Haven: Yale University Press, 1962); Thomas C. Schelling,
The Strategy of Conflict (Cambridge, Mass.: Harvard University
Press, 1960), highly relevant for tacit bargaining as well as negotiation; Martin Shubik (ed.), *Game Theory and Related Approaches to Social Behavior* (New York: John Wiley, 1964), a
collection of articles.

Analyses of the decision-making process are: Richard C. Snyder,
H. W. Bruck, and Burton Sapin, *Foreign Policy Decision Making*

(New York: The Free Press, 1962); Charles E. Lindblom, "The Science of 'Muddling Through,'" *Public Administration Review,* XIX (Spring, 1959), 74–88; and David Braybrooke and Charles E. Lindblom, *The Strategy of Decision* (New York: The Free Press, 1963), the latter two deal more with domestic policies.

Psychologists have developed the concept "level of aspiration," representing a level of future performance that an·individual explicitly undertakes to reach. Satisfaction (or dissatisfaction) results if this level is reached (or cannot be attained). The level tends to be revised in response to previous performance. Evidently there are some similarities between this concept and the ideas in this book of evaluations and of objectives that are adjusted to changing expectations. Selwyn W. Becker and Sidney Siegel, "Utility of Grades: Level of Aspiration in a Decision Theory Context," *Journal of Experimental Psychology,* LV, No. 1 (1958), 81–85, gives a bibliography. Jerome D. Frank, "Recent Studies of the Level of Aspiration," *Psychological Bulletin,* XXXVIII, No. 4 (April, 1941), 218–26, discusses the earlier literature. Sidney Siegel and Lawrence E. Fouraker, *Bargaining and Group Decision Making* (New York: McGraw-Hill, 1960), relates level of aspiration to bargaining situations. In the experiments on which most of these studies are based, however, the "level of aspiration" has frequently been artificially rigged (e.g., as a peak in rising rewards) so that modifications of this level in response to the bargaining process could not be adequately studied.

Unfortunately, there are few studies of how psychological or personality factors affect negotiations. Sidney Verba, "Assumptions of Rationality and Non-Rationality in Models of the International System," in Klaus Knorr and Sidney Verba (eds.), *The International System: Theoretical Essays* (Princeton, N.J.: Princeton University Press, 1961) offers an excellent abstract discussion of the problem of defining "rationality." Irving L. Janis, "Decisional Conflicts: A Theoretical Analysis," *The Journal of Conflict Resolution,* III, No. 1 (March, 1959), 6–27, is a most promising beginning where one wishes for more. An outstanding example is Alexander L. George and Juliette L. George, *Woodrow Wilson and Colonel House: A Personality Study* (New York: John Day, 1956).

LABOR-MANAGEMENT NEGOTIATIONS

There are a number of parallels between labor-management and intergovernmental negotiations, for instance the shifting evaluations, the effect of the negotiator's personality, and the influence of domestic affairs or intra-union and intra-management affairs respectively. One of the principal differences between intergovernmental and labor-management negotiations is that the latter take place under constraints enforced by higher authorities. Also, the issues in labor-management negotiations are much simpler.

The most comprehensive and systematic analysis is Carl Stevens, *Strategy in Collective Bargaining Negotiation* (New York: Mc-Graw-Hill, 1963), which puts proper stress on the fact that evaluations keep shifting (although the story might have been told just as precisely in simpler terminology).

Interestingly, there seem to be more studies of the bargaining process in labor-management negotiation than in international negotiation. Neil W. Chamberlain, *Collective Bargaining* (New York: McGraw-Hill, 1951), and J. T. Dunlop and J. J. Healy, *Collective Bargaining: Principles and Cases* (Homewood, Ill.: R. D. Irwin, 1953), both deal, in part, with the bargaining process. Ann Douglas, *Industrial International Peacemaking* (New York: Columbia University Press, 1962), contains case material. Elmore Jackson, *Meeting of Minds: A Way to Peace through Mediation* (New York: McGraw-Hill, 1952) on methods of mediation. James W. Kuhn, *Bargaining in Grievance Settlement* (New York: Columbia University Press, 1961); Edward Peters, *Strategy and Tactics in Labor Negotiations* (New London, Conn.: National Foremen's Institute, 1955).

INDEX

[N.B. Italic page numbers indicate direct quotations.]